The Book of Lost Books

The Book of
Lost Books

STUART KELLY

VIKING
an imprint of
PENGUIN BOOKS

VIKING

Published by the Penguin Group
Penguin Books Ltd, 80 Strand, London WC2R ORL, England
Penguin Group (USA) Inc., 375 Hudson Street, New York, New York 10014, USA
Penguin Group (Canada), 90 Eglinton Avenue East, Suite 700, Toronto, Ontario, Canada M4P 2Y3
(a division of Pearson Penguin Canada Inc.)
Penguin Ireland, 25 St Stephen's Green, Dublin 2, Ireland
(a division of Penguin Books Ltd)
Penguin Group (Australia), 250 Camberwell Road, Camberwell, Victoria 3124, Australia
(a division of Pearson Australia Group Pty Ltd)
Penguin Books India Pvt Ltd, 11 Community Centre, Panchsheel Park, New Delhi – 110 017, India
Penguin Group (NZ), cnr Airborne and Rosedale Roads, Albany, Auckland 1310, New Zealand
(a division of Pearson New Zealand Ltd)
Penguin Books (South Africa) (Pty) Ltd, 24 Sturdee Avenue, Rosebank 2196, South Africa

Penguin Books Ltd, Registered Offices: 80 Strand, London WC2R ORL, England

www.penguin.com

First published 2005
1

Copyright © Stuart Kelly, 2005
Illustrations copyright © Andrzej Krauze, 2005

The moral rights of the author and illustrator have been asserted

Set in 12/14.75 pt Monotype Bembo
Typeset by Rowland Phototypesetting Ltd, Bury St Edmunds, Suffolk
Printed in Great Britain by Clays Ltd, St Ives plc

A CIP catalogue record for this book is available from the British Library

ISBN 0–670–91499–1

This book is for Sam, who found me

Contents

Acknowledgements

Many friends and colleagues have endured incessant questions about their own specialities; many of them have also regularly sent me details about lost books they encountered in their own work. I would like especially to thank Gavin Bowd, Seán Bradley, Peter Burnett, Angus Calder, Andrew Crumey, Lucy Ellmann, Todd McEwen, Richard Price and James Roberston. Peter Straus, Leo Hollis, Kate Barker, David Ebershoff, David Watson and Sam Kelly were all unstintingly helpful in terms of the actual writing; and, of course, thanks to my parents, who started, and endured, my whole obsession with reading.

'Hence, perpetually and essentially, texts run the risk of becoming definitively lost. Who will ever know of such disappearances?'

Jacques Derrida, 'Plato's Pharmacy'

Introduction

'I'll burn my books – ah, Mephistophilis'

Christopher Marlowe, *Doctor Faustus*

My mother claims it started with the *Mr Men* series of children's books. In a well-rehearsed pantomime of parental exasperation, she recounts how, after a family relative had given me a copy of one of Roger Hargreaves' stories, every holiday jaunt, weekend outing and Saturday shopping trip became a single-minded trawl of bookshops until I had every single one of the series. Mr Bump needed Mr Nosey, Mr Tickle was lonely without Mr Chatterbox. After I had finished this first collection I swiftly became obsessed, I forget for what reason, with the *Dr Who* novelizations; this was followed by 'Fighting Fantasy' dice and decision books, and, as I approached my teens, Agatha Christie paperbacks.

A pattern began to develop; a pattern that would turn obsessive. Having *one* or *some* of the titles within any given series was not sufficient; I seemed to be afflicted with a relentless monomania for *all*, a near-compulsive necessity for closure and completeness. I even kept a 'Book of Lists', to double-check that I really did know every episode of *Dr Who*, with ticks against the ones I had bought and annotations about the ones that had never been novelized. When all of Agatha Christie's books were reissued with newly designed covers, the idea of having mismatched volumes struck me as unspeakably grotesque. I stalked the old stock, ferreted for the forgotten copies at the back of the shelves.

It must have been with some trepidation, on my fourteenth

Christmas, that my parents watched me unwrap a *Complete Works of Shakespeare* (Chancellor Press, 1982, printed in Czechoslovakia) and a selection of Wordsworth (by W. E. Williams, introduction by Jenni Calder, Penguin Poetry Library, 1985). I presume that they were hoping that Literature – with a capital L – was a large enough field in which my fixation might peter out.

Instead, Literature drove my zeal to new heights. The itch became a palpable rash when I started studying Greek (initially as a shameless ruse to avoid sports). Having saved up months of weekend-job wages, and having starved myself rationing lunch money, I binged on Penguin Classics of Hellenic drama: two volumes of Aeschylus, two of Sophocles, three of Aristophanes, four of Euripides and a solitary Menander. The first shock to my well-ordered system came as I peeled back the smart covers and began to browse through the introductions. I was under the impression that I had just bought *all* of Greek drama, yet the prefaces and commentaries doomfully tolled otherwise: Aeschylus, whose seven plays I was holding, had actually written eighty; there should have been thirty-three volumes of Sophocles, not a mere brace . . . and so on.

The second, more grievous realization came when reading note 61 to Aristophanes' play *Thesmophoriazusae*: 'Agathon, one of the most celebrated tragedians of the day, was forty-one when this play was produced. None of his works has survived.' None? Not a chorus, not a speech, not a hemistich? It seemed unthinkable.

This, I decided, at the age of fifteen, was a situation which I should rectify. I started compiling a List of Lost Books. It quickly superseded my Book of Lists with its 'Everyone in *Star Wars* That Wasn't Made into a Figure', '*Dr Who* Episodes Lost by the BBC' and even the list of books that I should read. This new list would be of the impossible and the unknowable, of books that I would never be able to find, let alone read.

It soon became clear that the subject was not limited to the Greeks, who, after all, had managed to keep on existing through Roman arrogance, Christian lack of interest and a certain Caliph's censorious view of libraries in general and the Alexandrian Library specifically.

From Shakespeare to Sylvia Plath, Homer to Hemingway, Dante to Ezra Pound, great writers had written works which I could not possess. The entire history of literature was also the history of the loss of literature.

It is intrinsic to the nature of literature that it is written: even work initially preserved in the oral tradition only truly becomes literature when it is written down. All literature thus exists in a medium, be it wax, stone, clay, papyrus, paper or even – as in the case of the Peruvian knot language, Khipu – rope. Since it has a material dimension, literature itself partakes of the vulnerability of its substance. Every element conspires against it: flame and flood, the desiccating air that corrupts, the loamy earth that decays. Paper is particularly defenceless: it can be shredded and ripped, stained and scrubbed away. Countless living things, from parasites and fungi to insects and rodents, can eat it: it even eats itself, burning in its own acids.

The simplest form of loss is destruction. Though the Roman poet Horace proclaimed, 'I have built a monument more durable than bronze,' he expressed a hope about his work, and not a certainty. The nineteenth-century poet Gerard Manley Hopkins burned all of his early poetry, as he dedicated his life to the beauty of God. James Joyce petulantly flung *Stephen Hero*, the first draft of *A Portrait of the Artist as a Young Man*, into the fire, but did not prevent his wife from saving what she could of it. Mikhail Bakhtin, exiled in Kazakhstan, used his work on Dostoyevsky as cigarette papers, after having smoked a copy of the Bible.

Some writings are absent, presumed destroyed: Socrates, while in prison awaiting his execution, wrote versifications of Aesop's *Fables*. None of these have survived, and we rely on Plato's remembered and invented dialogues to catch even an echo of what Socrates himself might have written. Similarly, at some point, the only text of Aristotle's second book of *Poetics* was lost, and even the first book is made up from students' notes. A similar fate happened centuries later to Ferdinand de Saussure's *Course in General Linguistics*. When the publisher John Calder had to hastily relocate his offices in late 1962, many manuscripts – including *The Sowing*, the third part of Lars Lawrence's trilogy, and Angus Heriot's *The Lives of the Librettists* – were left behind in the old premises. The building, unpublished works and all, was demolished. If any undiscovered genius had sent their sole copy to Calder, undiscovered they would remain.

There are other works which are lost in the sense of being misplaced. A suitcase containing Malcolm Lowry's *Ultramarine* was stolen from his publisher's car, and the version we have had to be reconstructed from what was left in Lowry's bin. Allen Ginsberg recollected hearing fellow beat poet Gregory Corso reading in a lesbian bar in the Village, though you can search in vain through Corso's published *oeuvre* to find a poem with the line he remembered: 'The stone world came to me, and said Flesh gives you an hour's life'. How Ginsberg knew that Flesh was capitalized is a moot point.

There are also those manuscripts that meet an untimely end, whose authors' mortal existence is concluded before their work. The medieval Scottish poet William Dunbar wrote a haunting elegy for many of his dead fellow writers: of the twenty-two poets he lists, there are ten about whom we know nothing whatsoever. Virgil left instructions for *The Aeneid* to be torched, since he had not polished it to perfection. Sir Philip Sidney wrote the *Arcadia* once, but his own massive expansion of the work was abruptly terminated by a bullet on the battlefield at Zutphen. Nathaniel Hawthorne's *The Dolliver Romance*, Robert Louis Stevenson's *Weir of Hermi-*

ston and William Makepeace Thackeray's *Denis Duval* are all partial classics. The SS put paid to the radical theologian Dietrich Bonhoeffer's disquisition on ethics. Robert Musil and Marcel Proust never quite perfected their similarly voluminous masterpieces; and though we have enough extant to make them 'classics', a doubt scratches around these incomplete, unfinished, permanently paused novels.

The final category of lost books is the eternally embryonic works that the author planned and worked on, but never actually got round to the business of writing. Solon, the Athenian legislator, was too busy introducing income tax to turn the story of Atlantis into verse. The philosopher Boethius never managed to create his proof that Plato and Aristotle were in strict agreement. Sheridan told everyone that the sequel to *The School for Scandal* was going to be called *Affectation*, but did not bother writing it. Daudet's *The Pentameron* and Victor Hugo's *La Quinquengrogne* are both perpetually forthcoming. Lewis Grassic Gibbon was prevented from even beginning the novel he described in a letter as 'McLorna McDoone', and who knows whether or not Sir Arthur Conan Doyle might not have planned to reveal the true story behind the Giant Rat of Sumatra, which Watson once alluded to whilst Holmes was engaged with more immediate cases? Would Thomas Mann's *Gaia* have been the masterpiece while it was unwritten he believed that it could be? Would Nabokov's never-written *Speak, America*, the follow-up to his volume of memoirs, *Speak, Memory*, have told us more about the composition of *Lolita* or his triumphs in butterfly-collecting? Often these works are so ambitious their completion seems intrinsically impossible: Novalis' *Encyclopedia*, covering all human knowledge, progressed little beyond his anxieties about whether the contents list would also serve as an index. Likewise, Leopardi's *Encyclopedia of Useless Information* is incomplete: one wonders what he would have made of the Internet.

One other category of lost books exists but, with an unreasonable optimism about the future, I have chosen not to discuss the illegible. Languages such as Linear A, Mayan and the Easter Island Script have not been deciphered, and might therefore be considered to contain whole lost literatures: however, after being thought incomprehensible for millennia, the decryption of the Rosetta Stone in the nineteenth century meant hieroglyphics could now, tentatively, be read. If this book is on the quanta-net in 5005, I would not wish my descendants to be troubled with having to make any deletions.

Loss has symptoms and predilections. Comedy displays many of the high-risk features, as do erotica and autobiography. The loss of Philip Larkin's diaries, combining all three of these genres, was almost inevitable. The censuring of the erotic also accounts for the loss of a book by the Abbasid court poet Ibn al-Shah al-Tahiri (whether panegyric, satire or handbook can never be known) entitled *Masturbation*. Over and above the content of the work, the multiplicity of theological and political regimes under which a piece of writing might find itself – its nurture, rather than nature, if you will – contribute towards extinction.

From Savonarola to the Ayatollah Khomeini, religions have expressed themselves through book-burning. Valentin Gentilis, who lived in Geneva, wrote a discursive piece on the idea that Calvin's Trinitarian doctrine inadvertently posited a Fourth Member of the Godhood. He was imprisoned for eight years, recanted and then was executed: his punishment (apart from the deprivation of life) was first to burn his own work. His sentence was considered light.

The fact that Mandelstam's blisteringly satirical 'Stalin Ode' survived at all is remarkable; many others of his papers, drafts and scribbles were burned, flushed and otherwise discarded. His compatriot Isaac Babel was not so lucky. When he was arrested by Stalin's secret police on 15 May 1939, agents removed every single piece of paper from his flat.

Certain authors, rather than certain works, become suspect. That there are not more entries on women writers, gay writers and writers from outwith Europe, and the English language, is partially my own fault, and partially the fault of those who systematically erased that work. Virginia Woolf famously tried to imagine Shakespeare's sister, but the inexorable and un-changeable nature of the past frustrates any attempt at giving a name to those who have been deprived of even a ghostly lost existence. In their place, with a few exceptions, I will concentrate on the so-called Canon. The much-vaunted Western Canon, trumpeted abroad for its wealth, happiness and strength, is not an Olympian torch or a thoroughbred horse; it exists by chance, not necessity, a lucky crag pro-truding from an ocean of loss. That melancholy parade of disfigured busts, crazed ceramics, blistered portraits and foxed photographs is here, in all its shoogly, precarious glory. They are our conditional, might-have-been-otherwise, sheer damn lucky tradition. Those overwhelmed by Time's corrosion are not so fortunate.

Is becoming lost the worst that can happen to a book? A lost book is susceptible to a degree of wish fulfilment. The lost book, like the person you never dared ask to the dance, becomes infinitely more alluring simply because it can be perfect only in the imagination.

We are, nowadays, almost incapable of believing in loss. As Project Gutenberg and databases like the Chadwyck-Healy continue to grow, and offer the idea of a perma-fixed cyber-space culture, it is important and humbling to recognize that there is no automatic afterlife for literature. Prizes and plaudits are awarded on a daily basis; yet the ultimate fate of those lucky recipients is no more secure than that of the great prize-winner Agathon. Even a repository like the British Library used to have old request slips with a box on the back, infrequently but occasionally ticked, stating 'Volume lost'. There is, equally, no guarantee that an intangible existence is also an unreachable state of being. If literature were a house, *The Book of Lost Books* would be Rachel Whiteread's *House*, a poured-into vacancy that is both tomb and trace. *The Book of Lost Books* is an alternative history of literature, an epitaph and a wake, a hypothetical library and an elegy to what might have been.

On the Absence of a Bibliography and Footnotes in this Work

Zora Neale Hurston, the American folklorist and black activist, who left a novel entitled *Herod the Great* unfinished at her death, defined research as 'formalized curiosity'. It is, I think, a liberating definition. There seems to me to be a terrible irony in trying to create a bibliography for *The Book of Lost Books*: the substance is, by its nature, not in any library or collection. I could, I suppose, display the chain of references that took me, for example, from Aeschylus' *Oresteia* translated by Robert Fagles to Gilbert Murray's *Aeschylus* to volume ten of the works of the theologian Athenaeus; but where would this chain end? Not, assuredly, in the actual lost book, but in the whisper of its disappearance. For a book like this, footnotes are a trail to an empty grave.

Rather than marshal the reader along the meanders and diversions that my own formalized curiosity led to, I would, however, prefer her or him to set out on their own adventure. There are obvious places to start: every moderately well-stocked public library should, at least, contain either the *Columbia* or *Britannica* Encyclopedia, which offer an array of further routes to choose. I would also recommend Margaret Drabble's *Oxford Companion to English Literature*, *The Cambridge Companion to Women's Writing*, *The Oxford Companion to Classical Literature*, Edward Browne's *Literary History of Persia*, Suchi Kato's *History of Japanese Literature*, Ian Hamilton's

Keepers of the Flame, Rosier's *Encyclopedia* and . . . but already this is looking like a reading list.

Most of the authors discussed in this book did leave behind extant works, and the reader can choose, for the most part, between numerous editions: Penguin Classics, The World's Classics, Everyman, the Modern Library. Lost books is a practically infinite subject; and there are many – Acacius' *Life of Eusebius*, Eusebius' *Life of Pamphilus*, works by Anna Boškovic and Denis Fonvízin – that, through reasons of space, obscurity or indolence, did not make it into this book. The curious reader will no doubt find many more, and may find many more interesting. They may even find a book hitherto thought lost: the Scottish poet John Manson recently discovered, amongst various papers and ephemera in the National Library of Scotland, an almost complete text of the modernist poet Hugh MacDiarmid's 'lost' *magnum opus*, *Mature Art*.

According to the Latin poet Horace, the function of writing was to instruct and delight. If *The Book of Lost Books* manages to whet and divert readers sufficiently that they begin their own peregrinations among the plenitude of books that remain, it will have done everything I hoped.

Anonymous

(c.75,000 BCE–c.2800 BCE)

The very origins of literature are lost.

An oblong piece of ochre, found in the Blombos Caves on the southern coast of present-day South Africa, is cross-hatched with a regular pattern of diamonds and triangles. It is 77,000 years old. Whether these geometric designs are supposed to be symbolic, whether they are supposed to mean anything at all, they present us with one irrefutable fact. A precursor of modern humanity deliberately engraved marks on to a medium. It was a long way yet to the word-processor and text messages, but a first step of sorts had been taken.

The period around 45,000 to 35,000 years ago in humanity's evolution has been called the Upper Palaeolithic Revolution or, more catchily, the Creative Explosion. More complex tools were fashioned, from fish-hooks to buttons to needles. Moreover, they are decorated, not only with schema of lines and dots: a lamp contains an ibex, a spear-tip transforms into a bison. There are also statuettes with no immediately discernible use; squat figurines of dumpy women. Is it possible to have slings but not songs, arrows but not stories?

Looking at the cave-paintings from Lascaux, Altamira and

Chavette, created some 18,000 years ago, it is overwhelmingly tempting to try and read them. Do these images record successful hunts, or are they imagined desires and hopes? Is this 'Yesterday we killed an aurochs' or 'Once upon a time there was an aurochs'? What do the squiggles and zig-zags, the claviforms and tectiforms over the animal images signify? Occasionally, looming out from an inconceivably distant time, a human hand print appears, outlined in pigment. A signature, on a work we cannot interpret.

Where did writing come from? Every early culture has a deity who invents it: Nabu in Assyria, Thoth in Egypt, Tenjin in Japan, Oghma in Ireland, Hermes in Greece. The actual explanation may be far less glamorous – accountants in Mesopotamia. All the earliest writing documents, in the blunt, wedge-shaped cuneiform style, are records of transactions, stock-keeping and inventories. Before cursives and uncials, gothic scripts and runic alphabets, hieroglyphics and ideograms, we had tally-marks.

But, by the first few centuries of the second millennium BCE, we know that literature has begun, has begun to be recorded, and has begun to spread. It was not until 1872 that the first fragments of *The Epic of Gilgamesh* resurfaced in the public domain after four millennia. The excavation of ancient Nineveh had been undertaken by Austen Henry Layard in 1839. Nearly 25,000 broken clay tablets were sent back to the British Museum, and the painstaking work of deciphering the cuneiform markings commenced in earnest. The Nineveh inscriptions were incomplete, and dated from the seventh century BCE, when King Assurbanipal of Assyria had ordered his troops to seek out the ancient wisdom in the cities of Babylon, Uruk and Nippur. These spoils of war were then translated into Akkadian from the original Sumerian.

Over time, the poem was supplemented by more ancient versions discovered in Nippur and Uruk, as well as copies from places as far apart as Boghazköy in Asia Minor and Megiddo in Israel. Gradually, an almost complete version of *The Epic of Gilgamesh* was assembled out of Hittite, Sumerian, Akkadian, Hurrian and Old Babylonian.

Who first wrote it? We do not know. Was it part of a wider cycle of myths and legends? Possibly, even probably, and there is a slim chance that further archaeological research will answer this. What, finally, is it about?

Gilgamesh is a powerful king of Uruk. The gods create an equal for him in the figure of Enkidu, a wild man, brought up among beasts and tempted into civilization by sex. They become firm friends, and travel together to the forest, where they slay the ferocious giant Humbaba, who guards the cedar trees. This infuriates the goddess Ishtar, who sends a bull from Heaven to defeat them. They kill and sacrifice it, and Ishtar decides that the way to harm Gilgamesh is through the death of Enkidu. Distraught, Gilgamesh travels through the Underworld in search of eternal life, and eventually meets with Utnapishtim at the ends of the world. Utnapishtim was the only human wise enough to escape the Flood, and, after forcing Gilgamesh through a purification ceremony, shows him a flower called 'The Old Are Young Again'. It eludes his grasp, and Gilgamesh dies.

The themes resonate through recorded literary endeavour. Gilgamesh wrestles with mortality, he declares he will 'set up his name where the names of the famous are written'. Death is inevitable and incomprehensible. Even the giant Humbaba is given a pitiable scene where he begs for his life. Prayers, elegies, riddles, dreams and prophecies intersperse the adventure; fabulous beasts sit alongside real men and women. The fact that we can discern different styles and genres within *The Epic of Gilgamesh* hints that unknown versions existed prior to it.

All the earliest authors are anonymous. A legendary name, an Orpheus or Taliessin, serves as a conjectural origin, a myth to shroud the namelessness of our culture's beginnings. Although anonymity is still practised, it is as a ruse to conceal Deep Throats, both investigative and pornographic. It is a choice, whereas for generations of writers so absolutely lost that no line, no title, no name survives, it is a destiny thrust upon them. They might write, and struggle, and edit, and polish, yet their frail papers dissipate, and all their endeavour is utterly erased. To those of whom no trace remains, this book is an offering. For we will join them, in the end.

Homer

(*c.* late eighth century BCE)

Homer was . . .

The verb's the problem here. Was there even such a person as Homer?

There was, or there was believed to be, a Homer: minds as sceptical as Aristotle's and as gullible as Herodotus' knew there was, of sorts, a, once, Homer.

'When 'Omer smote 'is bloomin' lyre . . . They knew 'e stole; 'e knew they knowed . . .' says Rudyard Kipling.

'But when t' examine ev'ry part he came, Nature and Homer were, he found, the same,' was Pope's interpretation.

Samuel Butler, in 'The Authoress of the Odyssey' (1897), proposed that at least half of Homer was a woman.

E. V. Rieu, in 1946, patriotically complained:

Homer's *Iliad* and *Odyssey* have from time to time afforded a first class battleground for scholars. In the nineteenth century in particular, German critics were at endless pains to show, not only that the two works are not the product of a single brain, but that each is a piece of intricate and rather ill-sewn patch-work. In this process Homer disappeared.

The imperishable Homer dwindles, a hum, an er, an incon-
clusive pause. Let's begin with what we know: *Il.* and *Od.*
Two long poems exist, *The Iliad* and *The Odyssey*, and somehow someone somebody called Homer became convoluted
within them.

The Iliad and *The Odyssey* were considered by the Greeks
to be the pinnacle of their literary achievements, and subsequent centuries and countries have concurred. Egyptian
papyrus fragments of the texts outnumber all other texts and
authors put together; they are the basis for many of the
tragedies and are quoted, almost with reverence, by critics,
rhetoricians and historians. It is tempting to extract information about the poet from the poetry, as did Thomas
Blackwell, who, in 'An Enquiry into the Life and Writings
of Homer' (1735), found such a happy similarity between the
work and the world. Or, like the archaeologist and inveterate
pilferer Schliemann, one might scour the coasts of Asia Minor
in search of hot springs and cold fountains similar to those in
the verse. But Homer, himself, herself, whatever, is irredeemably slippery.

Take customs. Bronze weaponry is ubiquitous in *The Iliad*,
and iron a rarity, leading one to assume the poem describes a
Mycenean Bronze Age battle. Yet the corpses are all cremated, never interred, a practice associated with the post-
Mycenean Iron Age. The spear and its effect are historically
incompatible. The language itself bristles with inconsistencies.
Predominantly in the Ionic dialect, there are traces of the
Aeolic, hints of Arcado-Cypriot. Are these the snapped-up
snatches of a wandering bard, linguistic sticky-burrs hitching
on to the oral original? Or the buried lineaments of disparate
myths corralled into a cycle, the brick from a Roman villa
reused in the Gothic cathedral? The artificer cannot be
extrapolated from the artefact.

To the Greeks, *The Iliad* and *The Odyssey* were not the

works of a poet, but the Poet. So impressed were the people of Argos with their inclusion in *The Iliad* that they set up a bronze statue of Homer, and sacrificed to it daily.

Seven cities – Argos, Athens, Chios, Colophon, Rhodes, Salamis and Smyrna – claim to be the birthplace of Homer, although, significantly, all did so after his death. When he was born is just as contentious: Eratosthenes places it at 1159 BCE, so that the Trojan War would have still been in living memory, though a plethora of birthdates up until 685 BCE have been offered. Most opt for the end of the ninth century BCE, a convenient average of the extremities. His father was called Maeon, or Meles, or Mnesagoras, or Daemon, or Thamyras, or Menemachus, and may have been a market trader, soldier or priestly scribe, whilst his mother might be Metis or Cretheis, Themista or Eugnetho, or, like his father, Meles.

One extensive genealogy traces him back to his great-great-great-great-great-great-great-great-great-great-great-grandfather, the god Apollo, via the mythic poet Orpheus and his wife, the muse Calliope (though she has also been advanced as his mother). Since, as a muse, she would undoubtedly have been immortal, this is possible, though unsavoury.

The Emperor Hadrian tried to untangle these contradictory accounts by asking the Pythian Sibyl for her tuppence, and was told, 'Ithaca is his country, Telemachus his father, and Epicasta, daughter of Nestor, the mother that bore him, a man by far the wisest of mortals.' If she was correct, and Telemachus, the son of Odysseus, was Homer's sire, *The Odyssey* becomes a biography of his grandfather as much as an epic poem.

At Chios, a group of later rhapsodes announced themselves as the Homeridae, or the sons of Homer, who solemnly learned, recited and preserved the works of the Poet. Were there literal as well as figurative offspring? Tzetzes mentions that a poem called *The Cypria*, dealing with the prequel to the Trojan War and attributed to one Stasinus, was for the most part written by Homer, and given to the poet Stasinus, along with money, as part of a dowry. One presumes that this means that Homer had a daughter. *The Cypria*, however, was also sometimes thought to be the work of Hegesias of Troezen; little of it survives, and it is thus impossible to confirm the conjectural daughter.

Accounts agree, however, on one important feature. The Poet was blind. The birthplace claim of Smyrna is bolstered by the contention that *homer*, in their dialect, means 'blind' (though not, as in the description of the Cyclops, in *The Odyssey*). A section in the *Hymn to Delian Apollo* is taken, by vague tradition, to be a self-description of Homer – or Melesigenes, as he was called before the Smyrnans christened him 'Blindy':

'Whom think ye, girls, is the sweetest singer that comes here, and in whom do you most delight?' Then answer, each and all, with one voice: 'He is a blind man, and dwells in rocky Chios: his lays are evermore supreme.' As for me, I will carry your renown as far as I roam over the earth to the well-placed this thing is true.

It seems that, rather than being born sightless, Homer went blind: cataracts, diabetic glaucoma, infection by the nematode *toxocara*. The later poet Stesichorus was struck blind by the gods for slandering Helen, and only had his sight miraculously restored when he rewrote his work, insisting that Helen had not eloped. Instead, she had been spirited away to Egypt and replaced with a phantom fashioned of clouds. Stesichorus blamed Homer, and Homer's version of events, for his temporary loss of sight. Presumably Homer's blindness was occasioned by a similar infraction. If, after *The Iliad*, he was struck blind, then the blinding of Polyphemus the Cyclops in *The Odyssey* must supposedly be drawn from personal experience.

The place of Homer's death, thankfully, is barely in dispute: the island of Ios. Indeed, Homer himself was informed by a Pythian Sibyl that he would die on Ios, after hearing a children's riddle. She referred to the island as the homeplace of his mother (but Nestor's daughter came from Pylos, a good 150 miles away! One of the priestesses must be mistaken). Eventually Homer went to Ios, to stay with Creophylus. What qualities or creature comforts this Creophylus possessed that would make the bard travel to exactly the place where he had been warned that he would die must be left to the imagination. On the beach he met with some children who had been fishing. When he asked them if they had caught anything, they replied, 'All that we caught we left behind and we are carrying all that we did not catch.' Nonplussed, he asked for an explanation, and was rewarded with the information that they were talking about their fleas. Suddenly remembering the oracle and its dire warning about riddling kids, Homer composed his epitaph, and died three days later.

At least we have the texts; the 27,803 lines that are 'Homer'. But even these are susceptible to error. Despite the best efforts of the Homeridae, the texts were unstable, misremembered, interpolated. The librarians of Alexandria, Zenodotus, Aristophanes of Byzantium and Aristarchus, all later endeavoured to fix the text, to staunch the ebb of letters. The two poems were divided into books, each poem in twenty-four books, exactly the number of letters in the Greek alphabet. No other recorded epics had such an elegant numerology. Earlier, Aristotle himself prepared an edition for Alexander, who placed it in a jewel-encrusted golden casket despoiled from King Darius at the battle of Arbela, with the words: 'But one thing in the world is worthy of so costly a repository.' But opulent boxes cannot preserve, nor can locks and keys keep back, the depredations of error. Before any of these scholars tried to secure *The Iliad* and *The Odyssey*, less reverent hands had handled the manuscripts.

The sixth-century BCE Athenian tyrant Peisistratus was generally held to be an enlightened man, who reformed taxes and developed the Solonic legal systems. He was also a patron of the arts and the founder of the Dionysia festival; and he was concerned with establishing a standard text of the works of Homer. To this end, he employed a writer called Onomacritus, who undertook the task.

On the surface, Onomacritus seemed to be an ideal choice; he had, after all, already edited the poems and oracles of Musaeus. But, Herodotus informs us, there was a less professional side to the man. Lasus of Hermione, who is credited with teaching the lyric poet Pindar, had accused Onomacritus of misattribution, and even forgery, in his edition of Musaeus – brazenly importing his own words.

Onomacritus may have been acting under a direct political imperative to alter the text. Peisistratus had recently undertaken a military campaign and successfully captured the port of Salamis from the Megarans. After a halt in the offensive, the state of Sparta had agreed to arbitrate between Athens and Megara over the true ownership of Salamis, and the Athenians clinched their case by quoting Homer, specifically, verse 558 of Book II, which described Salamis as traditionally being an Athenian dominion. The Megarans, outraged, later accused the Athenians of a brazen fabrication.

So the preservation of the poems which occupy the apex of literary achievement in Europe was entrusted to someone of questionable integrity, on behalf of a tyrant with a vested interest about border disputes. Was Onomacritus so awed by his position that he carried out the work scrupulously? Or did the recidivist urge to tinker and tamper, meddle and fiddle get the better of him – did he *improve* the text? Is even part of Homer – the slightest line, the tiniest adjective – forged? The critic Zoilus was thrown over a cliff by irate Athenians who objected to his carping criticism of the divine Homer, his snags at odd words and niggles at images: would they have been so precipitate if he had questioned the phraseology of *Onomacritus*?

In addition to *The Iliad*, *The Odyssey*, scraps of *The Cypria* and the so-called *Homeric Hymns*, we learn of other epics composed by, or attributed to, Homer. In the pseudo-Herodotus' *Life of Homer*, we hear of a poem entitled *The Expedition of Amphiarus*, composed in a tanner's yard. *The Taking of Oechalia* was mentioned by Eustathius; it was given to Creophylus or was actually written by Creophylus. We have one line, which is, unfortunately, identical to line 343 of book XIV of *The Odyssey*. There was a *Thebais*, which recounted the fate of Oedipus and the Seven Champions' attack on Thebes. It was 7,000 lines long and began: 'Goddess, sing of parched Argos whence kings', as well as its sequel, *The Epigoni*, when the seven sons of the Seven Champions finish the job. Again, the poem was in 7,000 lines, and began: 'And now, Muses, let us begin to sing of men of later days'.

But most tantalizing of all is the *Margites*. In the fourth chapter of his *Art of Poetry*, Aristotle said:

Homer was the supreme poet in the serious style . . . he was the first to indicate the forms that comedy was to assume, for his *Margites* bears the same relationship to our comedies as his *Iliad* and *Odyssey* bear to our tragedies.

The *Margites*, it is claimed, was Homer's first work. He began it while still a schoolteacher in Colophon (according to the Colophonians). The name of the hero, Margites, derives from the Greek μαργοσ, meaning madman. The Poet's first work was a portrait of a fool.

Alexander Pope, who never quite got over not being Homer, explained further:

MARGITES was the name of this personage, whom Antiquity recordeth to have been *Dunce the First*; and surely from what we hear of him, not unworthy to be the root of so spreading a tree, and so numerous a posterity. The poem therefore celebrating him, was properly and absolutely a *Dunciad*; which tho' now unhappily lost, yet is its nature sufficiently known by the infallible tokens aforesaid. And thus it doth appear, that the first Dunciad was the first Epic poem, written by *Homer* himself, and anterior even to the Iliad and the Odyssey.

This was reason enough for Pope to produce his own *Dunciad*, from the Preface to which the above words are taken.

Can we tell from the title what the book was about? The definition of madness is never fixed, but fluid, shaped by its culture and dependent on what is considered sane, reasonable or self-evident. A rational, scientifically minded Greek of the fifth century BCE could maintain that when a woman had a nosebleed, it meant her menstruation had got lost, that the Sun gave birth to maggots in dung and that a tribe of one-eyed men called the Arimaspi lived in the extreme North. Madness encompasses murderous rage and inappropriate levity, fearfulness and fearlessness, silence and babble. The title could suggest just about anything.

All that is left of Homer's comic epic are a few lines, pickled in other works. The Scholiast, writing on Aeschines, gives a thumbnail sketch that fits with his etymologically unfortunate name: 'Margites . . . a man, who, though fully grown, did not know if his mother or father had given birth to him, and who would not sleep with his wife, saying he was afraid she would give a bad account of him to his mother'. At this point, *Margites* seems to coincide with Nietzsche's description of the comedy of cruelty, as *Schadenfreude*. We laugh, because we know we are superior to poor Margites, for whom the birds and the bees are mysteries.

Plato and Aristotle each record a snippet of the poem. From Plato's fragmentary *Alcibiades* we learn that 'he knew many things, but all badly'. This Margites is a quack, a clown, a halfwit. It is not his innocence in a chaotic world that forms the comedy, but the chaos of his half-baked theories and half-assed ideas. Aristotle, in the *Nicomachean Ethics*, offers a different hint: 'the gods taught him neither to dig nor to plough, nor any other skill; he failed in every craft'. Odd. Odd indeed. Aristotle's Margites is an idiot, he has no function, no social reason. He's a spare part, an appendix. A vague imputation of laziness hangs over this creature who is confused by the difference between spades and hoes.

Is this a naive Stan or a flustering Ollie? Was he the stooge, the kid from the sticks, the fish out of water, the innocent abroad or the country cousin? Zenobius presents, again, an illustration. 'The fox knows many a ruse, but the hedgehog's single trick beats them all,' a phrase also attributed to Archilochus. Is Margites the fox or the hedgehog? Nowhere in the extant extracts is there the sense that Margites is a cheat, a con or a wily individual. Zenobius suggests something else: the wise little man. Chaplin. Forrest Gump. Candide. The Good Soldier Schweik. Homer Simpson.

The *Margites* is not the only comic epic that existed. Arctinus of Miletus, the author of the lost *War of the Titans* and a continuation of *The Iliad*, may be the author of *The Cercopes*. The *Suda* records that:

these were two brothers living upon the earth who practised every kind of knavery. They were called Cercopes (or 'The Monkey-Men') because of their cunning doings: one of them was named Passalus and the other Acmon. Their mother, a daughter of Memnon, seeing their tricks, told them to keep clear of Black-bottom, that is, of Heracles. These Cercopes were sons of Theia and Ocean, and are said to have been turned to stone for trying to deceive Zeus. Liars and cheats, skilled in deeds irremediable, accomplished knaves. Far over the world they roamed deceiving men as they wandered continually.

This form of comedy seems subtly different from the *Margites*: this is a pair of rogues, a couple of tricksters. We know they came an inevitable cropper. A carved frieze depicts Herakles with the scallywags trussed up by their ankles, hanging upside down.

With *The Cecropes* the audience is permitted a double empathy: we can enjoy their shameless pranks and outrageous antics, as well as the satisfaction of seeing their eventual come-uppance. Where the sympathies lie with *Margites* is far less clear. The heroes of *The Iliad* and *The Odyssey* are far from perfect. Achilles is petulant and inhumane, Odysseus is untrustworthy and vengeful. But a flawed hero can nonetheless be a real hero – a flawed schmuck seems, frankly, unimaginable. What could we have learned if the *Margites* had been spared! Did the Greeks laugh at or with or in a wholly different preposition? Did they yearn, in a rebuke to their entrenched sophistication, for a fool who muddled through? Did they mock the afflicted or smirk at the affected?

Of all the lost books, the *Margites* is the least explicable, the most tantalizing. Its author was esteemed beyond measure. It was unique among his works. But perhaps – just perhaps – its loss should not be mourned too deeply. What is gone must be reinvented. In the absence of a comedy by the greatest poet of all time, successive generations have been free to imagine sarcastic, sentimental, whimsical, serious, gentle and black comedies, wit and smut, slapstick and riddle. An explosion of new forms may be worth one extinction.

Hesiod

(seventh century BCE)

Homer is only ever glimpsed in his work. At the opening of the *Theogony*, one of the two extant works attributed to the Boeotian poet Hesiod, the poet himself appears. Although the bulk of the poem is an elaborate catalogue of the genealogy of the gods, it opens with a scene describing how, on Mount Helicon, the Muses taught the shepherd Hesiod how to sing, swiftly shifting their address to the first-person poet. 'They gave me a staff of blooming laurel,' he says, and 'breathed a sacred voice' into him.

But scholars from the earliest days have wondered how much of the work attributed to Hesiod was actually written by him. Longinus was so offended by a line about the snot-nosed goddess Trouble that he thought fit to exonerate the actual Hesiod from being the author of the lost work from which the line came, the *Shield of Herakles*. Of the two poems we have, the *Theogony* and *Works and Days*, most contemporary scholars would like at least one to be by Hesiod.

So the appearance of Hesiod in the *Theogony* might be thought to clinch the case. But on grounds of style, diction and the fact that it is occasionally rather gauche and boring, translators and critics have been loath to believe it can be by the same author as *Works and Days*. Nonetheless, the Greeks thought they were written by one author, and we shall proceed as if Hesiod wrote both poems.

Works and Days is strikingly dissimilar to the *Theogony*. It begins with two origin myths that account for the state of mankind. Firstly, the reader is told about Pandora's Box, and the unleashing of manifold pains, cares and diseases on humanity. Then we learn about Zeus' fivefold attempts at creation: the Gold, Silver, Bronze, Heroic and Iron Races, of which, Hesiod gloomily informs us, he belongs to the ferrous species, and would rather have died sooner or not be born yet.

The later parts of the work offer agricultural maxims, interspersed with autobiographical asides, and the whole is cast as an epistle to his cheating brother Perses, who would do well to listen to some homespun advice. No one can argue with 'Wrap up warm to prevent gooseflesh' or 'Invite your friends, not your enemies, to dinner', though 'Don't piss facing the sun' and 'Never have sex after funerals' seem more peculiar prohibitions.

The writer of *Works and Days* is not some autodidact, spinning his gripes and saws into a more mnemonic form. He tells us he won a poetry competition at the funeral games for King Amphidamas, and placed the prize (a tripod) on Mount Helicon, where he first started to write, on returning home. In *Works and Days* Hesiod does not tell us the title of his award-winning entry, and, since such works as *The Precepts of Chiron*, *The Astronomy*, *The Marriage of Ceyx*, *Melampodia*, *Aegimius*, *Idaen Dactyls* and *The List of Heroines* have all proven vulnerable to the corrosion of passing time, at least one academic has made a virtue of necessity and argued that Hesiod must have been reciting the *Theogony*.

But against whom was he vying in this competition? At the beginning of *Works and Days*, when surveying the effects of the goddess Strife, Hesiod conjectures that there must be two goddesses; since some forms of striving, such as warfare, are pernicious, and others, such as the healthy competition between tradesmen, farmers and even poets, are wholly beneficial. The ancients took this as a cue to link Hesiod (whoever he was) with the only other great early poet, Homer (whoever he was).

Another poem, called *The Contest of Homer and Hesiod*, is sometimes ascribed to Hesiod, even though the version that we have dates from nearly a millennium later. In it, Homer trounces Hesiod in every bout, and at one point seems to exasperate him into speaking nonsense. In the final round, they each read from 'their' greatest works: *The Iliad* and *Works and Days*. The judges eventually give the victory (surprise, surprise! It's a tripod!) to Hesiod, since the man who praises peace is better than the man who glorifies war. Blatantly apocryphal and clearly anachronistic, it is still the story that would be most charming, if true.

The Yahwist, the Elohist, the Deuteronomist, the Priestly Author and the Redactor

(*c.* sixth century BCE)

The Bible is frequently described as a library rather than a book: it is also a mausoleum of writers, a vast graveyard of authors. Who wrote the Bible? The orthodox answer is, assuredly, God; but even the most inflexible traditionalist does not believe that the Infinite condescended to ink. Through prophecy, inspiration and occasionally blatant dictation, God speaks but Man writes. God does have books – in particular, one which He is inordinately fond of editing. As He says to Moses, 'Whoever hath sinned against me, him will I blot out of my book.' But the books of the Bible as we have them are by God by proxy at best.

With the books of prophecy, it seemed logical to assign them to the prophets themselves as nominal authors. We are exhorted to 'Hear the Word of the Lord', regurgitated through human agency, as in the case of Ezekiel, whom God forced to swallow a scroll containing His message. The prophets sometimes employed their God's method of production: Jeremiah entrusted the actual transcription of his prophecies, which threatened the impending Babylonian conquest, to Baruch, who had to make multiple copies since the King, Jehoiakim, kept on burning the offending prophecies.

Jeremiah raged against false prophets, who were predicting an opposite outcome. Naturally enough, when Babylon did conquer Israel, the words of the worthless prophets were lost, and the correct foretellings of Jeremiah acquired the authenticity of oracular revelation. The scribes who collected the prophets were not above sleight of hand in this matter: the Book of Isaiah collates the words of an eighth-century BCE prophet with the words of another, unknown prophet who lived two centuries after Isaiah's death. Hindsight makes exceptionally good foresight.

Then there are the five first books, the Pentateuch, which contain the laws given to Moses and the prehistorical origin of the world. Tradition ascribed these books to Moses himself, which seems unlikely, given that they also contain an account of Moses' death, and his burial by God, 'no man knows where'.

Though apologists and ideologues are keen to present the scriptural texts as a unity (the Gideon Bible, for example, refers to the authors from different eras and backgrounds who nonetheless 'perfectly agree on doctrine'), the Bible is riddled with snags and stray threads. In particular, we can investigate the books *in* the Bible, rather than the books *of* it. King Solomon, for example, 'spake three thousand proverbs: and his songs were a thousand and five'. There are 1,175 verses in the Book of Proverbs, and only one 'Song of Songs'. Even in cataloguing the accomplishments of the ruler, the Bible also reveals the extent to which his achievements are lost.

Likewise, we have no idea what became of the 'book in seven parts' commissioned by Joshua, which described the cities that would be divided amongst the Israelites. Nor do we have the Book of Jasher, cited twice, and which, presumably, contained material on King David's archery lessons and the stilling of the sun in the valley of Ajalon. The 'Book of the Battles of Yahweh', mentioned in the Book of Numbers, chapter 21, is likewise lost. Throughout the First and Second Book of Kings and the First and Second Book of Chronicles, the writer refers the reader to the 'Book of the Chronicles of the Kings of Israel' and the 'Book of the Chronicles of the Kings of Judah', neither of which invaluable resource has survived.

In the Apocrypha, we learn that the Book of the Maccabees is a summary of the more complete, five-volume work by Jason of Cyrene. The Apocrypha also contains an account of the creation of the scriptures. 'For thy law is burnt, therefore no man knoweth the things that are done of thee, or the works that shall begin,' complains Esdras, and in response God commands him to recite the 204 books containing the Law, which are transcribed by five scholars over a period of forty days. The final seventy, the 'Books of Mystery', are held back from the people: still, it leaves eighty-two whole volumes unaccounted for.

The Bible appears again in its own history. In the Second Book of Kings, King Josiah intends to reconsecrate and re-furbish the Temple in 621 BCE, after its desecration by the Baal-worshipping sons of Athaliah. Hilkiah, the High Priest, is told to reckon up the amount of silver they have; and, in doing so, stumbles on the long-lost Book of the Law. With Shaphan the Scribe, they show it to the young King, who rends his garments on hearing of what will happen to those who do not follow in the paths of righteousness. Saint Jerome and Saint John Chrysostom in the fourth century CE both identified this Book of the Law with the Book of Deuteronomy. Josiah instructs them to seek out Huldah the Prophetess, to explain the work in detail. She confirms that if the King rectifies the behaviour of the people, God's anger will be deflected. Though Joash is told that God will 'gather him into his grave in peace', the Second Book of Chronicles claims he is murdered by his people, suffering from great diseases, after a Syrian incursion. The whole story of Hilkiah, Shaphan and Huldah is omitted from Chronicles. It is not the only, or most bizarre, contradiction between the pseudo-historical accounts; compare, for example, 2 Samuel 24:1 ('And again the anger of the LORD was kindled against Israel, and he moved David against them to say, Go, number Israel and Judah') with 1 Chronicles 21:1 ('And Satan stood up against Israel, and provoked David to number Israel').

Though the epithet 'People of the Book' was conferred on all the followers of the first Abrahamic religions, it appears that in the histories and prophecies we are more likely to encounter lost books, burned manuscripts and secret scrolls. Then, in the nineteenth century, a shocking new perspective on the question 'Who wrote the Bible?' was found.

The so-called 'Documentary Hypothesis' is an exercise in pure stylistics. We may not be able to know the names of the biblical authors, but, as Jean Astruc first demonstrated in 1753, we can trace their signatures and idiosyncratic constructions throughout the individual books. In effect, the Bible's text can bring us back to its putative authors.

The theory stems from a cluster of inconsistencies in the Book of Genesis. At times, God is referred to as 'Yahweh', and at others, as 'Elohim'. Moreover, in chapters 1 and 2, the same event – the Creation of Adam and Eve – is narrated twice; at Genesis 1:26–7 and at Genesis 2:7, 21–3. In chapter 1, we are told 'God created man in his own image, in the image of God created he him; male and female created he them'. In chapter 2, we are told of Adam being fashioned out of dust and breath, and Eve from Adam's rib. There are further curious anomalies. In chapter 1, God makes the birds and sea-creatures on the fifth day, and the land animals on the sixth, prior to Adam. In chapter 2, verse 19, God creates animals *after* Adam.

The Documentary Hypothesis suggests that there were

originally two Books of Genesis, one by 'J' – the Yahwist, the writer who calls God 'Yahweh' – and another by 'E' – the Elohist, who refers to 'Elohim'. These 'ur-texts' were synthesized into one version, with both contradictory sections aspicked together. 'J', for example, is fond of puns: it is to him that the etymology of 'Adam', meaning red earth, belongs. 'J' also is keen to give explanations for how things came about and why names are attached to particular places. 'E' is altogether more cryptic, an older version, perhaps especially considering his name for God is unaccountably in the plural.

To 'J' and 'E' were added the Deuteronomist ('D') and the Priestly Author ('P'). 'D' had a clear ideological theology; that God punished Israel for its intransigence and for straying from the Law, and that the history of the Jewish people was a moral lesson in the consequences of disobedience. The Priestly Author was liturgist and ecclesiast, defining the ramification of the Law, the categories of clean and unclean, the role of the Levites and the authority of the Torah. 'D' understood the reasons for the Exile; 'P' reaffirmed the centrality of the Temple.

It's a neat quartet, and an attractive theory. Unfortunately, it is only a theory. As much as one can almost hallucinate the differing qualities of 'D', 'E', 'J' and 'P', they are virtual authors at best, makeshift theories of possible writers. All of them collapse, especially at the advance of the fifth single-letter function: enter 'R', the Redactor.

'R' was the genius who spliced together 'J' and 'E' to give us the Old Testament. Only, 'R' was never singular; 'R' is a veritable host of textual editors, a dynasty of tinkerers, eliders, alterers, correctors, amenders and tidiers. Redactor, from the Latin *redigere, redactum*, is one who brings back. In effect, their shaping and framing never did recapture an aboriginal lost text, but tessellated a heap of fragments. The sublime Isaiah – or all three different writers who were merged together under that name – is jemmied next to a satire on the attitude of prophets (the Book of Jonah); the earnest imprecations that the good man has never been seen without sustenance in the Book of Proverbs is countered by the sadistic, inexplicable punishment of the good man Job (although admittedly, he does get 14,000 sheep in compensation). As a theologian friend once said to me, in utter exasperation, 'It's all just redacted to buggery.'

A sepulchre of possible authors, a catafalque of contradictory texts: the Bible is a library, but one in ruins.

Sappho

(sixth century BCE)

The Greek lyrical poet Sappho of Lesbos furnishes us with the most extreme example of what happens when any author is read. An interpretation does not filter out versions of history to distil some inalienable truth; it duplicates the past into the present. Like science-fiction attempts to clone an extinct species, the ancient DNA is fused into a contemporary cell and fostered in some suitable matrix. The reader recreates the writer into his or her own world.

With an author like Sappho, most of whose nine books of poems have been lost, the very lack of a tangible text encourages her imaginative resurrection. Like a figure in a hall of mirrors, she is distorted, refracted, skewed and twisted by the reader's particular curvature. The bare bones of her biography are fleshed out with numerous myths, wishes and archetypes, as well as some outright oddities. According to the *Suda*, she invented the plectrum.

Some fragments of a play called *The Girl from Leukas*, by the comic playwright Menander, display one of the earliest and most persistent of the legends about Sappho: that she committed suicide by flinging herself from a cliff because of her unrequited love for a ferryman called Phaon.

Sappho had written poems in the persona of the deity of love, Aphrodite, lamenting being spurned by the beautiful Phaon. In a curious instance of back-reading, based on the presumption that a female poet firstly, could not impersonate, and secondly, was irredeemably solipsistic, the imagined words of the goddess of love became the autobiographical outpourings of Sappho herself. Another tradition asserted that her husband was called Cercylas of Andros, and this union persists in some encyclopedias, even though, since the name means 'Mr Cock from Mansville', it is most likely an invention of the comedians.

The Latin poet Ovid frequently recommended reading Sappho's poetry to those who would become adept at courtship (and told those seeking alleviation from romance to strenuously avoid her). She was the pinnacle of female accomplishment in poetry and, as such, is the only non-legendary heroine in his *Heroides* (although this may be a typically knowing wink). Ovid's Sappho, supposedly writing to Phaon, 'burns like Etna', and her songs will be known throughout the whole world. When Seneca satirized ludicrous speculations in his *Epistles to Lucilius*, he wryly typified such endeavours as being like trying to find the birthplace of Homer, or resolve whether or not Sappho was a prostitute. Nonetheless, the joke was taken seriously by subsequent scholars.

In the Renaissance, the blame for the disappearance of Sappho's poems was put on the church. Tatian, in the second century CE, had referred to her as an erotomaniac, and it seemed apposite that work which kindled the flames of love should itself be committed to the fire. At some point before the Fall of Constantinople, the actual poems were eradicated.

But Sappho herself continued to be a byword for the female poet. In the eighteenth century she was a bluestocking, presiding over a coterie of acolytes. In the nineteenth, Christina Rossetti imagined her 'living unloved, to die unknown/unwept, untended and alone', a neurotic, suffocated martyr.

The Modernists, such as Ezra Pound and H.D., made a virtue of necessity, and imitated the terse shards of what remained; and the postmodernists, not to be outdone, preferred the beauties of the blanks, gaps [. . .] and absences. Sappho was the laureate of the torn, the fissured and the cavity.

Despite this parade of projections, in *The Book of Lost Books*, Sappho could be considered one of the lucky ones.

⌣ / – ⌣ ⌣ – / ⌣ –
⌣ ⌣ / – ⌣ ⌣ – / – –

These scansion marks are practically the whole legacy of Telesilla of Argos. They represent the verse form, called the Telesillean, which she invented; a few scraps of her own verse survive, and a larger number of examples by male authors. She supposedly encouraged resistance to Spartan expansionism. Tatian informs us she was 'silly' and 'wrote nothing of worth'.

Myrtis of Boeotia, according to the *Suda*, was the tutor of the acclaimed poet Pindar, and another of her pupils, Corinna of Tangra, beat him in competitions, and rebuked him for adopting the Attic dialect. Neither has survived.

Praxilla of Sicyon, who wrote drinking songs; the 'female Homer' Amyte of Tegea; Nossis of Locri; Moero of Byzantium and Erinna have all been eradicated, with the exception of a few quotations and fifty-four lines of Erinna's poem *The Distaff*.

Perilla, whom Ovid thought second only to Sappho, has joined the mute muses of antiquity, along with most of the work of Sulpicia and the *Miscellaneous History* of Pamphila. Whether it was Plutarch or his wife Timoxena who wrote the book *On Cosmetics* does not matter, since it no longer exists.

Instead of an array of possible roles, from political activist to theoretician of practical beauty, we are left with Sappho, most famous, as the *Edinburgh Review* noted, for 'her love, her leap, her looks and her lyrics'. It is not an image without its pernicious, darker side; an insinuation that self-destruction is the natural corollary of female creativity. With Sappho: Letitia Landon, Constance Fenimore Woolson, Charlotte Mew, Virginia Woolf, Marina Tsvetaeva, Sylvia Plath, Anne Sexton, Sarah Kane.

K'ung Fu-tzu

(551–479 BCE)

'From the birth of mankind until now, there has been none to equal him.' So said Mencius, an early interpreter and one of the foremost followers of K'ung Fu-tzu, known in the West as Confucius. The historian Ssu-ma Ch'ien in the first century BCE claimed that ten generations had venerated Confucius, a commoner, while the memory of countless princes had vanished. The academic William Theodore de Barry in 1960 could likewise assert that 'if we were to characterise in one word the Chinese way of life for the last two thousand years, the word would be "Confucian".'

He is an endearingly unlikely revolutionary. Although countless fables have accreted to his name, we can safely say that he was born into a low-ranking family in the state of Lu, did not hold high office, travelled for a while and attracted disciples. After his peregrinations, he eventually returned home, and edited the 'Six Works': *The Book of Poetry*, *The Book of Rituals*, *The Book of Music*, *The Book of History*, *The Book of Changes* and *The Spring and Autumn Annals*. He did not claim a divine provenance for his pronouncements, nor did he justify his propositions from an investigation into first principles. His work is not a manifesto, nor a prophecy, nor a tractatus. The closest possible analogy is a curriculum. Knowledge of the so-called 'Confucian Classics' was central to the examination system, in which one's results determined one's place in the bureaucracy of China for 2,000 years.

At the centre of Confucius' vision is a concept which defines his difference from other epochal figures: *jen* or 'humaneness'. Translating concepts from Chinese is a perilous business, and various authors have suggested perfect virtue, magnanimity, altruism and goodness. Confucius, when asked about *jen* by his pupil Fan Ch'ih, defined it as 'to love others'. It connotes a virtue embedded in being human, which expands to encompass how one should behave towards others.

A closely aligned and similarly slippery concept is *li*. Originally, *li* meant 'correct ceremony', but again, the term enlarged to include the secular as well as the religious: somewhere between politeness and propriety, ritual and decorum, is *li*. Moreover, it was a fundamental aspect of good government. It was not merely a diplomatic stance, but a reflection of the smooth order between ruler and subject.

On another occasion, Confucius advanced a refinement on the inter-relation between these attributes. 'What has a man to do with the *li* if he lacks *jen*?' At the simplest level this is a clear indictment of hypocrisy. No amount of solemn observation of social niceties, civil responsibilities and religious etiquette can compensate for a hardened heart. But Confucius continues, linking *jen* to another concept. 'If a man is without *jen*, what has he to do with music?'

Music and *li* were paired in Confucius' teaching. As well as possessing wisdom, courage and self-control, the paradigmatic man would be refined by *li* and music. The man 'whose mind was already awakened by understanding the *Book of Poetry* would be established by *li* and perfected by music'. What this perfection would consist of, we cannot know, as the *Book of Music* is lost.

Throughout the *Lun yü* or *Analects*, there are, however, numerous instances that testify to the importance of music in the scheme of Confucius' thinking. On his travels, when Confucius heard the music of Shun, he did not eat meat for three months, saying, 'I never dreamed that the joys of music could reach such heights.' After he returned to his home state of Lu, he set about reforming its music. An apocryphal story from the *Shih chi* of Ssu-ma Ch'ien claims that, as a young man, Confucius studied a piece of music with the Master Hsiang. He worked so assiduously that he could see the composer in his mind's eye, and startled the Master by declaring (correctly) that the piece was written by King Wen, the so-called Cultured King.

Moreover, twice in the *Analects*, Confucius draws attention to the deleterious effects that improper music could have. The tunes from the state of Cheng were wanton, and comparable to specious orators. They had corrupted classical music, like the debased mixed colour of purple that was replacing the pure colour of vermilion, or like the self-interested and ambitiously clever men that treacherously deposed noble families.

Music, good government, humaneness and ritual were all part of a seamless vision of an ordered universe. As Ssu-ma Ch'ien said, all of the six books help to govern: '*The Book of Rites* helps regulate men, *The Book of Music* brings about harmony, *The Book of History* records incidents, *The Book of Poetry* expresses emotions, *The Book of Changes* reveals supernatural influences and *The Spring and Autumn Annals* show what is right.' Confucius' reforms of music sought to restore the pentatonic balances, stripping away innovation and mere decoration. Corrupted music could infect the whole universe with discord. Confucius clearly believed there was a political benefit to be gleaned from cultural *savoir-faire*: he berated the official who knew the 300 odes in the *Book of Poetry* by heart, but could not use them strategically when sent to foreign states.

★

Given its importance, it seems surprising that *The Book of Music* was lost. What is more surprising is that any of Confucius at all survived.

By 221 BCE, King Cheng, the overlord of a semi-barbarous state known as Ch'in, finally conquered the remaining states of Chao, Yen, Ch'i, Ch'u and Han (Lu, alongside many others, having been incorporated during the 'Warring States' period). Under the name of August First Emperor Shih-huang-ti, he set about turning the disparate states into an empire.

He was assisted in this by his chancellor, Li Ssu, the theoretical architect behind the military might of the Emperor. Li Ssu belonged to a school of thought known as Legalism, which was fundamentally opposed to much of Confucian thought.

For example, Confucius' ideal ruler led by being a moral exemplar to the people: his virtue would affect the populace in much the same way as grass could not help but be bent by the wind. Legalism had a very different approach to the business of governance. The Emperor's key function was punishment and reward; he made examples of the people.

Whilst Shih-huang-ti became increasingly reliant on alchemists, searched for an elixir of eternal life and commissioned his elaborate mausoleum, Li Ssu resolved to do something about 'the men of letters who do not model themselves on the present, but study the past in order to criticize the present'. In tandem with Shih-huang-ti's megalomaniac ambition to ensure that history would begin with his reign, the consequences were inevitable.

The result was the Burning of the Books, when the Chinese bureaucracy turned destructively against itself. Except for a single copy of each work, to be stored in the Emperor's personal library, Li Ssu initiated a purge. It was a crime to harbour books, and town squares were soon choked with the smoke of massive pyres. People heard discussing books were publicly executed, along with their immediate family. Officials who did not implement the new rules were punished in the same manner as the offenders. Two hundred and sixty Confucian scholars were buried, alive, in a mass grave, in order to prevent them reconstructing the classics from memory.

The First Emperor died in 210 BCE. Li Ssu and the chief eunuch, Chao Kao, conspired to destroy the Emperor's decree that his eldest son should succeed to the throne, replacing the order with one in favour of the more pliable Hu-hai. Chao Kao then eliminated Li Ssu, forced Hu-hai to commit suicide (after slowly driving him mad with elaborate deceptions), and declared a grandson of Shih-huang-ti to be Emperor. New internecine conflicts broke out, which ended with a former police officer establishing the Han dynasty.

The Han, however, were keen to curb the worst excesses of Legalism and encouraged a resurgence in the Confucian system. Scholars re-edited, and occasionally even rewrote, the five remaining Classics. *The Book of Music* was lost entirely during the Burning. Eventually, in 175 BCE, a decree was issued that the surviving texts, which for nearly half a century had persisted in the hearts and minds of men, should be engraved on stone.

Aeschylus

(c.525–456 BCE)

Ptolemy III (247–222 BCE) had a lot to live up to. His grandfather, Ptolemy I, had accompanied Alexander the Great on his campaigns and, on the conqueror's death, acquired the government of Egypt. There he had constructed a new wonder of the world: the Alexandrian Library. The repository grew out of Aristotle's personal library. In addition, Ptolemy I brought such scholars as Euclid the Geometer and the grammarian Zenodotus to create the most distinguished academy of literary, historical, philosophical, mathematical and astronomical knowledge in the known world. The Preserver's son, Ptolemy II, secured and expanded the Library. According to tradition, to satisfy his desire that the Library should be the most complete as well as the most prestigious, he employed seventy Jewish scholars to translate the Hebrew Scriptures into Greek. Such endeavours require peace, and Ptolemy II brokered a treaty with the Romans and forged a dynastic alliance with the erstwhile enemy of the Egyptians, Antiochus II of Syria, by giving his daughter Berenice in marriage.

So, in time, Ptolemy III inherited a legacy of military security and intellectual esteem, along with the urge to out-do his ancestors and further extend the glory of Egypt. As luck would have it, Antiochus II callously divorced and poisoned Berenice as soon as Ptolemy II died, and Ptolemy III waged a war of vengeance, subduing Asia from Mesopotamia to Babylon and recapturing statues of deities stolen throughout the wars between Egypt and Persia. He conquered deep into the south, as far as Ethiopia, and developed a powerful maritime fleet. The garlands of victory were all very well, no doubt, but his predecessors were praised as men of letters as well as heroic conquerors. Ptolemy III turned his attentions to the Library.

Cataloguing the Library's 200,000 scrolls began in earnest, and an anomaly of unthinkable proportions was discovered. Pharaoh had no Aeschylus. That the 'Cage of the Muses', as some referred to the Library, lacked a complete text of the most revered Athenian dramatist seemed an unforgivable oversight. Obtaining it would provide the perfect demonstration that Ptolemy III had accomplished what Ptolemy II and Ptolemy I had failed to do. Alexandria would have its Aeschylus.

The Athenians had the only copy of *The Complete Works of Aeschylus* in existence. After, one assumes, protracted negotiations, it was agreed that these revered scrolls might be transported to Alexandria for scholars to make an accurate copy, and then returned to Athens. To ensure that this agreement was honoured, Ptolemy III would deposit fifteen silver talents with the Athenians, repayable when the text was brought back intact. This was a phenomenal amount of money: the entire annual Jewish tribute payment amounted to only twenty silver talents, and that had driven them close to rebellion. Following the agreement, the manuscript arrived in Alexandria.

Did the idea arise in Ptolemy's own mind? Did a librarian impress upon his Pharaoh exactly what they had? This was the sole complete copy of Aeschylus in existence. It was a unicum, a non-pareil, a one and only. It was the Golden

Fleece, it was Helen of Troy's wedding ring, it was the ball of string that Theseus unravelled in the Labyrinth. It was worth losing fifteen silver talents. How could the Athenians protest against the Vanquisher of Syria?

The scripts stayed in Alexandria, with a strict injunction that no copy should ever be made. And then Ptolemy III died. Later, Ptolemy XIII died. Finally, the Empire died. Their religion died. But the original manuscript remained: it, and its singularity, preserved. Since its transcription was forbidden, scholars flocked from around the known world and from every intellectual background to read it: Plotinus the Neo-Platonist, Clement of Alexandria, Diodorus of Sicily, Nepotian of Africa, even Ælian, who notoriously hated travel. Some came to marvel at the poetic majesty; others came to ponder whether, in a line from *Prometheus Bound*, 'Nothing will make me reveal the name of the God to come who is greater than Zeus', Aeschylus had had an out-of-time inkling of Christianity. None of them quibbled with the centuries-old piece of self-important petulance that kept the manuscript there.

On 22 December 640 CE, a reader with a very different agenda was in control of Alexandria. His aesthetics were strict: 'Those which disagree with the Word of God are blasphemous, those which agree, superfluous.' Amrou Ibn el-Ass, on direct orders from the Caliph, decreed that the Library be burned. The scrolls opened a final time, unfurled before the unscholarly eyes of flame, and *The Complete Works of Aeschylus* became lost for ever.

One of the more astonishing examples of acquired behaviour in the animal kingdom occurs in the eagles of south-east Europe. As documented by the ornithologist Grubač, these birds have not only adapted to their habitat, but also make active use of their environment. One of the primary sources of nutrition in harsh, rocky climates, along with hedgehogs, Boback marmosets and large-toothed Susliks, is the tortoise.

The eagles have been observed, gliding at low altitude, to drop suddenly into a plunging attack, and curl their talons around the rim of the tortoise's shell. They then soar to upwards of 100 metres, and drop their catch on to round, exposed stones in order to split the shell. With the protective armour of its quarry shattered, the eagle can then eviscerate its prey with relative ease.

Just such an incident occurred in 456 BCE, outside the city of Gela, on the island of Sicily. The eagle would have glimpsed its prey and swooped. Still scanning the terrain, it located a suitable rock on which to crack the casing. As the bird's claws withdrew, the tortoise would have briefly experienced a hitherto-unimaginable sense of acceleration, before being splintered and mangled. One variable, however, turned this instance of sophisticated predation into a much more remarkable occasion. It was no rock that the tortoise hurtled towards, but the bald head of an elderly Greek named Aeschylus. He was killed outright. History does not record the fate of the tortoise.

Luckily, Aeschylus had already written his epitaph. Like most Greeks of his age, he was proud of his status as a 'Marathonomachos', a veteran of the battle in 490 BCE where the Athenians repelled the Persian king Darius' invasion.

> This tomb the dust of Aeschylus doth hide,
> Euphorion's son and fruitful Gela's pride,
> How tried his valour, Marathon may tell,
> And long-haired Medes, who got the point full well.

He failed, however, to mention he was also the most revered playwright of his age, and that he had single-handedly transformed the nature of drama.

Aeschylus was born around 525 BCE near Eleusis, a site sacred to the goddess Demeter, to which pilgrims would travel to be initiated into her cult, known as the Mysteries. As a counterbalance to the shrouded secrecy of the chthonian rites at Eleusis, Peisistratus, the relatively enlightened tyrant of Athens, had established forms of public worship, including an annual dramatic festival, sacred to Dionysus and performed in the heart of the city. By the time of Aeschylus, the Dionysian festival had mutated into a theatrical competition, and though to an extent it had become secularized, it was nonetheless rooted in religious significance.

According to the geographer Pausanius, Aeschylus had been commanded to become a writer by the god Dionysus. Apparently, on one occasion, the young dramaturge had been given the rather bemusing task of keeping an eye on some ripening grapes. As might be expected, he nodded off, and the wine god-cum-careers adviser appeared in a dream to inform him of his new vocation. The next day he wrote a tragedy, with, so Pausanius claims, remarkable ease. His first plays were performed in the 480s; by 484, he had been awarded first place in the dramatic competition.

In Aristophanes' play *The Frogs*, the irreverent satirist presents a debate in the Underworld between Aeschylus and the younger playwright Euripides. Although one must allow for a degree of caricature, and given that Aristophanes was born after Aeschylus had died, it still provides a glimpse into what was perceived to be his personality. He was irascible and conservative, a staunch believer in the power of drama to inspire military glory and civic duty. In contrast to Euripides, Aeschylus was the laureate of masculine heroism rather than feminine psychopathy. Some mocked his language for being grandiloquent, high-falutin' and abounding in such recondite concatenations as 'hippococks' and 'goatstags'. To others, Aeschylus' style was rugged yet ornate, chiselled with gravitas.

In his lifetime, Aeschylus wrote over eighty plays. Only seven have survived, with copious fragments either persisting on papyrus or preserved in commentaries. The anonymous, though not conspicuously unreliable, *Life of Aeschylus* makes clear his significance:

Whoever thinks that Sophocles was the more effective composer of tragedies, thinks correctly, but let him consider how much more difficult it was in the time of Thespis, Choerilus and Phrynicus to bring tragedy up to such a level of greatness than it was for one entering the scene at the time of Aeschylus to bring it to the perfection of a Sophocles.

Before Aeschylus, drama had been more akin to a quasi-liturgical recitation or an oratorio. Thespis, according to Plutarch, was the first to add a *hypokrites*, an actor impersonating a character, who stood on a raised platform above the orchestra, where the Chorus would dance and sing hymns. Drama began when Thespis stood apart from the Chorus and announced, 'I am the God Dionysus.'

The next development has been documented in the lost works of Phrynicus. Here, the solo actor would play a number of different roles, though the action was still predominantly performed through soliloquy. The major innovation introduced by Aeschylus was the presence of a second actor. The effect of this cannot be underestimated: monologue became dialogue, and with it the possibility for dramatic conflict, argument, irony and reconciliation arose. It is for this reason Aeschylus is called the father of modern drama.

Aeschylus was also acclaimed as an innovator in his addition of elaborate stage machinery and painted effects. His actors were decked out in flowing robes, raised buskin shoes and more ornate masks. He changed the role of the Chorus from passive commentators to integral participants in the drama, and, although his capacity for innovation may have waned, his willingness to respond to new theatrical practices did not. Sophocles introduced a third actor on to the stage, and in Aeschylus' final, most acclaimed work, *The Oresteia*, he used this new triangle of players rather than the former limitation to protagonist and antagonist.

For all his radical advances, Aeschylus owed a debt to his predecessors. No genius emerges *ex nihilo*, and it is possible to discern the hints of influence from Phrynicus on his development. Phrynicus wrote works set in the sphere of contemporary history: one example, *The Capture of Miletus*, apparently so distressed the Athenians, and needled their sense of shame for allowing the Persian destruction of that city, that it was forbidden to be restaged, all copies were destroyed and Phrynicus was fined. Out of pocket but unbowed in principle, he went on to write another, *The Women of Pleuron*, and another, *The Persians*.

Only one line of Phrynicus' *The Persians* remains. Aeschylus used exactly the same opening line for his identically titled play – 'Behold, most of the Persians have already set forth for Greece!' – yet the play that follows goes on to become his own. Aeschylus' experience at Marathon and Salamis added telling details, such as the bodies of the drowned Medes held afloat by their oriental robes.

At the first performance of Aeschylus' *The Persians*, the role of Chorus leader was taken by Pericles, the aspiring democrat who would rise to govern Athens at the height of its cultural, political and military significance. Pericles and Aeschylus were both aware that Themistocles, the victorious and aristocratic general at Marathon, had taken the role of Chorus leader for Phrynicus' *The Persians*. The play may not have been conceived as agitprop: that did not prevent it being deployed for political ends. Throughout Aeschylus' career there is a creative tension between myth and contemporary relevance.

Aeschylus was invited by the tyrant Hieron, ruler of Sicily and one of the few leaders whose military capability and cultural clout could rival that of Athens, to produce *The Persians* in Sicily in 471 BCE. It was not the playwright's first visit to the court. Five years previously, he had moved there, furious at having been defeated by the young Sophocles. On that occasion, he wrote *The Women of Etna*, now lost, to commemorate Hieron's construction of a new city. A description of Mount Etna's eruption may have acted as a source for the conclusion of *Prometheus Bound*, where 'dust dances in a whirling fountain' and 'fiery lightning twists and flashes'. Hieron wished to be remembered as a patron of the arts, and cultivated men of genius. It was under his despotic rule, rather than in democratic Athens, that Aeschylus chose to live out his retirement, after the success of his masterpiece, *The Oresteia*.

At the dramatic festival, each playwright presented four plays: a trilogy followed by a satyr play. The trilogy originally described three linked aspects of a single myth: for example, Aeschylus' earliest surviving work, *The Suppliants*, concerned the fifty daughters of King Danaus, who plead for sanctuary with King Pelasgus of Argos, to avoid an enforced marriage to the fifty sons of Aegyptus. It was followed by the lost *The Egyptians* and *The Danaids*, which presumably described how they relented, how their father then plotted that each daughter should kill her husband on the wedding night, and how one, Hypermestra, refused. A long speech by Aphrodite, goddess of Love, survives from *The Danaids*.

Prometheus Bound represents more of a problem. It was followed, naturally enough, by *Prometheus Unbound*. The third part, all sources concur, was entitled *Prometheus the Fire-bringer*. This is odd, since it is the theft of fire from Zeus that precipitated the original binding. Despite the profusion of Christian scholars unpicking the pagan premonition of Christ in *Prometheus Bound*, none of them record how the trilogy ended. The answer to the conundrum may never be known, the crucial evidence atomized in the Egyptian sand.

The satyr plays which concluded the trilogy were farcical dramas about serious themes, with a chorus of goat-legged satyrs led by their master Silenus. One example, the *Cyclops* of Euripides, remains, with sufficient fragments of Sophocles' *The*

Trackers for it to be reconstructed. Aeschylus was acclaimed as the master of the satyr play, and yet not one of his has escaped the insistent erosion of time. A smattering of lines – 'The house is possessed by the God, the walls dance to Dionysus', 'he who hurt shall heal', 'Whence comes this woman-thing?' – are all that are left. We do not even have the *Proteus*, the satyr play that completed *The Oresteia*, except for the decidedly uncomical lines 'a wretched, struggling dove looking for food, is crushed by winnowing rakes, its breast torn open'.

Aeschylus' sole complete trilogy is *The Oresteia*, comprising *Agamemnon*, *The Libation-Bearers* and *The Eumenides*. In the first play, Agamemnon returns home from the Trojan War, only to be murdered by his wife as punishment for sacrificing their daughter Iphigenia. Agamemnon's son, Orestes, is then faced with a moral dilemma: he has to avenge his father's death, but to do so must commit the heinous crime of matricide. When he does, the insoluble problem unleashes the Furies, and the second play ends with Orestes hallucinating their approach, 'shrouded in black, their heads wreathed, swarming with serpents'.

The Eumenides opens with those Furies now visible to the audience as the Chorus. This scene was so indescribably shocking that various members of the first audience miscarried, went mad or ran out of the amphitheatre. The goddess Athena intervenes in the action on stage to rebalance the moral equation. She institutes the first murder trial for Orestes on a hill called the Areopagus; the location, for the Athenian audience, of their court. Athena's casting vote sets him free and transforms the vindictive Furies into beneficent Kindly Ones, or Eumenides.

The Oresteia moves from a chain-reaction of revenge to a society determined to implement justice through reason, from savagery to civilization. The mythological subject-matter is again replete with political resonance. The trilogy was staged in Athens in 458 BCE, when Pericles had become the leader of the democratic faction and was regarded as the major statesman of the period. The Areopagus had changed since the acquittal of Orestes, and become more of a legislative body for the aristocratic faction rather than merely a criminal court. Pericles had, therefore, taken steps to limit its authority, restricting it to murder trials.

Later critics have sought to argue that *The Oresteia* presents a patrician critique of Pericles: the Areopagus is divinely ordained and is central to Athens' role as the paragon of civic virtue and enlightened behaviour. Others have argued that Aeschylus is reminding Athenians of the original function of the Areopagus, and is thus tacitly supporting Pericles' reforms. Whatever our interpretation, Aristophanes tells us that Aeschylus had a rather combative and critical relationship with his fellow citizens.

The enigmatic Eleusinian Mysteries of his birthplace offer a different reason for the bad blood between Aeschylus and the Athenians. From Ælian and Clement of Alexandria we learn that he was charged with revealing the Mysteries on the stage. At some point – aggravatingly, the sources do not record which, exactly – the audience was so enraged by the blatant infraction that Aeschylus was nearly murdered on stage and had to seek refuge in the temple of his one-time mentor, Dionysus. Sicily may have been altogether safer for someone who had, in Aristotle's words, 'spoken those things of which it is impious to tell'.

What secrets had he let slip? The Eleusinian Mysteries, supposedly, promised an afterlife. Homer had depicted the listless wasting-away that awaited even the heroic dead: the Mysteries offered an alternative. Just as Demeter had rescued her daughter Persephone from the Underworld, an initiate would not be trapped with the melancholic wraiths in the kingdom of Hades, but reach a paradisiacal place called the Elysian Fields. In *The Frogs*, Aeschylus boasts that although he is indeed confined to Hades, his name lives on in his work:

of all the playwrights, only his plays are still staged after his death. Did the idea of literary immortality make him lax or dismissive about the orthodox paths to Eternal Life? Poets have always claimed that their work guarantees a kind of immortality. Aeschylus may have taken this boast more literally than the religious arbiters of his day thought fit.

Aeschylus did not know that his artistic canonization only occurred by the narrowest of margins. He had been warned in a prophecy that his own death would come by a blow from heaven, and, one presumes, made sure he did not sit under trees in Sicily's countryside, and run the risk of the appointed lightning bolt suddenly striking home. He probably even enjoyed the sunshine on his wrinkled, hairless head, musing about dear old Phrynicus; the excellence of Homer; Orpheus; who made the first lyre from a tortoise shell; and how he would be remembered.

He was not cremated – the epitaph tells us as much. But could he imagine that *The Priestesses, Bassarides, Phineus, The Carding Women, The Sphinx, Europa, Hypsipyle, Niobe, Nereids, Oedipus, Laius, The Archer Maidens, Semele, The Nurses of Dionysus, Lycurgus, Atalanta, Nemea, The Award of the Arms, Mysians, Myrmidons, Sisyphus Rolling the Stone, Sisyphus the Runaway, The Net Drawers, The Bacchae, The Kabeiroi* (or *Drunken Heroes*), *Palamedes, Penelope, Pentheus, Perseus, Philoctetes, Phorcides, Psychostasia* and *Polydectes, The Young Men* and *Glaucus of the Sea, The Women of Salamis* and *The Women of Thrace* and many, many others would end as ash?

Aeschylus may have suspected his works deserved pride of place in a magnificent library. He knew enough about war to know temples were looted and palaces despoiled. He was acquainted with the whim of tyrants, and their penchant for surrounding themselves with genius. But no one could predict that the sole copy of his plays would become a casualty in a religious war between two theologies a thousand years in the future.

Sophocles

(495–406 BCE)

The Greeks venerated Aeschylus and were challenged by Euripides: Sophocles, however, they loved. Even the rebarbative Aristophanes, in his lit-crit comedy *The Frogs*, gave a heartfelt tribute to the recently deceased playwright, saying that 'Sophocles is getting on with everyone in Hades just as he did on earth.' Another comedian, Eupolis, eulogized him as 'the happiest of men'.

Born in 495 BCE in the provincial town of Colonus, Sophocles first comes to attention in 480, when he was chosen to sing, play the lyre and, on account of his beauty, lead the victory procession naked, to commemorate the Greek defeat of Xerxes at Salamis. At the age of twenty-seven, he won his first dramatic victory against the renowned Aeschylus, who left Athens, mortified at the result. The decision was taken by Cimon, the military leader who had recently returned from Scyros with the bones of the legendary King Theseus. In an unexpected departure from normal procedure, the Archon insisted that Cimon and his nine officers be appointed as the arbiters of the dramatic festival. Such a break with tradition was mirrored in the sudden toppling of the pre-eminent Aeschylus by the fledgling Sophocles.

Sophocles went on to write 120 plays, and was only ever awarded first or second prize in the festivals. Of these, only seven survive, with substantial fragments from one of his satyr plays, *The Trackers*. He was a close friend of Pericles. Like Pericles, Sophocles had a foreign mistress, Theoris, as well as an Athenian wife. His legitimate son, Iophron, was apparently infuriated by his father's favouritism towards Sophocles the Younger, his grandson through Theoris' child. The family feud ended in court, with Iophron claiming his father was senile. The ninety-year-old Sophocles read from his as yet unperformed *Oedipus at Colonus*: the judges summarily dismissed the case and punished Iophron for his unfilial behaviour. It was perhaps at the same time that Sophocles made the pronouncement attributed to him by Plato: 'I bless old age for releasing me from the tyranny of my appetites.'

We do not have in Sophocles' seven plays an intact trilogy, as we do with Aeschylus' *Oresteia*. Although *Oedipus Rex*, *Oedipus at Colonus* and *Antigone* all deal with the ramifications of a single story, they were written at different times of his life, and were originally linked to other plays. Aristophanes mentions a play called *Tereus*, of which Aeschylus' nephew Philocles wrote a derivative imitation. There is the lost *Orithyia*, a single line of which survives. Longinus, in his essay on literary style *On the Sublime*, favourably compared the death of Oedipus with the ghostly appearance of Achilles at the end of the lost *Polyxena*. (The scene was apparently only bettered in a poem by Simonides, which is lost as well.) There was an *Athamas*, about a father who vowed to sacrifice his children, and was himself nearly sacrificed when they escaped, and a *Meleager*, which may have dealt with the prophecy that the hero's life would last only as long as a burning branch. His mother, after having preserved and treasured the charred wood, destroys it in a vengeful fury.

Our knowledge of Greek dramaturgy would no doubt be greatly enhanced if Sophocles' essay *On the Chorus* had survived. As it is, all we know is that he increased the Chorus from twelve to fifteen, and that they acted as a substitute audience, rather than as a character (as in Aeschylus) or as an interlude (as in Euripides). Sophocles also wrote a paean on the god of medicine, Asclepius, and was known to be such a devout adherent of that divinity that the statue of Asclepius was left in his safekeeping. This too has perished.

Given that he was so successful, and so well loved by the Athenians, it may seem mysterious that more of Sophocles' plays, let alone his prose or his poems, have not survived. One possible reason may be that of the plays that did, one was considered perfect. Only the best was saved.

Coleridge wrote that *Oedipus Rex*, along with Jonson's *The Alchemist* and Henry Fielding's *Tom Jones*, were the three perfect plots in existence. A similar opinion was held by Aristotle, who frequently used *Oedipus Rex* as an exemplar in his treatise *The Poetics*. When discussing the importance of the epiphany and peripeteia, or revelation and reversal, or when expounding on the role of fear and pity, it is to the *Oedipus Rex* that Artistotle instinctively refers. Longinus, too, quotes approvingly from the play.

Despite the fact that other writers have given variations on the story of the unwittingly incestuous king and his rash promise to bring justice to the person whose sin is tainting the city, Sophocles' version remains *the* Oedipus. To what can the enduring fascination be attributed? In literary terms, one might point to the extreme economy of the plot; the embedded irony that the villain is revealed to be the hero. Even the protagonist's name is slick with double meaning: the Greek *oida* means 'I know'; and yet the King is in the dark until the denouement, when he blinds himself. The play raises, without answering, profound questions about fate and free will. Oedipus cannot avert his destiny, nor can he merely submit to his doom.

Sigmund Freud, of course, famously claimed that there was

something about the play that 'a voice within us [is] ready to recognize', namely the repressed incest-urges of the subconscious. But, as Robert Graves wittily observed, though Plutarch mentions that the hippopotamus is unique in the animal kingdom for murdering its father and impregnating its mother, Freud did not call his theory the hippo complex. *Oedipus Rex* is more than its story.

Though critics can cavil about the unfeasibility of the various messengers adhering to the drama's unity of time, it is very close to perfection. If we had any number of Sophocles' other, lost, dramas, the preponderance of second-bests and inferior offerings might make him less, not more, respected. As Longinus said, 'Yet would anyone in their right mind put all of Ion of Chios' tragedies on the same footing as the single play of *Oedipus*?'

Euripides

(480–406 BCE)

At the time of the battle of Salamis, Aeschylus was fighting, Sophocles was preparing to sing in the victory procession and Euripides was being born, or so the legend goes. Most biographical details about the third member of classical Greek drama's mighty triumvirate have to be taken with a pinch of salt. Take, for example, the *Life and Race of Euripides* by one Satyrus. This work was thought to be lost, and our only traces of it were contained in commentaries, lexicons and other authors, until a near-complete papyrus from Oxyrhyncus was pieced together in 1911. Until then, it would have been acceptable for any critic to quote these marginalia without too much worry about the source.

Amongst the titbits we learn in the intact work, about Euripides' mother being a vegetable seller and his often stormy relationship with his wife, we also learn that at one point the women of Athens became so frustrated with Euripides' supposedly misogynistic depiction of heroines that they convened a meeting to decide upon his punishment. Euripides persuaded his father-in-law, Mnelisochus, to attend the assembly, disguised as a woman, to learn what they were scheming. On the surface, an amusing, if improbable, anecdote, until we remember that this is exactly the plot of Aristophanes' comedy the *Thesmophoriazusae*. The name 'Satyrus' may well indicate we should not take the text too seriously.

Though Aristophanes put Euripides on stage at least twice, and peppered his own plays with parodic versions of *Melanippe the Wise*, *Stheneboea*, *Oeneus* and other plays now known only through their travesty, some writers thought the two men more similar than divergent. Cratinus slated an aspiring poet character in one of his plays as 'a hair-splitting master of niceties, a regular Euripidaristophanist'. They moved in the same intellectual circles. Both Aristophanes and Euripides grew up during Athens' cultural and political heyday, and became opposed to its increasingly imperial policies as the war in the Peloponnese lingered and festered.

Aristophanes' criticisms of Euripides' plays exaggerate, but they do not invent. Euripides had shocked his audience by showing kings dressed as beggars, in the lost *Telephus*, for example. The *Bellerophon* had another ruler reduced to ignominious circumstances, and – well, so says Aristophanes – scandalized the audience so much that every decent member swallowed poison immediately afterwards. Sophocles said that he showed men as they ought to be, but Euripides showed them as they are. In the short term, this 'realism' was no doubt considered a defect; in time, it becomes a virtue. Euripides also showed women, for the first time, as intelligent, vengeful, complex beings. His *Medea* still stuns, with the murderous foreigner rising like a goddess at the end, and no doubt, the *Daughters of Pelias*, *Cretan Women* and *Alcmaeon in Psophis* would too, if they still existed. Most controversially, Euripides used the drama as a vehicle for philosophical speculation.

The young Euripides was taught by Anaxagoras, the adviser to Pericles and a natural scientist of intense perceptiveness; for example, he conjectured that the sun was not a god, but a mass of burning stone, 'several times the size of the Peloponnesian peninsula', and that the moon reflected light from the sun. Euripides was also well acquainted with the sophist Protagoras, who read his work *On the Gods* in Euripides' house. It opens: 'About the Gods, I have no means of knowing whether they exist or not, since there are many obstacles to knowledge, the subject is obscure and man's life is short.' An echo of the sentiment can be heard in a line from Euripides' *Orestes*: 'We are the slaves of the gods, whatever gods may be.' Both men were accused of impiety, and *On the Gods* was ordered to be burned, though the *Orestes* survived. Both ended their lives in exile from the increasingly intolerant Athens. According to Philodemus, when Euripides left Athens it was to the malicious celebrations of the citizens.

It is therefore ironic that more plays survive by Euripides than by Sophocles and Aeschylus put together: eighteen, including our only complete satyr play, out of over ninety. Even more surprising is the survival of plays which openly attack the Athenian policy. In the 430s and 420s, he wrote plays which honoured the mythical founder of Athens, Theseus; nonetheless, the *Aegeus*, the *Theseus* and the *Erechtheus* are all no more. In 420, Euripides wrote the Olympic Victory Ode for Alcibiades. At the time, Alcibiades was beginning to display the venality, vanity and self-seeking impulses which would lead him to turn traitor, then return as a once-again victorious general. Beautiful, arrogant, beloved by Socrates, and riddled with contradiction, Alcibiades organized for the Spartans to be banned from attending the games, in part to bolster his own chances of success.

Euripides' attitudes changed profoundly in 416 BCE, when Athens forcibly colonized the island of Melos. The city once hailed as the 'Saviour of Hellas' was now murdering the indigenous inhabitants of a minor island, and selling their women and children into slavery. When Euripides' *The Trojan Women* was staged, few could have been in doubt that it contained a political subtext, given that it showed a grandmother holding the corpse of a murdered grandchild, executed because he might one day, hypothetically, develop into a threat. In case we are in any doubt, the opening chorus rings out, 'Such is the handiwork of Athena, daughter of Zeus.' The one-time propagandist of the state had become its implacable conscience. We have lost much of Euripides; though, on balance, it may be preferable to have lost his panegyrics and not his protest plays.

'Have all the nations of the world since his time created a dramatist worthy to hand him his slippers?' opined Goethe. Euripides was a patriot betrayed by his country, who combined traditional stories with the most advanced investigation into what it meant to be human and ethical. He was caricatured as a misanthropist, gynophobe and blasphemer because he dared to look at the complexity of the world. Goethe's question applies as much to his person as to his art.

Agathon

(*c*.457–*c*.402 BCE)

At the close of the fifth century BCE, King Archelaus of Macedonia was gradually realizing his ambitions to transform the northern Greek kingdom into something more substantial than a semi-barbarous satellite state. He wished to form a nation that did not have to second-guess the strengths of Athens and Sparta and side with whichever seemed in the ascendant. Admittedly, he had had to murder his half-brother to gain the throne. Nonetheless, since the last decade of the century, an influx of exiles from Athens had greatly contributed to the ongoing programme of civilization. His palace was decorated by the painter Zeuxis, whose *trompe-l'œil* were so convincing that birds reputedly attempted to snatch grapes that were no more than pigment on plaster. He listened to the intricate instrumental music of Timotheus, who had increased the number of strings on the *cithara* in order to turn his mental compositions into actual sounds.

As Athens became ever more militaristic, its much-vaunted intellectual freedoms became curtailed. Around 404 BCE, both Euripides and his friend and colleague in the theatre Agathon decided that not only their finances, but their lives, were imperilled by Athens' drift into doctrinaire repression. They were right – in 399 BCE, the philosopher Socrates, with whom they had both been intimate, was sentenced to death for corrupting the young. The Court of King Archelaus must surely have appeared a relatively enlightened place to retire.

Agathon had suffered carping and derision from the Athenians. Even the comic playwright Aristophanes, whose wit notoriously spared neither friend nor foe, had lampooned his method of composition in the *Thesmophoriazusae*. Agathon had been presented, dressed as a woman, justifying his odd vestments by saying that to write a female role, one had to think *as* a woman; and some moderate transvestism helped that process no end. Sly digs at his preference for homosexual to heterosexual relationships were accompanied by pastiches of his precious, ornate style.

Agathon's over-refined and rhetorically embellished poetry had been criticized often enough, and his retort to the critic who suggested excising those purpler passages had erred on the side of self-absorbed arrogance: 'Would you purge Agathon of Agathon?' Other innovations introduced by him had been equally sceptically received. Aristotle, years later, would remember that 'even Agathon' had been censured for trying to incorporate too much of an epic sweep into a single play. He had even severed the link between the Chorus and the action of the play, reducing their role to mere interludes.

Most contentiously, he had introduced an element into tragedy that had broken with every tradition: originality. His play *Antheus* (or *The Flowers*) had been based on a plot of his own devising. It is hard to fully imagine the shock to the audience: instead of an Oedipus, whose incest and blinding would be fully expected, or a wounded Philoctetes, or a passion-struck Phaedra, there were characters whom nobody recognized. Nobody knew what was going to happen next, let alone at the end. The lost *Antheus* is the only original tragic plot we know of; later Greek authors returned to the well-worn myths.

All that said, Agathon had been successful. He had won the first prize in 416 BCE, and the celebration afterwards would later be the setting for Plato's *Symposium*. Even in that imaginative reconstruction, lineaments of Agathon's character emerge. His lover, Pausanius, is present, and gives a defence of homosexual love affairs. Agathon's speech attests to his powers of invention and slightly florid tone. Although Phaedrus begins the debate by citing Hesiod and the lost author Acusilaus, who both maintain that Love is one of the oldest of the gods, Agathon begins by declaring conversely that Love is the youngest. He quotes the lost *Stheneboea* of Euripides, saying that Love can turn men into poets, and argues with sophistication that since Love is the strongest of passions, all other passions must be subordinate to it. Socrates gently unpicks the muddle of ingenuity.

As Agathon and Euripides, having finally decided to skip to Macedonia, headed towards the northern fastness of Archelaus, they may have discussed how best to write works that would flatter and challenge their new ruler. They may have compared notes on the veteran tragedian Sophocles, and his recent remarkable *Oedipus at Colonus*. What opportunities and advancements lay ahead? After all, they had already done enough to guarantee their immortality.

Put 'Agathon' into an internet search engine. Weed out the copious commentaries on Plato's *Symposium*. You will find a lot of information about precision tool manufacturing, with a special emphasis on ball sleeves, tool guiding and plastic moulding. There is a kennel club, a web-hosting service and an academic publisher, specializing in political science. There are details about a northern European rock band, Agathon's Favorite, who played in Liverpool once, and synopses of the 1975 movie *Assault on Agathon*, directed by Laslo Benedek (about a Greek Second World War veteran, thought dead, who returns to fight again). In January of the same year,

Marvel Comics *Haunt of Horror* #5 featured Agathon the Tempter, a servant of Kudros, a.k.a. Satan, who was impaled on a spiked sculpture by Satan's daughter, Satana. Jonathan Edwards played Agathon in season 3 of *Xena, Warrior Princess*, where he is now a warlord with magic armour from Hephaestus, the god of metalworking. *The Wreckage of Agathon* (Harper and Row, 1970), by John Gardner, a philosophical satire, was compared by one Amazon reviewer to Borges.

There are no extant plays by Agathon.

Two fragments of Agathon's work were used by Aristotle to emphasize and illustrate his arguments. 'Art loves Chance and Chance loves Art,' reads one, and chance has snatched any art Agathon was once thought to have had. 'Not even the Gods can change the past,' reads the other: a fitting epitaph, perhaps, for all the lost books.

Aristophanes

(*c*.444–*c*.380 BCE)

At the end of Plato's great debate on the nature and purpose of love, *The Symposium*, three of the guests remained awake: Socrates, the philosopher, Agathon, the tragedian, and Aristophanes, the comedian. The conversation had moved on from metaphysical investigation into the precise inter-relations between passion, devotion and friendship, and, as the wine was passed round, and the men passed out, they discussed drama. Unfortunately, with the exception of Socrates' contention that a man capable of writing tragedy would necessarily be able to write comedy, and vice versa, we do not know what occurred.

How did two of the most notable practitioners of their respective genres react to Socrates' theory? What theory of literature did they themselves subscribe to? And, with their tongues sufficiently loosened by the wine, did either Socrates or Agathon upbraid their comedic colleague for having satirized them on the stage?

Aristophanes would certainly have agreed that comedy had a function every bit as serious as that of tragedy. In the eleven plays we have, out of the forty he is said to have written, there is a consistent emphasis on the castigation of vice, the promotion of harmony and the proper responsibilities of the ruling class. 'What do you want a poet for?' Dionysus is asked in *The Frogs* as he attempts to liberate one of the great dramatists from the Underworld. 'To save the city, of course,' is the answer. That such noble intentions were quite compatible with knockabout farce, sexual innuendo and even personal invective is in part explained by the heterogeneous, hybrid nature of the comedy itself. Aristophanes is the earliest comic dramatist whose works have survived, yet he incorporated many of the registers, methods and propensities of his shadowy, lost predecessors.

According to the inscriptions on the Parian Marble, the comic chorus was invented by a writer called Susarion in the sixth century BCE. Almost nothing is known of this Thespis of comedy except his name. Archilochus of Paros (*c.*714–*c.*676 BCE) is credited with the invention of the lampoon, in iambic metre. His barbed, vituperative poetry was notoriously so cutting that it drove its subjects to suicide. Aristotle maintained that the first person to develop comic plots was a Sicilian, Epicharmus (*c.*540–*c.*440 BCE), and Plato refers to him as comparable to Homer in the field of comedy. He was supposedly a student of Pythagoras, and only a few fragments and titles have survived.

Two figures dominate the scene just prior to Aristophanes' debut in 427 BCE. Cratinus (519–422 BCE) was famous for the extremely vicious diatribes which he launched on public figures of the day. The statesman Pericles, with his 'squill-shaped head', was a frequent target, as was his mistress Aspasia, and his advisers. Tragedians and lyric poets were satirized in the *Euneidae*. Though none of his plays survive, the fact that one was called *The Followers of Archilochus* amply attests to where Cratinus derived his lashing style. The *Dionysalexandros*, the *Nemesis*, *Chiron*, *Drapedites* and *Thracian Woman* all reiterate his accusations.

Crates, who flourished around 470 BCE, had originally

appeared as an actor in Cratinus' plays; however, he became increasingly uncomfortable with the torrent of vitriol he was forced to enunciate. According to Aristotle, he adopted the more philosophically nuanced plots of Epicharmus: a fragment from Crates' play about the Golden Age, *The Beasts*, depicts fishes willingly basting and cooking themselves. If Aristotle is correct, then Cratinus followed Crates' example with his own Utopian play *Riches*. Aristophanes eulogized Crates' wit and dry humour, though, as ever, he qualified this by stating that he rarely won any prizes for it.

Although Aristophanes praises Cratinus' choruses in *The Knights*, he also launches an equally unsparing attack on the satirist; in short, Cratinus was a drunk. The Chorus in *The Knights* proclaims its truthfulness by claiming that if they are lying, they would rather be Cratinus' bedclothes, saturated with the results of his incontinence. Likewise, it is wholly appropriate that he sits next to the statue of Dionysus, god of drama, and alcohol. These jibes did not go uncountered: Cratinus took the daring step of producing a work entitled *The Bottle*, showing his bibulous self torn between his wife, the Muse and his mistress, Booze. It won the prize in 423 BCE, relegating Aristophanes' satire on Socrates, *The Clouds*, to an ignominious third place.

Aristophanes' early career quickly became embroiled in controversy. His lost play, *The Babylonians* of 426 BCE, attacked Cleon, the demagogue who had risen in influence after the death of Pericles. Cleon, unlike Pericles, attempted to use the law to quell criticism, and it would appear that Aristophanes was fined. Nonetheless, by 422 BCE, Aristophanes was so successful that the only reason his play *The Wasps* came second in the dramatic contest was that he had anonymously entered another, *The Preview*, as if it were the work of one Philonides. Despite winning, *The Preview* is lost. The attacks on Cleon continued.

Aristophanes' plays combined Crates' philosophical speculation with Cratinus' energetic satire. Aristophanes was a very literary comedian, and the loss of *The Poet, The Muses, Sappho* and *Heracles the Stage Manager* not only robs us of examples of the earliest theatrical self-consciousness, but also prevents us seeing, askance, the literary world that indubitably furnished him with ample targets for ridicule.

Today, Aristophanes' work seems for the most part unaffected by the obsolescence that so often engulfs comedies from the past. The founding of 'Cloud Cuckoo Land' in *The Birds* or the sex strike in *Lysistrata* seem just as fresh, even if puns about figs and informers, or *double entendres* about piglets, disappear in translation. Of all the Attic Greek writers, Aristophanes exhibits the highest frequency of *hapax logomenon*: the one-off use of a word. Only in Aristophanes could we read an adverb like *archaiomelisidonophrynicherata*, meaning 'in the old, sweet style of Sidonian Maidens in the work by Phrynicus'. What makes him difficult also makes him unique.

Towards the end of his life, in *Wealth*, his last extant play – and apparently in the two, lost subsequent plays, *Aeolosicon* and *Kokalos* – Aristophanes paved the way for the 'New Comedy' of Menander, simplifying the plots and reining in much of the fantasia and verbal pyrotechnics of his earlier work. He had written another play called *Wealth* twenty years previously, but the earlier work no longer exists to contrast with the later, less flamboyant style. His son, Araros, continued the family tradition of comedy, though under the constraints of the new anti-libel laws.

There were, of course, some critics for whom Aristophanes' particular brand of comedy was anathema. Plutarch, writing in the first century CE, fulminated that 'his use of words combines the tragic and the comic, the grandiose and the prosaic, the obscure and the commonplace, bombast and elevation, verbal diarrhoea and outright sickening rubbish' – in many ways, the very qualities we still admire.

Xenocles and Others

(fourth century BCE)

Poor Xenocles! All we know of him comes from Aristophanes' comedies, in which he becomes almost a byword for weak writing. His only lines, from the tragedy *Tlepolemus*, are held up for mockery in Aristophanes' *The Birds*. All that has been retained for posterity is

> O cruel goddess, O, my chariot smashed
> Pallas, thou hast destroyed me utterly!

But he is not alone in having himself been destroyed utterly: what of

Aristea's *Who the Jews Are*;
Aristaeus of Proconnesus, whose three-volume *Arimaspeia* dealt with the far north;
Astydamas, the grand-nephew of Aeschylus whose self-promotion was so blatant the Athenians tore down his statue;
Callipedes, the Roman comedian who specialized in running on the spot;
Carcinus' *Thyestes*, with its birthmark recognition scene;

Chaeremon, author of *The Centaur*;

Choerilus, the poet whose epic on Alexander only had seven good lines;

Cinaethon's epic, *Oedipus*;

Cratippus, the inventor of *Everything Thucydides Left Unsaid*;

Dicaeogenes, whose *Cyprians* involved Teucer bursting into tears at a portrait;

Ennius, the father of Roman poetry, who wrote, 'No sooner said than done; so acts the man of worth' in his *Annals*;

Eupolis, the comedian rumoured drowned by Alcibiades;

Accius, one of the first tragedians in Latin;

Epimarchus, the cookery writer;

Eugammon of Cyrene, who wrote the sequel to *The Odyssey*;

Lesches of Mitylene, author of the *Little Iliad*;

Magnes, the comedian who put talking animals into plays;

Neophron, who introduced on-stage torture and child-minders for young actors;

Nicochares, who showed men in a bad light;

Pytheas, author of *On the Oceans*;

Stesichorus, whose father was reputedly Hesiod and whose soul was Homer's, who wrote, in twenty-six volumes, *The Boar Hunter*;

Teleclides' version of *Cloud Cuckoo Land*; or

Varro of Atax's adaptation of Apollonius' *Argonautica*?

It is only through **Suetonius** that we have an account of the reign of Caligula, since **Tacitus'** version is lost, along with **Suetonius'** *Royal Biographies, Roman Manners, Roman Festivals, Roman Dress, Greek Games, Grammatical Problems, Methods of Reckoning Time, Essay on Nature, Critical Signs used* *in Books*, *The Physical Defects of Mankind* and the wonderful *Lives of the Famous Whores*.

Technology is no bulwark. Crashed software, surreptitious viruses, an unthinking click or a toppled drink can dispense with writing quicker than flames, waves or the stale air of library cellars. At least **Xenocles**, in a sad, etiolated and pitiable way, is still known to have been a writer. Thousands had a far more absolute extinction.

Menander

(c.342–291 BCE)

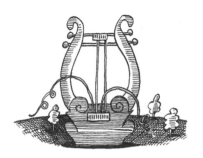

Aristophanes of Byzantium, who held the prestigious position of chief librarian at Alexandria, thought that the works of the comic playwright Menander were second only in talent to those of the divine Homer. Whereas the epic excelled in depicting the deeds of gods and heroes, the outcome of which shaped whole civilizations, Menander's work was the pinnacle of a different order of magnitude. In plays like *The Hated Man* and *The Arbitration*, he had shown people just like his audience, speaking as they did, in situations they recognized: in short, his plays established a sparkling new form of realism. Or, as Aristophanes of Byzantium enthused, 'O Menander! O Life! Which of you is imitating the other?'

Critical veneration of Menander's 'New Comedy' was a commonplace in antiquity. No less a person than Julius Caesar dismissed the writer Terence as being merely 'a half-pint Menander'. The Roman rhetorician Quintilian recommended all aspiring orators to study the plays assiduously, since 'the picture of life he presents to us . . . is so brilliant, there is such an abundance of invention and turns-of-phrase, he is so adept in every situation, characterization and emotion'.

Plutarch's encomium of Menander in the *Moralia* becomes

dizzy, encapsulating the widely held sense of his dramatic pre-eminence:

Menander's charm makes him utterly satisfying, for in these works that present with universal appeal the splendours of Greece, society finds its culture, the schools their study, the theatre its triumph. The nature and possibilities of literary elegance were first revealed by him: he had conquered every quarter of the world with his invincible glamour, bringing all ears, all hearts, under the sway of the Greek language. What reason does any educated man have for entering a theatre, except Menander?

This paradigm of refinement was born in Athens around 342 BCE. His family seems to have been well-to-do, and his father, Diopeithes, may have been a general. His uncle, Alexis, was a remarkably prolific writer of comedies – the *Suda* suggests 245, and Plutarch claims he died while being given the triumphal laurels on stage at the age of 106. Except for titles, Alexis' only literary remains are fragments recorded in anthologies of wise or witty proverbs – such priceless pearls as 'There is only one cure for the illness known as love: prostitutes,' 'How come cook-books outsell Homer?' and 'Human life is completely mad.' In these *bons mots*, Alexis parodied the teachings of both ascetic Pythagoreans and the abstruse Platonists. His nephew may have imbibed some of his intellectual prejudices, and was known to be a friend of Epicurus.

Menander's choice of vocation may also have been influenced by his teacher, Theophrastus. Theophrastus had been a pupil of both Plato and Aristotle, and succeeded Aristotle as head of the Lyceum, inheriting his library and his private papers. Aristotle himself nicknamed him 'Theophrastus', meaning 'divine speaker'. Theophrastus became a much-loved and respected teacher; and, when Ptolemy Soter was beginning to assemble the Great Library at Alexandria, it was to the libraries of Aristotle and Theophrastus that he turned.

Theophrastus' book *The Characters* is the clearest indication of his influence on Menander. Although it was published a few years after Menander's first recorded play, it seems likely that the young playwright was aware of Theophrastus' classification of humans into clearly recognizable types. These observations of boasters, bumpkins and boors are translated into stock characters of the 'New Comedy' stage; the archetypes segue into theatrical stereotypes. The text we have of *The Characters* is, unfortunately, itself incomplete, covering only the negative personality traits.

Menander's first victory at the dramatic festival was in 317 BCE, with a play called *Dyskolos*. There would be few repetitions of the event, and the later epigram-writer Martial took some comfort in the idea that true genius is unappreciated during one's lifetime. How Menander felt may be surmised from an anecdote where he berated Philemon, his great dramatic rival, asking, 'Why don't you blush every time you beat me?'

Like Alexis, Menander wrote voluminously and, apparently, with ease. The use of generic characters in formulaic circumstances allowed for near-infinite variations. Once, when being badgered by a friend about not having completed his contribution for that year's festival (and hampering impatient actors, scene-painters and musicians), Menander breezily retorted, 'The play is done. All that remains is to write the dialogue.' If you have one play, so his logic runs, you pretty much have them all.

The theatre in Menander's day was changing. His friend Demetrius of Phalerum, the Macedonian viceroy of Athens, had, amongst other tax-breaks for the aristocracy, discontinued the payment of *theorica*, a fund which reimbursed artisans who wished to attend the festival. It was therefore a new, more 'middle-class' audience which could enjoy plays like *The Shoemaker*, *The Goat-herds* and *The Farmer*. Although Anaxandrides was reputedly the first to make 'love and seduction' the staple of the comedy, Ovid tells us that Menander 'never wrote a play without romance in it'.

Menander died, drowned, while swimming, or failing to, at Piraeus. He was to become so famous that a later writer, Alciphron, had a modest success with a fictitious correspondence between Menander and his mistress Glycera (whose name Menander had immortalized in *The Girl Who Gets Her Hair Cut*). The Athenians erected a statue to him, as they had done for the great tragedians.

Menander's fame grew and grew. Diphilus, Ephippus, Xenarchus, Antiphanes, Aristophon and Anaxilas fell from favour. Even Philemon and Alexis were lost. And the works of Menander, bolstered by the posthumous panegyrics of orators, poets and moralists, eventually accompanied them. Just over a thousand lines were kept as proverbs in commonplace compilations. When Goethe praised the 'unattainable charm' of Menander, he chose his adjective carefully. The last known manuscript had disappeared in Constantinople 200 years previously.

Hold on, hold on. Cut. Imagine, for a moment, reader, the sound of a stylus ripped hastily across the surface of a record.

We got him back.

Nineteen hundred and five, Aphroditopolis, Egypt, and the house of a lawyer, Flavius Dioskoros, was being excavated. In a large jar, a sheaf of fifth-century CE papyrus documents was discovered. Securing the bundle were fragments of five plays by Menander. Amongst parts of *The Woman from Samos* and *The Arbitration* were twelve shorter extracts from a play called *Dyskolos*.

The 'Cairo Codex', as it was called, caused ripples of appreciation and murmurs of approval in the world of classical studies. But when Professor Victor Martin of the University of Geneva announced nearly fifty years later that he had acquired a rare third-century papyrus from Martin Bodmer, the Swiss bibliophile and book collector, it was a sensation. The 'Bodmer Codex' had nearly all of the rest of *Dyskolos*. The play, translated as *The Bad-tempered Man*, *The Misanthrope* or *Old Cantankerous*, could be staged for the first time since antiquity.

Then the trouble really started.

Contemporary critics were well aware of their classical counterparts' lofty evaluation of Menander: expectations would naturally run high. Textual critics struggled to produce a workable version; after all, as the manuscript stood, there were neither stage directions nor line attributions. The script was reassembled, like Frankenstein's monster, edited, translated, and on Friday 30 October 1959, broadcast by the BBC.

'Tell me why Menander is anything but a wet fish?' G. S. Kirk, the Regius Professor of Greek, was reported to have said when visiting Yale. Christopher Fry was less outspoken, referring to it in the introduction to the English translation as 'slight and predictable'. Even Philip Vellacott, the translator, admitted it was 'not a work of . . . calibre' and 'remarkably unambitious'. Special pleading, especially since it was known to be a juvenile work, did little to enhance the reputation of the newly discovered play. Euripides, the last great tragedian, had experimented with tragicomic plays with magical resolutions: Erich Segal, author of *Love Story* and Professor of Humanities, now referred to Menander as 'a suburban Euripides'.

Moreover, as more of the papyri were deciphered, more problems with the 'comic genius' became evident. The author whose 'lifelikeness' was proverbial appeared to have a curious penchant for incredible revelations about orphans' parentage and other hackneyed dramatic devices. Some brave critics suggested that the Greece of Menander's day, recovering from civil war and Alexandrian belligerence, did, indeed, have an inordinate number of orphans. Whether many of them were reconciled with their family, who turned out to be the very individuals they had, unaware, grown up amongst, is not known.

One of the other favourite plots could be summarized as: 'Whoops! I raped someone last night', which normally ended with perpetrator and victim realizing they are the love of each other's lives, and getting married. The 'narrowly avoided incest' set-up attracted equally few admirers.

Menander had been regarded as the hypothetical progenitor of a dramatic line that culminated in Shakespeare, Molière and Feydeau. Introducing him back into the theatrical repertoire now seemed as sensible as cloning a caveman and asking him to cook for a dinner party. Lost, Menander was a genius; found, he was an embarrassment.

There was one other important, and unlikely, figure in antiquity who appreciated the plays of Menander: St Paul. Verse 33 of chapter 15 of the First Epistle to the Corinthians is, though unacknowledged in the letter, a quotation from Menander. 'Be not deceived,' says Paul. 'Evil communications corrupt good manners', a line from Menander's play about a courtesan, *Thais*. St Paul does not quote from any other non-biblical source, and the thought of the erstwhile persecutor of, Damascene convert to, and martyred sufferer for Christianity – the very individual who did most to change a Jewish apocalyptic sect into a world-governing religion – enjoying a little light comedy is boggling enough in itself.

Menander might well have preferred to stay lost, rather than be deflated by posterity. But although he never made it on Broadway, he may have approved of his work, hidden like a stealthy mine, endangering the edifice of the Doctrine of Scriptural Authority.

Callimachus

(*c*.320–*c*.240 BCE)

To be called 'sophisticated' is an ambiguous plaudit. The lustre of polish contains a suspicion of superficial veneer; suave urbanity raises the shadow of oleaginous artifice. Sophisticated authors may well be complex, but their cleverness is always denounced as mere cleverness. They may be charming, refined, chic and stylish, but the hint lingers that they lack a soul. Sophistication is a taunt and a triumph, an accomplishment and a snub.

Callimachus would have easily appreciated the manifold, contradictory meanings bound up in that single word. Born in Cyrene, he rose to a position of eminence in the Alexandrian Library, which he catalogued in 120 scrolls called the *Pinakes* (or Tablets) *of the Illustrious in every branch of Literature and What they Wrote*. His own output purportedly exceeded 800 volumes, and covered a polymathic plenitude of interests: as well as satires, tragedies and comedies, he wrote *On the Changes of the Names of Fish, On Winds, On Birds, On the Rivers of Europe, The Names of the Months according to Tribes and Cities* and even *A Collection of Wonders of the Entire World according to Location*.

All we have left of this encyclopedic oeuvre is six hymns

and a collection of fragments and epigrams. Two poems, the *Aitia*, or *Origins*, and the epyllion *Hekale*, can be partially reconstructed: the fifty-eight slivers of *Hekale*, some from papyri and others preserved by commentators, comprise around a fifth of the entire poem. It is enough for us to glimpse not only Callimachus' character, but also his literary ideology.

Callimachus preferred finely honed, elegant poems. Brevity was a virtue, and poetry, he wrote, should be judged by the art, not the mile. He abhorred the bombast of the 'cyclic' epic writers, comparing their work to a sluggish, muddy river, and wryly suggesting that whereas Zeus might like thundering, he did not. In the Hymn to Apollo, he puts his partialities in the mouth of the god of poetry himself: sacrifices should be fattened animals, but the Muse was best when slender. Intellectually precocious and linguistically deft, his poetry announced itself as a break from tradition.

He not only promoted his own aesthetic, but lambasted his opponents, calling them the Telchines, after a primitive race of invidious spirits from Rhodes. A longstanding legend pits Callimachus against his one-time pupil and the future head librarian of Alexandria, the poet Apollonius of Rhodes, whose four-volume epic *The Argonautica* was presumed to be the object of Callimachus' derision. Ovid translated a poem by Callimachus called *The Ibis*, though the original Greek is lost. It is a fearsome pasquinade about the carcass-eating stork, a bird 'full of filth'. Ancient scholars read the poem as another sustained attack on the author of *The Argonautica*. The sneering association between Apollonius, the Telchines and their mutual homeland of Rhodes seems clear, but the reason why an ibis might remind readers of Apollonius is unclear.

'A big book is a big evil,' was one of Callimachus' maxims. His penchant for the literary miniature did not, however, increase his chances of survival. The feud – even if it is a later fiction – between the modernist sophisticate and the orthodox traditionalist proved more immortal than his works.

The Caesars

Julius (100–44 BCE), Augustus (63 BCE–14 CE), Tiberius
(42 BCE–37 CE), Caligula (12 CE–41 CE), Claudius
(10 BCE–54 CE) and Nero (37 CE–68 CE)

From Shakespeare to Racine and Robert Graves to Albert
Camus, we are more accustomed to the earliest Roman
emperors being the subjects, not the authors, of books. But
in addition to ruling the known world, Julius Caesar and the
five descendants who took the title Emperor all harboured
literary ambitions. Most of their compositions, however, went
the same way as their Empire.

For generations, the first contact schoolchildren had with
a Latin author was Caesar himself, and his *Conquest of Gaul*.
This was not the atrophied hangover of centuries of syco-
phancy; Julius Caesar's prose style was generally held by his
contemporaries to be exceptional. Cicero praised it as 'chaste,
pellucid and grand, not to say noble', and enthused to Cornelius Nepos that no one else had 'a vocabulary so varied and
yet so precise'.

Like most cultured young Romans, Julius tried his hand at
drama; however, his successor, Augustus, decreed that such
juvenilia as the *Oedipus*, as well as *Collected Sayings* and *In
Praise of Hercules*, should not be circulated. The *Conquest of*

Gaul was completed by his friend Hirtius, and other volumes of 'memoirs' detailing the campaigns in Alexandria, Africa and Spain were soon appearing from opportunistic authors. Caesar was also a poet: his lost verse travelogue *The Journey* detailed his travels over twenty-four days between Rome and Spain, and an *Essay on Analogy* was said to have been composed while he was crossing the Alps.

Under Augustus, Roman literature flourished: Virgil dedicated his *Aeneid* to the Emperor, Horace praised him in exquisitely ironic, nuanced *Odes* and Ovid entertained with risqué humour, until he overstepped the mark. Surrounded by such talents, it is unsurprising that the Emperor scrapped his tragedy *Ajax*, and contented himself with a brief poem on Sicily (though it too was lost) and his thirteen-volume *My Autobiography*. This early example of a politician's self-assessment was not considered sufficiently pertinent to preserve, though his grandiloquently entitled *Actions of the Divine Augustus*, carved rather than entrusted to friable scrolls, allows us a little insight into his sense of his own achievements. No doubt *An Encouragement to the Study of Philosophy* was a very worthy endeavour; however, it has not been handed down to posterity.

Tiberius Caesar completed Augustus' *Reply to Brutus' Eulogy of Cato*, and wrote his own *Elegy on the Death of Julius Caesar*. According to Suetonius, his prose style was affected and ponderous, and his taste in literature rather limited. He preferred the works of Euphorion, Rhianus and Parthenius, none of which have survived, even though academics attempted to outdo each other in producing editions of the Emperor's favourite writing. As he declined into bloated, lecherous decrepitude, he spent more time patronizing toadies than bothering to do anything himself. Asellius Sabinus appreciated the 2,000 gold coins he received for a dialogue where a mushroom, an oyster, a fig and a thrush argue who is tastiest.

Gaius Caesar, nicknamed Caligula, was 'no man of letters', according to his biographer. He thought Virgil overrated, and dismissed Seneca: but then again, he found the idea that gods might be superior to him infuriating. In one notorious act of literary criticism, he not only burned the work of an Atellan comedian, but then had the author burned in the theatre. The only flashes of eloquence conspicuous in Caligula are in his sadistic wit. 'If only the Roman people had a single neck!' he screamed, when the crowd cheered for the wrong team. His uncle, the stammering Claudius, destroyed two manuscripts of Caligula's that he found in the private apartments on his accession: one entitled *The Dagger* and another called *The Sword*, detailing his insane nephew's programme of conspiracies and intended victims.

Claudius, like Augustus, wrote an autobiography, which, according to Suetonius, suffered from 'lack of taste' rather than 'lack of style'. The work he was most proud of was a typically eccentric scheme. Claudius decided to reform the Latin alphabet, introducing three new characters;) to represent the Greek *psi*, ⊢ for a vowel between u and i, and ⊢ for the consonantal v. Both the *Official Gazette* and state monuments adopted the new letters, and dropped them soon after the Emperor's demise.

In Greek, rather than Latin, Claudius compiled twenty volumes of Etruscan history and eight volumes of Carthaginian history. His Roman history stretched to forty-three volumes, heavily censored by his family. So voluminous was his output that the Library at Alexandria had to build a new wing, the Claudian, to commemorate his historical writing. Even this testament to a state leader's literary bent was less steadfast than might have been expected.

Claudius was the first emperor since Augustus to be deified. Nero, who succeeded Claudius, ordered his tutor Seneca to mock the apotheosis in verse, as *The Pumpkinification of the Divine Claudius*. The Stoic philosopher struggled in vain to inculcate a sense of self-control and mental discipline into his wayward ward, and eventually committed suicide as Nero's murderous regime sought out new traitors. His nephew, the poet Lucan, similarly killed himself, leaving his poem about Julius, *The Pharsalia*, incomplete.

Nero fancied himself as an artist, and acted in various plays and farces, sometimes scandalizing the court by playing the female roles. His attack on Claudius Pollio, *The One-Eyed Man*, has perished alongside the rest of his oeuvre. 'What an artist dies with me!' he had lamented as the troops hunted him down. History disagreed.

Gallus

(*c*.70–26 BCE)

In the fifteenth poem of his first book of *Amores*, Ovid makes
a bold claim for the immortality of poetry: 'carmina morte
carent', 'songs from death are free'. To prove his point he
catalogues the imperishable names of Homer, Sophocles and
Virgil, concluding with the lines

> Gallus et Hesperiis et Gallus notus Eois
>   et sua cum Gallo nota Lycoris erit.

> Gallus, from the West and even to the East, Gallus will be famed
>   and with Gallus will be famed his Lycoris.

Gallus' literary perpetuity was more precarious than that of
the illustrious company in which Ovid places him; and Ovid
may have had a suspicion this was the case. Inscribing his
name three times in two lines is almost laying it on a little
thick, especially when Homer is only referred to as 'the son
of Maeonia'. Ovid's insistence on Gallus' greatness extended
across his career: he is mentioned again in book III of *The
Amores*, in *The Art of Love* (where young men are advised to
memorize poems by Gallus) and thrice in his *Tristia*.

Nor was Ovid the only poet to commemorate the achievements of Gallus. Propertius links his name with the earliest Latin love elegists, and two of Virgil's *Eclogues* feature Gallus. In *Eclogue VI*, he appears with no less than Orpheus and the god Phoebus in a cantata of poetic themes. *Eclogue X* is both dedicated to Gallus and descriptive of him. 'Who would refuse poetry to Gallus?' asks Virgil. The answer was the Emperor.

Servius, the commentator on Virgil, tells us that Gallus composed four books of amatory elegies for Lycoris, whose real name was Cytheris, an actress rumoured to be the mistress of Mark Antony. He was one of the *neoteroi*, or 'new poets' (modernists might be an acceptable comparison), who drew their inspiration from the allusive, finely polished poetry of Callimachus and the Alexandrians. As well as being an eminent poet, Gallus was a soldier. He fought alongside Octavian (who became Augustus Caesar) against Mark Antony, and was rewarded for his loyalty and bravery during the capture of Alexandria by being made Prefect of Egypt in 30 BCE. Some unspecified indiscretion or rumour of ambitions or unacceptable conduct led to his fall from Imperial favour: he committed suicide in exile in 26 BCE.

Though Augustus could be forgiving – Horace, his panegyricist and ode-writer, had fought alongside Mark Antony – he could also be implacable. Servius claims that the Emperor demanded that Virgil remove a section praising Gallus from the fourth *Georgic*, but it seems as if the commentator had confused the final, fourth poem of the *Georgics* with the final, tenth poem of the *Eclogues*. Absence of evidence often being mistaken for evidence of absence, several scholars were later on embroiled in trying to hypothesize about the missing accolade, whilst ignoring the evidence that Virgil did not remove a reference.

We do not know if Gallus' work was actively suppressed: nonetheless, no manuscripts have come down to us. Servius claimed that the words which Virgil puts in Gallus' mouth were actually Gallus' own: if so, the phrase 'Love conquers all' would be attributable to him. However, the lines could as easily be completely fictitious, and given Virgil's close relationship with the Emperor, it is unlikely he would flaunt the talent of someone who had incurred Augustus' displeasure.

Only one line that is without a doubt by Gallus has been preserved. In Vibius Sequester's book on geography, he quotes the line 'uno tellures dividit amne duas': 'it is divided by one river into two lands'. It is hardly a fitting tribute to posterity for a poet whose expressions of the pains of love had inspired a generation.

Ovid

(43 BCE–18 CE)

Being a poet in Ancient Rome was a perilous business. Catullus had lauded his friend C. Helvius Cinna for his epyllion *Zmyrna*, sure it would be read by future generations. The poem has not survived, and Cinna met an exceptionally sticky end, when a mob mistook him for his namesake L. Cornelius Cinna, the conspirator against Julius Caesar, battered him to death and paraded his head on a spear through the city. A century later, Petronius would be driven to suicide at the hands of Julius' descendant, Nero. Publius Ovidius Naso, called Ovid, was luckier; although his career too was blighted, 'by a poem and a mistake'.

Ovid's first book of poems, the *Amores*, opens with a dedication telling the reader that he has slimmed it down from five volumes to three. He was candid about the necessity of reworking and revising, mentioning 'the flames which emend'. The *Amores* is a waggish take on the Roman love elegy, in which he praises, pleads with and vilifies his mistress Corinna. Unlike Lesbia, whom Catullus alternately hated and loved, or Propertius' Cynthia or Tibullus' Delia, all of whose *noms-de-plume* have been unravelled by commentators,

Corinna is a mystery. Whilst the earlier elegists had struggled to convey, convincingly, their earnest passion, Ovid, with delicious glee and urbane wit, confutes expectations and winks at the audience. There is no 'real' Corinna at all; she exists only because a love poet needs an object for his affection.

Ovid was a virtuoso, also composing a tragedy on Medea (which Quintilian thought best displayed his talents, but which has not survived), a gloriously abundant compendium of myths, *The Metamorphoses*, and inventing the dramatic monologue, in his *Heroides*, where he gives a voice to legendary heroines. The poem which blasted his fortunes, however, was the *Ars Amatoria*, *The Art of Love*. In debonair and sardonic fashion, he advises the youth of Rome how to flatter, avoid suspicion from jealous husbands, deport themselves at the chariot games and variously wheedle their way into the beds of Rome's women. It is a cosmopolitan extravaganza, conjuring up the alleys and banquets of the city. As a manual for seduction, it earned the ire of the Emperor.

Augustus, whose impatience at the moral laxity of his subjects was manifesting itself in strict legislature against extramarital affairs, was less than amused. *The Art of Love* was the poem, but the error which accompanied it is shrouded in speculation. Suggestions range from the idea that Ovid was conducting an affair with the Emperor's granddaughter, or that he had seen the Empress naked, or had defiled the rites of Isis: whatever it was, Ovid was discreet enough, and perhaps humbled enough, never to make the charge specific. All he would let slip was that he 'had eyes'.

His punishment was severe. Ovid was banished from the Rome he so lovingly described, to Tomis, on the Black Sea, the outermost edge of the Empire. The suavest of poets would live with barbarians. He continued to write, sending letters and regretful poems back to his friends. The gravity of his sentence has often been heightened by comparison: imagine

Byron in Saskatchewan, or Oscar Wilde in Iceland. During his ostracism, he started to compose a celebration of the Roman calendar, *The Fasti*, commemorating the way time used to be governed in a place where it was fixed by the flow of tides, seasons and equinoxes. He completed only six months of his evocation of the etiquette and mythology of the holidays and holy days in Rome.

In the *Epistulae ex Ponto*, however, Ovid tells us of one remarkable feat he accomplished in exile. He learned the Getic language of the savages, and even composed poems in it. His subject was a eulogy for Augustus, and the tribe were impressed enough to call him a bard. But, they insisted, since he sang the praises of the Emperor, surely he would be restored to civilization? He never was, and the lines in which he celebrated the divine Caesars in the rough tongue of his despised compatriots were left unpreserved. As, for that matter, was the entire Getic language.

Longinus

(*fl.* first century CE)

The treatise entitled *Peri Hypsos* or *On the Sublime* is not only a reliquary for lost books, but is itself a lost book. The Paris manuscript has pages missing; it ends on a remark about another literary discussion the author wrote called *On the Emotions*. The author is about to summarize its contents, when the pages suddenly cease. Its lacunae create weird disjunctions: Alexander's retort to Parmenio, 'I would have been content . . .', segues into 'the distance between heaven and earth; it may be said this is the stature of Homer'.

Almost every aspect of *On the Sublime* flickers with a sense of instability. The opening page names one Postumius Florentianus as the dedicatee of the essay; he is not mentioned again, and it is to one Terentianus that the subsequent points are addressed. The author is called Dionysius Longinus, though on the contents page this becomes Dionysius *or* Longinus. Earlier scholars presumed Longinus to be Cassius Longinus (*c.*213–73), the Neoplatonic philosopher and rhetorician, who advised Queen Zenobia to secede from the Roman Empire and was executed by the Emperor Aurelian when he quashed the move towards independence. Most critical opinion now gravitates towards *On the Sublime* being rather earlier, and the author is given the clumsy title of 'Pseudo-Longinus'.

Pseudo-Longinus defines the sublime as 'the echo of the greatness of spirit', and quotes widely, and sometimes wildly, to prove his definition. It is thanks to *On the Sublime* that we have fragments of Aeschylus' *Orithyia*, Sophocles' *Polyxena* and Euripides' *Phaethon*. Conversely, there are lines which cannot be attributed to any known author. Whoever wrote, 'His field was smaller than a letter', or, 'Immediately, along the beaches, a countless crowd called out Tuna!' was once so famous he or she did not need to be named.

The most remarkable preservation in *On the Sublime* is an almost completely intact poem by Sappho. Indeed, of her nine volumes, the only complete poem is contained in the Longinus manuscript. Though the book itself was to inspire aesthetic theories by Pope, Burke, Kant and Coleridge, its conservation of these priceless lines would guarantee its readership.

But this stroke of luck should not obscure those shivering uncertainties in the text. Longinus elsewhere quotes Homer, but inaccurately. A description of the god Poseidon splices together lines from Books XIII and XX of *The Iliad*; another account, of the Olympian gods in battle, conflates parts of Books XX and XXI. In an extremely curious throwaway line, Longinus also claims that the 'lawgiver of the Jews' displays the characteristics of the Sublime; he quotes the opening of Genesis which apparently reads 'God said Let there be Light and there was Light, Let there be Land and there was Land'.

Pseudo-Longinus has safeguarded our sole intact poem by Sappho; however, given his other discernible errors and misquotations, the awful spectre rises that our one poem might not be as genuine and immaculate as we might have hoped.

Saint Paul

(Saul of Tarsus) (first decade–*c*.65 CE)

Around 200 CE, an unknown Christian bound together a codex containing ten epistles by Saint Paul (known to us as P⁴⁶, the Chester-Beatty Papyrus, the earliest extant manuscript of Paul's work). It includes Romans, Hebrews, 1 and 2 Corinthians, Ephesians, Galatians, Philippians, Colossians and 1 and 2 Thessalonians. Did the compiler pause as he or she inscribed the text of 2 Thessalonians 2:2, where the saint warns the church at Thessalonica to be troubled 'neither by spirit, nor by word, nor by letter as from us'? Since Paul himself had been vexed by forged letters purporting to be his, the scribe's task took on the onerous responsibility of regulating divine revelation. Unfortunately, 2 Thessalonians is not by Paul.

Saul, born in Tarsus, the capital of the Roman province of Cilicia, was a Jewish-Roman citizen. He was educated by the Pharisee Gamaliel and came from a family of tent-makers (though given the importance of canvas shelters to the Roman army, military procurement might be a more apt description of his profession). He tells us in the Epistle to the Galatians

that he was 'exceedingly zealous' in his faith, to the extent
that he persecuted the apocalyptic sect founded by a Nazarene
called Jesus, which his followers called 'the Way'. When
Stephen, the first martyr, was stoned to death by a mob, the
witnesses laid their clothes at the feet of Saul. According
to the Acts of the Apostles, this Saul 'made havock of the
church'.

The convert Marcion, whose heretical beliefs were subdued
in the middle of the second century, knew of Paul's letters,
but did not include in his canon the Second Epistle to
Timothy. An alert reader, Marcion believed only Luke's Gospel was necessary for salvation (though even that benefited
from some judicious pruning), and he must have been struck
by the contradiction between the letter supposedly by Paul
and the accounts of Paul's travels in Acts, Luke's continuation
of the history of the earliest church. In 2 Timothy, the author
impersonating Paul says that he has left Trophimus sick at
Miletus: nonetheless, a perfectly healthy Trophimus is with
Paul in Jerusalem after the saint's departure from Miletus in
Acts of the Apostles. Was it this inconsistency that suggested
to Marcion that the letter was not, in fact, by Paul? Or was it
the overly vehement assertion that 'All scripture *is* given by
inspiration of God'?

On his way to Damascus, to continue the extirpation of the
Jesus–cult, Saul was confronted with the object of his hatred.
In a blinding vision, the risen Christ asked 'Saul, Saul, why
persecutest thou me?' Saul's sight was restored by a follower
of the Way in Damascus, and the erstwhile intimidator performed the most famous volte-face in the history of religion.
Saul's name did not immediately change; it was only when
he struck the sorcerer Elymas blind through the power of the
Holy Spirit that we learn he was now also called Paul.

Paul's mission was not to convert the orthodox Israelites

whose rejection of Christ he had so recently enforced, but to proselytize amongst the Gentiles. His evangelical itinerary took him to Antioch, Athens, Ephesus (where he burned 'books of curious arts' worth 50,000 pieces of silver) and eventually Rome. He was mistaken for the god Mercury in Lystra, and was told by the Roman Governor Festus at Caesarea that 'too much learning doth make thee mad'. He was whipped thirty-nine times on five occasions, beaten thrice with rods, stoned once and shipwrecked three times. Although the Book of Acts informs the reader of numerous miracles, including even the raising of the dead, his own Epistles are remarkably coy about supernatural powers, preferring instead a catalogue of his physical sufferings.

In 367, Athanasius, the Bishop of Alexandria, decreed that the New Testament had twenty-seven books. Paul, of course, had not been writing a testament, and would have been surprised that his letters dealing with specific crises in various churches now had universal relevance (though he would have been equally surprised that the world still existed). Although Athanasius commanded, 'Let no one add, let nothing be taken away,' the newly crystallized 'Bible' still retained the traces of its less than monolithic conception. In 1 Corinthians 5:9, Saint Paul had said, 'I wrote unto you in an epistle not to company with fornicators.' The '0 Corinthians' letter is lost, presumably because its anti-libertine agenda was adequately dealt with elsewhere (or, an admittedly remote possibility, because it was rather too specific about the sexual proclivities of the Corinthians. The demotic expression 'to corinthicate' – κορινθιαζεσθαι – meant to whore around).

Paul hoped to preach the gospel as far as Spain. Conflicts and tensions between converted and traditional Jews, however, meant that he was forced to return to Jerusalem and defend himself against a charge of sedition. A conspiracy of forty men loyal to the Sanhedrin had sworn an oath not to eat before they had murdered Paul, and it was therefore in Paul's own interests to allow the Roman overlords to decide his case, rather than the Jewish Temple authorities; moreover, being a Roman citizen, Paul had the right to appeal to the Emperor himself. Unluckily, in this case the Emperor was Nero.

Agrippa, the client-king, and Festus, the Roman overlord of Judaea, agreed to Paul's request, ruefully noting that if he had not invoked this right, they were minded to set him free anyway. Paul was transferred to Rome, and while the boat was buffeted by tempests and stymied in doldrums, he impressed the crew by prophesying that none of them would come to harm, for it was decreed that he would stand before Caesar. They safely reached Rome, and, practically at that point, the Acts of the Apostles unexpectedly ends. The whole narrative has been moving to this encounter, yet the final climactic showdown between Nero and Paul is either lost or was never even written.

We do not know how Paul died. One tradition asserts that he did reach Spain, but, given the Emperor's notorious sadism and insanity (he used Christians dipped in pitch to light the streets), it would be nothing short of miraculous for Paul to have persuaded Nero to let him go free. But miracles had been known to happen, if we trust the author of Acts.

Paul disappears from the narrative like Enoch or Isaiah ascending into Heaven. One ingenious speculation reads the text of Acts of the Apostles as a kind of legal briefing for the lawyer who would defend Paul: it insists, for example, that he has always been deferential to political authorities. The ending was not written because it had not yet happened. This hypothesis cannot, however, explain why no later writer appended the details of what transpired, the arguments for faith put forward by Paul or the Emperor's retort. There is no ancient account of the death of Saint Paul.

The very fact that Paul's name was later used to bolster missives by other authors attests to his phenomenal standing among his peers. Never having met the physical Jesus, never even using the word Christian, Paul invents Christianity. If the whole of philosophy is merely footnotes to Plato, then the entirety of Christian theology is an attempt to unravel the insights of Paul.

Origen

(*c.*185–254)

Origen, the greatest of the early exegetes of Christianity, freely admitted that even he had, on one occasion, grievously misinterpreted the Bible. Reading the Gospel of Saint Matthew, chapter 19, verse 12, he had taken rather too literally the phrase 'and there be eunuchs, which have made themselves eunuchs for the kingdom of heaven's sake. He that is able to receive *it*, let him receive *it*', and castrated himself. In terms of his career this was bad enough, as his admission to the priesthood was repeatedly questioned on account of this self-mutilation; in terms of his scriptural hermeneutics, it was an embarrassing lapse into reading as verbatim a text that was deeply allegorical, anagogical, metaphorical and mystical in its import.

Origen was born in Alexandria into a Christian family. From an early age, he displayed an almost excessive zeal for reading scripture, to the extent that his father, Leonides, in a rather touching anecdote recorded by Eusebius, would kiss his son's chest as a sanctuary of the Holy Spirit. Leonides was executed in 202 under the purges of Emperor Severus: no doubt this deeply affected Origen's theology. At the age of only eighteen he became the head of the catechetical school in Alexandria, preparing candidates not only for baptism, but for the possibility of martyrdom. He sold his beautiful editions of the Greek philosophers and poets in order to support the family; a decision he may later have rued.

His intellectual skills were soon applied to weightier matters than the simple induction of new converts. 'I was sometimes approached by heretics and people educated after the Greek model, particularly in philosophy', he wrote. 'I therefore thought it advisable to make a thorough study both of heretical doctrine and of the philosopher's views about the truth.' A school began to form around Origen, where he encouraged the students to 'read all philosophy without preferring one . . . or rejecting another'. Except for the atheist Epicureans, 'nothing was kept from us, nothing concealed or made inaccessible. We could learn any theory, barbarian or Greek, mystical or moral,' recorded one student, Gregory of Nyssa.

Some students converted to Christianity, others merely improved their moral conduct. In effect, Origen was embarking on a massive, liberal, programme of education that would have far-reaching consequences for the church, and equip him for the most intensive theological battle of his career. Listening to other philosophies had an immediate pragmatic goal: as Origen sagely observed, the established schools – Stoicism, Platonism, and so forth – found it difficult to effect change. 'They never listen to those who think differently . . . that is why no old man ever succeeded in persuading any of the young.' In the intellectual melting pot of early third-century Alexandria, Origen had the opportunity to immerse himself in vastly different philosophies. 'All wisdom is from God,' and the Christian scholar winnowed the errors from the inspired pagans.

Origen's fame as a philosopher, textual critic and preacher won him praise from his adversaries, even from Julia Mamaea, aunt of the Emperor Heliogabalus. Seven amanuenses transcribed his sermons, although his *Commentary of Saint John* was preserved in an imperfect Latin translation by Ruffinus, who often 'supplied the missing threads . . . readers would not stomach his habit of raising questions and leaving them in the air, as he often did when preaching'. Origen's eight-volume *Commentary on Genesis* is lost, as is Ruffinus' text, and the *Commentary on XXV Psalms* is a handful of fragments.

Origen left Alexandria in 230, because of a dispute with his bishop, Demetrius. He was accused of preaching without being a priest, and then of becoming a priest in Palestine despite being a *castrato*. Finally excommunicated, he settled in Caesarea, where he participated in ecclesiastical councils, corresponded with other scholars, and, eventually, was tortured under the resurgence of anti-Christian edicts of the Emperor Decius.

There, he also completed his major work, *Against Celsus*. Celsus was a prominent Platonist scholar, who, around 180, had written a major philosophical diatribe against Christianity entitled *On the True Doctrine*. Although seventy years old, the attack was still sufficiently pertinent for Ambrosius to encourage Origen to consider a rebuttal. Without Origen's retort, we would know nothing of Celsus at all.

Christianity had been attacked beforehand, by satirists like Lucian of Samosata and the orator Fronto, but the basis of the criticisms had been so hyperbolic (ritual murder, atheism, cannibalism) that the earlier theologians, Irenaeus, Tertullian and Clement, had concentrated on suppressing internal division, heresy and unorthodox teachings, rather than parrying criticism from outsiders. Celsus' polemic was of a different order, and required a more substantial retort. *Against Celsus* is the first true work of Christian apologetics.

Celsus' *On the True Doctrine* is lost, but its substance can be inferred from the frequent quotation Origen deploys throughout his counter-attack. Scholarly estimates have presumed that anything between 50 and 90 per cent of Celsus' treatise has been ossified in Origen's work, though it would seem uncontentious that Origen would not choose to quote any hypotheses he could not disprove.

What is evident is that Celsus had a certain gift for vituperation. In deliriously caustic prose he castigates the new religion: it is for 'sinners, the stupid, the childish and, not to mince words, outcasts of all kinds . . . if you wanted to form a gang of thugs, who else would you ask to join?' Jesus was a two-bit street magician, the apostles were 'miserable publicans and sailors' and the only evidence of the resurrection came from a 'fanatical woman'. Entertainingly arch though this is, it allows Origen to undermine him with considerable elegance. Each mocking exaggeration is held up to calm correction. Christians may evangelize sinners; does Celsus believe that there is anyone who has not sinned? Though Celsus mocks Jesus for allowing his own betrayer to become a disciple, Origen counters that even Celsus' beloved Plato was intellectually betrayed by Aristotle.

When Celsus points out parallels between classical and Christian mythology, such as the similarity between Deucalion and Noah, arguing that this new religion is merely derivative, Origen retaliates with an impassioned defence of the allegorical nature of scripture. 'Adam' is not just a literal forefather, but the condition of all mankind. The new religion has more truth, even if the Greek versions have more beauty.

Even if Origen did not introduce the concept of non-literal reading into biblical exegesis after the incident with the knife, he certainly perfected it. In his commentaries on Saint John, he addresses head on the contradictions between John and the other evangelists. Such inconsistencies were deliberately present in the text like hermeneutic distress flares. The Holy Spirit allowed them to shock readers out of acquiescence and force them to consider the symbolic levels of the narrative. This manner of reading the Bible is an unquestionably profound legacy.

Origen did not die during his torture, but soon afterwards; thereby denying him his beloved status as a martyr. After his death, many of his works were banned and destroyed, particularly since he seemed to subscribe to an unorthodox belief (that God's power was so great that, should He wish it, He could even redeem Satan) which ran against notions of election. Having been excommunicated in life, he was eventually deemed heretical in death. His works were destroyed, and the most substantial remnant twins him perpetually with the pagan Celsus, each for ever preserving and subverting the other.

Faltonia Betitia Proba

(*c*.322–*c*.370)

In her one extant poem, Faltonia Betitia Proba informs us of the other poems she had written:

> Once I wrote of leaders violating sacred truths
> Of them who cling to this terrible thirst for power.

She had concerned herself with 'the spectacles of trivial themes . . . horses, arms of men and their wars'. More specifically, she had written a panegyrical epic on the defeat of the usurper Magnetius by Emperor Constantius II. It was at a time when her husband, Adelphius of the Anicii, would have appreciated her public show of support. The Emperor and his brothers and co-rulers, Constantine II and Constans, had found that dividing the Empire led to a multiplication of problems: in the early 350s, Constantius II had faced four separate rebellions. When Adelphius was elevated to the post of prefect in 351, loyalty was at a premium.

But we cannot be sure about Proba's description of her lost works, since the poem in which she alludes to them is an example of a very peculiar genre: the cento, which means that Proba did not actually write any of the lines of her poem.

A cento is a patchwork, where the writer rearranges lines by another poet to create a wholly new poem. Proba's *Cento* shuffles 694 lines of Virgil to narrate a Christian history of the world, from the Creation to Christ's resurrection. Tradition has it that she composed the work in an attempt to convert Adelphius, showing the immanence of God's truth even in his beloved pagan authors. She describes a deity who:

> When He saw them all shining steadfast in the clear skies
> (Virgil, *Aeneid*, book 3, line 518)

> The Almighty gave his name and numbers to the stars
> (Virgil, *Georgics*, book 1, line 137)

> And the year was divided into four equal parts
> (Virgil, *Georgics*, book 1, line 258)

Centos were a popular form. Ausonius composed an epithalamion version for the nuptials of Valentinian – H. J. Rose describes how 'by a process of collocation, totally innocent phrases of the poet are twisted into indecent meanings'. The poet Hosidius Geta, according to Tertullian, had created a whole tragedy, about Medea, using the method. Theoretically, if any cento's ur-text exists, we knew the length of a lost cento, it would be possible to recreate it from the works of Virgil.

Suppose, for example, that Proba's *Cento* had joined her other works in oblivion; though a passing mention in a minor commentator retained the information that it had been 694 lines long. The number of possible permutations is given by the factorial formula:

$$\frac{n!}{r! \times (n-r)!}$$

where n denotes the size of the sample from which the lines are drawn, and r is the length of the finished work. A factorial – for example, factorial 3 (3!) is a way of expressing $3 \times 2 \times 1$; similarly factorial 7 (7!) is $7 \times 6 \times 5 \times 4 \times 3 \times 2 \times 1$.

Using the dimensions of Proba's *Cento*, we would have to calculate very large factorials – 12915! divided by the product of 694! and 12221!.

Thus, the number of combinations is:

347929660538362150481004377012484366904387893314
505631212505761344529509095817488351499463966638
083761482141545937161855025291535265360398303317
637973251934334064484022021772303841847889590041
976470797646635409091252766371818190514478337 82
921326374371664993479075151455156943589129054 59
982469163724485013160856559751194379143468692 75
593188857625522987828727622872220820359846701 18
511479310931909925572931116195614766694577649 96
699085451499898712916599028489256834875493998 36
278668918361192207751571647059165087260717662 87
359744582208070029999128708904187282013759801 91
714685563548689675865035210323847875887082592 98
415987141919576064167991334924487003872690000 62
916521413642305565828887041788490110815363389 05
395291756365387776656061387641966306026409220 50
045470959853463238442672088101679355525414785 10
152934290889715609552004256860954872394894077 61
535894471818166344858989062317680538188071209 69
399262490954606036091539748996036330212974583 17
435736406850001576947772742162440502034468027 82
113460649318976091778626040814269506943221071 07
901457290761264141751829235047162980136609220 77
518113147204861754928628983890902317279336781 87
453546691079292634048924371655954382904640000

which hugely exceeds the numbers of atoms in the universe. Moreover, our formula does not take into consideration that the *order* of the lines is also important: it treats the combinations (a, b, c), (a, c, b), (b, a, c), (b, c, a), (c, a, b) and (c, b, a) as being identical. The actual number of permutations is a number longer than the rest of this book. But still, if only we knew the extent of any lost cento and had sufficient Latin scholars to weed out the versions where the verbs do not agree, or the rhythm syncopates, or which are just meaningless, and had enough paper: a lost work could be found!

As for Proba, we do not know if her poetic deck-shuffling had the desired effect of converting her husband. Scholars have speculated that it was written around 362, when the Emperor Julian, called the Apostate, had declared that classical texts were not sacrilegious: however, he also forbade Christians to teach and resurrected the old religions, so it would be daring, to say the least, for a writer to negotiate the political, cultural and theological paradoxes of bending paganism to the ends of Christianity.

Proba's tragedy stems from her use of this singular form. Unlike the majority of female Roman authors, we still possess a work by her, although we have none of her words. Without knowing the date of composition, it is impossible to decide if the *Cento* is a wry parlour-game or a sly act of subterfuge. She shimmers, trapped on the cusp of becoming lost.

Kālidāsa

(*c.* mid-fourth–*c.* early fifth century)

Kālidāsa tells us almost nothing of himself. He is traditionally associated with the court of Vikramāditya, the 'Sun of Valour'; however, this title was adopted by King Chandra Gupta II in the fourth century CE, as well as referring to a semi-mythical king who defeated the Śaka, or Scythians, in the first century CE. The earlier Vikramāditya had his court at Ujjayinī, a city praised by Kālidāsa in his lyrical poem *The Cloud Messenger* (*Meghadūtam*). Conversely, it has been suggested that the poem was written for Kālidāsa's wife, during a separation when he was advising the widow of Chandra Gupta II. Dates from the fifth century BCE to the seventh century CE have been advanced for Kālidāsa, and evidence from Greek astronomical terms to Chinese manuscript acquisition has been proposed and countered. All that is certain is that he is the most highly regarded of all Sanskrit poets, the *Kavi-kula-guru* or Master of Poets, as a later writer was to call him.

In the absence of any firm biographical facts, a gloriously apocryphal body of legends has entwined itself with his name. Kālidāsa means 'Servant of the Goddess Kali', and the fact that the –dāsa suffix was thought pejorative by orthodox Hindus has been taken to suggest that he was a foreigner and convert. He was, by all accounts, very handsome, and some traditions claim he was also inordinately stupid as a child. They say he was seen up a tree, cutting off the bough on which he was sitting.

He was inveigled into marrying a haughty princess, who had decreed she would only marry her intellectual superior. Some wags at court persuaded her to take part in a silent debate with Kālidāsa. She put up one finger, to state that 'Shakti is one', Shakti being the personification of primal energy, and the consort of the god Shiva. He thought she was going to poke him in the eye, so put up two fingers, which she accepted as the answer 'Shakti is in duality as well'. She extended her palm, to symbolize the elements earth, water, fire, air and void. Fearful of getting a slap, he put up his fist. The princess agreed to marry him, as he had successfully shown that the elements constitute the body. When the ruse was discovered, he was banished, and, mortally ashamed, he offered his tongue to Kali, who in return made him a poet.

Although the titles of 500 Sanskrit plays have been recorded, only three can be attributed to Kālidāsa with any certainty. In addition he is known to have written the afore-mentioned lyrical poem, a meditation on the seasons and 'The Birth of the War God'. He also left unfinished an epic poem entitled *Raghuvaṁśam*, or *The Dynasty of Raghu*, on the genealogy and descendants of Rama, comprising material also found in the *Ramayana*.

It was principally as a playwright, though, that Kālidāsa became known in Europe. Sir William Jones translated his play as *Sacontala, or the Fatal Ring* in 1792, coining the epithet 'the Sanskrit Shakespeare'. Goethe was deeply impressed when it was translated from English into German, and lauded it for 'blending youthful blossoms with the fruits of maturity, uniting heaven and earth in one'. Goethe began his *Faust* with a debate between the author and the theatre manager, after the model of Kālidāsa, such prologue scenes being a notable feature of Sanskrit drama.

The Recognition of Śakuntalā, to give it its original name, has many of Kālidāsa's dramatic preoccupations: romantic misfortune, magical intervention, enchantment and disenchantment. It opens with King Dushyanta on a hunting expedition, meeting with the maiden Śakuntalā. They marry in secret and he gives her a ring, but is called back to court, and promises to send for her. A curse makes him forget, and when the pregnant Śakuntalā finally finds him, he cannot recognize her, nor can she prove she is his beloved, since the ring has been lost. It is found in the belly of a fish, and the couple are reunited.

A synopsis can hardly do justice to the charm of the piece, nor can a translation ever capture the subtleties of alliteration, homonymy and word-play. Moments in another of his plays, *Urvaśi Won by Valour*, have the feel of an exotic, late-period Shakespeare: the nymph Urvaśi is won by the King Pururavas only after he descends into madness, and she must escape a curse which will turn her back into a celestial being at the moment she sees her child's face. Given the scant nature of the Kālidāsa canon, alongside the undeniable problems of translation, it is unremarkable though unfortunate that he has also been misprized. Max Muller famously damned his work with faint praise, saying his 'plays are not superior to many plays that have been allowed to rest in dust and peace on the shelves of our libraries'.

Muller may well think so, but his opinion does not explain Kālidāsa's high esteem by his native peers. An anonymous panegyric said, 'Once, when the poets were counted, Kālidāsa occupied the little finger; the ring finger remains unnamed true to its name [the Sanskrit for ring-finger means, literally, without name]; for his second has not been found.'

His stature is confirmed by another weird story from the legendary accounts of his life. Kālidāsa died in Sri Lanka, supposedly murdered by a prostitute. The King, overcome with remorse that the greatest playwright ever should have been 'annihilated from the round of births' under his jurisdiction, set himself on fire.

Fulgentius

(467–532)

Bishop Fulgentius, who opposed the Arian heresy, is sometimes considered to be the author of allegorical interpretations of Graeco-Roman mythology, as well as one of the most curious works in the classical repertoire.

(Ahem.)

Humanist authors assign to this bishop (or not) a singular work, to wit, his history of all things past and upcoming, which diachronously charts, from birth and youth to coffin and tomb, a living individual's span. An ambitious topic by most authors' standards, but our Latin wordsmith flung on his opus an astonishing constraint, viz. that in turn, from A at first to Z lastly, his books would forgo a customary graphic sign for a sound, cyclically; thus it was similar in its plan to that of Tryphiodorus, who, in his account of Calypso's wily inamorato, had to miss out glyphs in a chain or, to put it simply (in contrast to this paragraph), his triumph (in common with this paragraph) was a lipogram.

Enough already! Joseph Addison railed against the lipogram in *The Spectator* for Tuesday 8 May 1711, denouncing Tryphiodorus' *Lipogrammatical Odyssey*, where 'the most apt and elegant word in the whole language was rejected, like a diamond with a flaw in it, if it appeared blemished with a wrong letter'. Fulgentius' *De Aetatibus Mundi et Hominis* likewise omitted A from book I, B from book II and so on, a technical stricture preventing, for example, Adam from appearing in an account of Genesis. The work was to cover the entire history of the world. The Bible (except the Book of Revelations) is covered in the first nine books, followed by the reign of Alexander, the Roman Republic, the life of Christ and the Acts of the Apostles, and it ends abruptly with the lives of the Roman emperors up to Julian the Apostate in book XIV.

Fulgentius' preface says that the work should be twenty-three books long (the Latin alphabet doubling I and J, and V and U, and omitting W altogether). It would seem likely that a Z-less Apocalypse would end the book. Apart from finding synonyms for the tribe of Zabulon and the gemstone topaz, which makes up the ninth foundation of the New Jerusalem, it seems a less onerous task than the beginning.

What, one is tempted to ask, is the point? For postmodernists, like the twentieth-century lipogrammist Georges Perec, the submission to an outrageous linguistic limitation may be an end in itself, though this is unlikely in this case. An early Christian writer must have had reasons other than a demonstration of dexterity. Fulgentius had a serious purpose. The truth will out, rough hew it how we will. His God was the God of St John, the Word that was in the beginning. Language itself – not individual languages – was Godlike; eternal, creative, human and yet beyond the encompassing of any individual. Adam was in God's image most when he was allowed to name creation. If God was in the language and with the language, then whatever evasions, shenanigans or wilful schemes were thrown on Him, He would find a way to be expressed. Far from being an arrogant demonstration of creative superiority, Fulgentius' linguistic game was a proof of his share in the divine, and a humbling before the eternally elusive, always present God.

Widsith the Wide-travelled

(?late sixth century CE)

Widsið, maðolade,   wordhord onleac
se þe monna mæst   mægþa ofer eorþan,
folca geondferde

'Widsith spoke, unlocked his word-treasury, he who of all men had most widely travelled among all the nations and peoples of the world.' The poem *Widsith* introduces the poet, Widsith, an Anglo-Saxon *scop* (or minstrel). The rest of the work narrates the various kingdoms and rulers he has performed before, a panoply of places and poetic subjects that Widsith has encountered.

Despite the vague lineaments of a biography – he comes, apparently, from the Myrgingas, a Saxon enclave in Schleswig-Holstein, and has, in his time, received a golden torque worth six hundred gold coins from King Eormanric for his songs – we should not be so naive as to suppose this poem is an accurate 'About the Author'. Widsith claims to have journeyed from the lands of the Picts and the Scots to the Medes, Egyptians and as far as India. He has sung before Caesar, as well as for the chieftains of Huns, Goths, Swedes and Geats. His travels are extravagantly cosmopolitan; even more surprising is his assertion to have performed both for Eormanric (who died in 375) and the munificent Ælfwine (who was alive in 568). His name, 'Widsith', tautologically means, 'Wide-travelled', and similar epithets have been ascribed to Viking *skalds* as well.

Widsith verges into the mythical. He might be an almost supernatural figure, like Orpheus, or a once-real poet on to whose life numerous, contradictory stories have been grafted, like Homer. It is as fruitless to ascribe even the words in *Widsith* to Widsith as it would be to attribute papyrus fragments to the god Thoth.

But the poem does allow us a glimpse into the repertoire of the Anglo-Saxon poet. Tacitus, in his survey of Germanic customs, said that the only poetry they had was a historical record of their great deeds, and this seems borne out by Widsith's roll-call of rulers. Among his catalogue of characters he mentions Finn Folcwalding, the ruler of the Frisians, Hnæf the Hocings and Sæferth the Secgan. All three of these heroes appear in the epic poem *The Battle of Finnsburh*, of which only a few score lines survive. 'Widsith' also mentions Hrothgar and Hrothwulf, who will be familiar to readers of the only extant Anglo-Saxon epic, *Beowulf*, as well as their hall, Heorot, which is assailed by the monster Grendel. In total, 'Widsith' mentions over sixty names, and, given that some of them are known to be the subjects of heroic lays, it is not beyond the bounds of possibility that most of them are the heroes of lost works. As Christianity slowly converted Britain, the value of these old sagas was called into question. Alcuin, the director of Charlemagne's educational programme, berated the monks of Lindisfarne, saying, 'What has Ingeld to do with Christ?' Ingeld, too, is mentioned in *Widsith*.

The 'Widsith' poet is keen to let the audience know the range of his materials, and how he was handsomely remunerated for singing the great deeds of wise leaders. The *Widsith* poem is a prospectus, a repository of well-known classics and the promise of future deathless songs. In its own way, it is the Dark Ages equivalent of a Frankfurt Book Fair Rights Guide.

The Venerable Bede

(*c*.673–735)

Bede was canonized, and acquired his 'Venerable', in 1899. His reputation for holiness, however, was established nearly a millennium beforehand. In 1020, his skeleton was purloined from the monastery at Jarrow in Northumberland where he had spent most of his life and moved to the cathedral at Durham, to rest near the remains of Saint Cuthbert. Durham, it seems, was keen to corner the market in English relics. But by the nineteenth century, despite all the necessary evidence of his exceptional goodness, it was as the 'Father of English History', rather than as a dedicated monk, that his name was known.

Bede's *History of the English Church and People*, completed in 731, surveys the establishment of Christianity, and its subsequent tribulations, in the British Isles, among the 'perfida gens', or 'faithless people', as he frequently castigated its inhabitants. So recalcitrant were the British that God found it necessary to punish them, even raising up a new scourge, Muhammad, in Arabia, to terrify them. Bede's five books are a unique source for historians of the Anglo-Saxon period, Bede being as diligent in his researches as he was in his devotions.

Thanks to Bede, the mists of anonymity disperse and the melancholy roll-call of bards whose works have perished pauses. After glimpses of semi-mythic Widsiths and speculations about who might have written *Beowulf,* we reach a real name. Chapter 24 of book IV introduces Cædmon, the earliest English poet to be known by name and whose verse survives. In 680, Cædmon was an elderly shepherd, with no gift for the communal singing of his peers, until a visitation in a dream demanded that he sing. He demurred, saying that the reason he left the feast was his lack of skill; but the vision insisted. Cædmon then refused, on the grounds that he had no topic to sing about anyway. 'Sing about the Creation of all things,' he was told. Cædmon sang:

Now we must praise the Guardian of the heaven-kingdom, the might of the Lord and his mind's wisdom, the work of the Father of Glory; he, the Eternal Lord, commanded the beginning of each wonder. He, the Holy Creator, first fashioned heaven as a roof for the sons of men; after, the Guardian of mankind, created the middle earth below, the world for men, everlasting Lord, almighty Leader.

Bede gives only the 'general sense' in Latin, and apologizes that poetry cannot be translated without losing its dignity and power. But another, anonymous hand thought fit to inscribe in the margins the actual words Cædmon used:

Nu scylan hergan hefaenricaes uard,
metudæs mecti end his modgidanc,
uerc uuldurfadur sue he uundra gihuaes,
eci dryctin, or astelidæ.
He aerist scop aelda barnum
heben til hrofe, haleg scepen;
tha middungeard moncynnæs uard
eci dryctin æfter tiadæ
firum foldu, frea allmectig.

Cædmon went on to compose a great deal more poetry, including, according to Bede,

the whole story of Genesis . . . Israel's Exodus from Egypt and the entry into the Promised Land, and many other events of scriptural history. He sang of the Lord's Incarnation, Passion, Resurrection and Ascension into Heaven, the coming of the Holy Spirit, and the teachings of the Apostles. He also made many poems on the terrors of the Last Judgement, the horrible pains of Hell, and the joys of the Kingdom of Heaven.

All he had learned Cædmon could turn into poetry, after reflection, 'like one of the clean animals chewing the cud'.

Cædmon may have had some experience of translating before he worked biblical Latin into Anglo-Saxon verse. His name does not appear to be of Anglo-Saxon or Germanic origin; and it may be that the 'first known English poet' was composing in his second language, not his mother tongue. When, much later, Anglo-Saxon scholars turned their attention to the Junius, Vercelli and Exeter Manuscripts, it seemed a natural assumption that the poems on Genesis, Exodus, Christ II (on the Ascension) and the 'Fates of the Apostles' were the very poems that Bede had attributed to Cædmon. But the nine lines remain all we can certainly attribute to him. Without rehearsing the arguments on dialect and date, a simple irrefutable proof denies two of these pieces of Cædmon: another poet signs the lines.

Cynewulf lived more than a century after Cædmon. Four Anglo-Saxon poems contain his signature, always in the form of the runes that made up his name, and with the rune's hieroglyphic significance embedded into the poem. As well as the aforementioned works, 'Elene' and 'Andreas' contain the distinctive, riddling sections, where *cen* ᚻ (torch), *yr* ᛜ (bow/trumpet), *nyd* ᚾ (necessity), *eoh* ᛇ (horse), *wynn* ᚹ (happiness), *ur* ᚢ (ox/our/strength), *lagu* ᚱ (ocean) and ᚠ *feoh* (wealth) are interpolated. Cynewulf adds a biographical ending to 'Elene', where he says he was a man of wrath before the Lord redeemed him.

Playing with words, runes and initials, it was clearly tempting to ditch the assumption that Cædmon wrote these poems and place all these works under the ascription of Cynewulf. But only four poems have the oblique moniker, and even these cannot have been actually put to parchment by the poet himself. 'Christ I' and 'Christ III' lack the mark, if not the talent. Despite the understandable desire to make Cynewulf the recognizable genius behind a whole tradition, we can only know for sure that he was the author of four poems.

Cædmon was falsely given Cynewulf's oeuvre, then Cynewulf was thought to have supplanted Cædmon as the Anglo-Saxon meistersinger, but neither misattribution nor misprizing obliterates Cædmon's claim to fame. A predecessor might, and two candidates present themselves: Drycthelm and Aldhelm.

Little is known about Drycthelm apart from his appearance in Bede's *History*. The head of a religiously observant family in Northumberland, he died, and apparently came back to life after three days. During his temporary mortification, he had a vision of Heaven and Hell, which induced him to become a monk in Melrose. He spoke very little about the afterlife: a monk called Haemgils transcribed and stitched together an account akin to those of Dante and Milton; but Drycthelm was more concerned with the quality of his immortal soul than any temporary celebrity as a bard. He would frequently stand in the freezing river, singing psalms, as a bodily penance. When other monks marvelled at his endurance, he responded tersely, 'I have known it colder.'

Aldhelm was much more famous. He was the Abbot of Malmesbury and Bishop of Sherbourne, and wrote a Latin panegyric on virginity, which Bede says was 'composed in a double form in hexameter verse and prose on the model of

Sedulius', as well as a treatise on metrics, illustrated by 100 riddles. King Alfred stated that Aldhelm's English poems were his favourites, though none at all has survived. The *Gesta Pontificum* contains the lovely story that he began writing verses as a response to his congregation's aversion to sermons. The Abbot would disguise himself as a minstrel outside of the church, and begin to perform, 'mingling words of scripture among the more entertaining matter'. Drycthelm and Aldhelm show that there was an indigenous tradition of creative exposition of Christianity before Cædmon, and, even though William of Malmesbury could assert that Aldhelm's work was still being recited in the twelfth century, neither writer's English work has reached the twenty-first.

Bede himself was more than just a historian. At the time of his death, he was translating St John's Gospel into Anglo-Saxon; it would have accompanied the impressive bibliography of his work which concludes the *History*. As well as the two books on *The Building of the Temple*, *Thirty Questions on the Book of Kings*, *On the Book of the Blessed Father Job* and fifty-six other theological expositions, he wrote a *Book of Hymns*, a *Book of Epigrams*, *On the Nature of Things*, *On Orthography*, *On Times* and an *Art of Poetry*, all of which are lost.

The last title shows that Bede was a theoretician of poetry: he was also a practitioner. A letter from Cuthbert, one of Bede's pupils and latterly the Abbot of Jarrow, to his school-friend Cuthwin narrates Bede's final days. On his deathbed, he composed a poem: 'Before setting out on the fated journey, no man is so wise that he need not reflect, before his soul departs, what good and evil he has done, what judgement he will receive after his death-day.' As with Cædmon's verses, Bede's English poetry is only preserved as marginalia to the Latin text.

Muhammad Ibn Ishaq

(704–67)

Ibn Hisham, who died in Baghdad in 833, was a respected grammarian and scholar. His most challenging work was to prepare a definitive edition of the *Sirat Rasul Allah*, the biography of the Prophet Muhammad, written over sixty years previously by Ibn Ishaq. In doing so, and in doing it so diligently, he destroyed Ibn Ishaq's work.

Islamic historiography involved a complex analysis of oral and written sources. In 610, Muhammad, a forty-year-old merchant of the Quraysh tribe, had been performing his annual meditations outside of Mecca, when he was seized by the angel Jibra'el, whose presence filled the whole sky wherever he turned. The angel commanded, 'Recite,' and, despite his faltering, Muhammad began to compose the Qur'an. A much later historian, al-Tabari, claims that the Prophet was so frightened, and convinced he was possessed by a djinn, that he nearly committed suicide. Over the next twenty years, Muhammad would be regularly overwhelmed, as the *ayas* and *suras* that comprised the Qur'an were given to the world through his lips.

The pagan Quraysh worshipped a god called al-Llah, alongside his three female consorts, al-Lat, al-Uzza and Manat.

Through trading contacts with Jewish and Christian communities, whom they referred to as 'the people of the book', the Arabians became acutely aware that they had never received a similar, immediate revelation from God. The Qur'an's haunting, beautiful verses could have no other source than the divine: Muhammad himself retorted to sceptics who asked why he could not perform miracles that the Qur'an was miracle enough. As well as providing them with a holy text, as the Qur'an developed it provided the Arabs with an aetiological myth, an origin story that linked them to the historical presence of the 'One God'.

Jews and Christians both traced their relationship with God back to Abraham, through his son Isaac. Abraham, however, had an older son, Ishmael, the offspring of his Egyptian concubine Hagar. Ishmael and Hagar were expelled by Abraham's wife Sarah, and God had twice given them his blessing: like Isaac's generation, Ishmael will 'form a great nation', and the Lord will 'multiply his seed'. He then disappears from the Pentateuch, his nation and seed forgotten. The Qur'an spun out this loose thread, and cast the Quraysh as the aboriginal Abrahamic tribe. The plot the authors rejected, as Jesus might have said, has become an epic.

As this new, monotheistic religion grew in strength, Muhammad's followers would commit the verses and chapters to memory. After the Prophet's death, the first and second Caliphs (Muhammad's lieutenant and father-in-law, Abu Bakr, and Umar, who had been ready to kill Muhammad at first, before a Damascene conversion) collected the text together and had it written. The third Caliph, Uthman, standardized the Qur'an and destroyed all variant versions.

At the same time, a large number of sayings about the Prophet and his life were in circulation. These *hadith* were scrupulously examined by scholars, who were keen to establish the authenticity of the aphorisms that had been recorded by those closest to Muhammad. Similarly, the first written records of the life of Muhammad were bolstered by *isnads*, cited authorities that told where the historian had found each particular incident, like a precursor of the footnote. Ibn Hisham would have compared the *isnads* in Ibn Ishaq's work to relevant sources, weighed the testimony of *hadith* and ensured that nothing ran contrary to the revelation of the Qur'an.

Ibn Hasham took his editorial duties very seriously. He removed those things which were offensive to Muslims, and produced a recension of Ibn Ishaq's original text: he expanded it where there were alternative, valid traditions and deleted aberrant fables. So we have Ibn Ishaq's biography, but skewed and squeezed through Ibn Hasham's academic endeavours. Naturally, one wonders what was removed.

The *Sirat Rasul Allah* may be hagiography, but it does not stress Muhammad's greatness by stripping him of his humanity. The Prophet laughs, plays with children, is terrified, furious and benevolent. He loves, jokes, suffers and schemes. Second-hand ideas of what constitutes a religiously 'offensive' section are challenged at every turn. Ibn Ishaq / Hisham records some comments by Muhammad's third wife, Aisha, Mother of the Faithful, that approach mordant irreverence. When a Qur'anic verse justified the Prophet's actions, she is supposed to have commented, 'Truly thy Lord makes haste to do thy bidding.' On face value, the story of Abdallah Ibn Sa'id, who deceitfully altered transcriptions of the Qur'an to test Muhammad's inspiration, seems a model of lenience. Under the protection of his foster-brother Uthman, he begged for mercy. The Prophet was silent for a long time and then lifted the death penalty, then berated his Companions for not taking the pause as a sign to execute Ibn Sa'id.

Opponents' adverse comments are equally commemorated. When the Quraysh first heard of the new monotheism, they were fairly tolerant, and some even offered to pay for medical treatment for the Prophet. As relationships between the Quraysh and the new religionists deteriorated, and economic sanctions against the converts deepened, the wife of Abu Lahab shouted obscene poems at the believers, and children pelted Muhammad with sheep's uteruses. Ibn Ishaq also retained some of the defamatory verses by the Jewish poet Ka'b Ibn al-Ashraf, whom Muhammad had assassinated.

The most tempting subject for the censored section must be the notorious Satanic Verses. The much later writers Ibn Sa'd and al-Tabari record that on one occasion, the evil spirit Shaitan managed to interpolate verses that seemed to make concessions to the polytheism of the Quraysh. These verses in *Sura* 53 sanctioned the worship of al-Lat, al-Uzza and Manat as intermediate intercessory gods. Despite the fact that such an accommodation would have settled affairs between the Quraysh and Muhammad, he recanted, and the revised *sura* had an explicit denunciation of the goddesses as 'naught but names yourselves have named'. *Sura* 53 is mostly in short lines, but contains odd sections in a longer, less embellished style. This may indicate that it was composed at two different times.

It is a good story, but it is only a good story. Given the political tensions at the time of Ibn Ishaq's writing between the followers of the family of the fourth Caliph, Ali (the Shi'a), and the Ummayad dynasty (the Sunni) which had come to power, there could be countless, subtle shadings that Ibn Hisham might have deemed imprudent to preserve.

What we do have, though, is a collection of stories that have an immediacy to the Western reader that the Qur'an, in translation, can appear to lack. Although Thomas Carlyle's criticism – 'a wearisome, confused jumble, crude, incondite; endless iterations, long-windedness, entanglement; most crude, incondite insupportible stupidity' – is characteristically overblown and intemperate, even for the blustering voice of nineteenth-century British imperialism, it unfortunately reflects many readers' lack of empathy.

Contrast this one sublimely startling legend. A poor man was brought before Muhammad, guilty of a misdemeanour. He was told to give alms to the poor, but pointed out he had nothing to give. Muhammad requisitioned some dates and told him to give them to someone worse off than himself. He replied that no one was as impecunious. So Muhammad laughed and commanded him to eat the dates as a penance. Whatever Ibn Hisham cut out from Ibn Ishaq's text, that which remained still challenges Western notions of piety.

Ahmad ad-Daqiqi

(932–76)

Although the poet Ahmad ad-Daqiqi took the Islamic name Abu Mansur Muhammad after the Arab conquest of Persia, tradition has long asserted that he persisted in the Zoroastrian faith. One of the fragments attributed to him claims that there are only four things Daqiqi deemed necessary for happiness:

> The ruby lip, the flute's lament,
> Crimson wine and the creed of Zoroaster.

As a court poet in Baghdad, his name became synonymous with excellence. 'To praise him is to bring dates to Hajar' – or coals to Newcastle – claimed one critic, but ad-Daqiqi did not allow this to go to his head. 'My whole life has been spent being patient; I would need another to enjoy reaping its fruits'. Yet his elegant ghazals and quatrains were dwarfed by a project which would have crowned his career.

Daqiqi was commissioned to compose an epic, but his ambition was crudely curtailed by the knife of his Turkish servant, whose reasons for murdering his master have been left unrecorded. Daqiqi's epic might well have drifted into oblivion like his contemporary Rudaki's *Kalíla and Dimna*, had it not been for the dream of the young poet Firdausi (940–1020).

Daqiqi had completed a thousand lines of his epic before his murder, which told the story of the Iranian kings from Gushtasp to Arjasp, interleaved with lines on the beginnings of the prophet Zoroaster's mission. Firdausi acquired these remains, and relates how, in a dream, Daqiqi appeared, seated in a lush garden, with a goblet of wine. The ghost of Daqiqi gave Firdausi permission to continue the epic on Iranian history, and to incorporate the lines he had written into the poem. Thus, Daqiqi's fame would not perish.

'Now I will tell what Daqiqi said, for I am alive and he is as one with the dust.' It took Firdausi a further thirty-five years to complete *The Shah-nameh*, or *Book of the Kings*. He was not wholly reverent to the memory of the poet whose task he adopted and superseded, criticizing the weakness of Daqiqi's lines, which did not 'renew the ancient times'. Firdausi's outspokenness would have serious consequences when it was directed at those not yet in the grave.

When Sultan Mahmoud of Ghaznavid received all 60,000 couplets of *The Shah-nameh*, his promise to pay a gold coin for each seemed rather rash. Moreover, whilst Daqiqi had been a courtier, the provincial Firdausi had laboured at his work in the backwater of Tus, and was perhaps unaware that his praise of the Shi'a tradition was unlikely to win favour with the Sunni ministers. The Sultan offered instead an equivalent number of silver coins, which Firdausi disdainfully rejected. He gave the money to the first people he came across, a bath-keeper and a sherbet-seller.

Incensed, the Sultan decreed Firdausi was to be executed by being trampled on by an elephant. He fled to Herat, dedicated the poem instead to Ispahbad Shahriyar bin Shir-win, and prefaced it with a hundred lines of satirical venom against Mahmoud, calling him the son of a slave. Shahriyar, aware that no good would come of this libel, offered to buy the diatribe at 1,000 dirhans per line, and immediately destroyed it. An attempt to reconcile the Sultan and Firdausi would have been successful, if Firdausi had received the 60,000 dirhans the Sultan sent to him. Instead, the messenger with the money met Firdausi's funeral cortège as it entered the city.

The Shah-nameh became the national epic of Persia, a work that 'rescued from oblivion and preserved for all time our national history ... and the Persian language', as Mirza Muhammad Ali Fernghi said, and it simultaneously saved Daqiqi. Had he lived, Daqiqi might even have eclipsed Firdausi; as it is, he is engulfed in him.

Dante Alighieri

(1265–1321)

Jacopo and Pietro Alighieri had a serious problem. Their father had been working on a poem for nearly thirteen years, an encyclopedic allegory describing his vision of Hell, Purgatory and the Heavens, entitled the *Comedy*. An exile from his home town of Florence, where he had been sentenced to death *in absentia*, he had wandered round the feuding and fractious states of Italy, from Verona to Tuscany to Urbino and finally to Ravenna, where he came under the protection of the Can Grande della Scala. There, Dante sent for Jacopo and Pietro.

The youthful Can Grande was an exceptional military tactician and a generous patron of the arts. He commissioned the building of churches and employed the painter Giotto to decorate them. His chancellor, Benzo d'Alessandria, was a famous Humanist scholar. Although he was occasionally as raucous and bawdy as the basest of his infantrymen, Can Grande held Dante Alighieri in profound respect. As the cantos of his masterwork were finished, they were sent to Can Grande, who had them copied and circulated.

Soon after Jacopo and Pietro arrived, their father died, and the final thirteen cantos of the *Comedy* could not be found.

The *Paradiso*, the culmination of the entire poem, was missing. Dante's fame as a poet was unparalleled in Italy. The last thing that Can Grande would want was an imperfect and unfinished epic. The last thing their father would have wanted was to be cheated of posterity in the same way that his life had been blighted by banishment. There was only one thing for it. Jacopo and Pietro themselves were going to have to complete the *Comedy*.

How to begin? The poem was so densely structured that at least the lineaments of their projected forgery were easily discernible. They knew for certain that there were thirteen missing cantos. The poem was divided into 100 cantos: an introduction and then thirty-three each for *Inferno*, *Purgatorio* and *Paradiso*. It was written in *terza rima*, a form equally imbued with the significance of the number three: each stanza had three lines, with the second line rhyming with the first and third of the next stanza – a b a, b c b, c d c . . . The 100 cantos represented the perfect number, ten, multiplied by itself; or rather the mystical number three, indicative of the Trinity, multiplied by itself, plus one, to signify the Unity of God.

Numerology and personal history suffused the entire work. Their father had fallen in love, at the age of nine, with a girl called Beatrice Portinari. She had spurned him, and married another, before dying in 1290; nonetheless, and despite his marriage to Jacopo and Pietro's mother, he had lauded Beatrice's indescribable mortal and moral beauty in a sequence of *canzoni* called *The New Life*. In the *Comedy*, she had become a symbol of celestial intervention.

She appeared in the sixty-fourth stanza (6+4=10), which had 145 lines (1+4+5=10), and announced her identity in line 73 (7+3=10). She should be mentioned by name 63 times (6+3=9), and her name used as a rhyme only nine times.

The text of the *Comedy* the brothers possessed broke off at the twentieth canto of the *Paradiso*. It stranded their father in the Sixth Heaven, that of Jupiter, guardian of the Just. This left the Seventh (the realm of the Contemplatives, governed by Saturn), the Heaven of Fixed Stars, the Primum Mobile and finally the Empyrean. They had still to write in encounters with Thrones, Cherubim and Seraphim, and disquisitions on the Theological Virtues of Faith, Hope and Love (Beatrice, of course, figuring prominently therein). With such a rigorous and regimented form, the lines would hopefully flow fairly logically. They also, rather more troublingly, had to describe God.

Did their father's other works suggest any clues, or lines of thought, or possible images? He had written to Can Grande explaining that the poem was called the *Comedy* since it 'began in sorrow' – i.e. Hell – and 'ended in joy'. He had intended to write a description of the rules of the literary genre of comedy in his work defending writing in vernacular Italian rather than antique Latin, the *De Vulgare Eloquentia*. Unfortunately, he never completed the work, though his sons did have his strict taxonomy of types of adjectives.

Dante had also planned to write a work describing the virtues that crowned the Heavens. In the *Convivio*, or *The Banquet*, Alighieri Snr provided commentaries and glosses on the *canzoni* he had written after *The New Life*. The work was to have comprised an introduction, and then fourteen essays on fourteen poems. They had copies of the poems, including 'Tre donne', a lament for the justice so conspicuously lacking on earth, and 'Doglia mi reca', a panegyric on liberality. Again, however, he had never finished the work, leaving eleven of the essays unwritten. Leaving work unfinished seemed to be a habit.

As for God . . . well, the Bible appeared of little help. Even Saint Paul, in the Second Epistle to the Corinthians, told of a man – himself – 'caught up to the Third Heaven' where he 'heard unspeakable words, which it is not lawful for a man to utter'. How much of Saint John's vision in the Book of Revelations should the brothers include, given that the saint had warned that if anyone left out parts of his vision of Heaven, they would be struck from the Book of Life and cast out of the Holy City?

In Florence, at Easter in 1300, their father had had some kind of vision. He had cryptically written to Can Grande of 'aliqua "quae referre nescit et nequit rediens"' – 'things "which he who returns has neither knowledge nor power to relate"'. The tongue faltered. Language itself was too human to articulate the divine. The memory was too fleshily fallen to retain the imprint of such an ecstatic insight. Dante had known – right the way through the perverse and insidious tortures of Hell, where he had consigned and condemned his own teacher, cousin and Pope, right the way up the pining, refining punishments of Mount Purgatory, where all this mortal pain and confusion was whittled away – where it must all end. But that Vision of Heaven had been Dante's, and not his sons'.

Jacopo seemed less daunted than Pietro about the task in hand. They would have to describe the ineffable in more ways than one; perpetrate a daring act of ventriloquism, throwing their voices as if it were whispering from their father's sepulchre. And then he spoke.

According to Boccaccio's *Life of Dante*, he appeared in a dream to Jacopo, eight months into their elaborate invention. Jacopo asked if he was alive. 'Yes, but of the true life, not of ours,' Dante replied. With due filial devotion, Jacopo asked if the *Comedy* had been completed, and was led to his father's old bedroom. The shade pointed to the wall, and disappeared. Jacopo and his father's friend Piero di Giardino investigated, and found a hanging covering the spot that had been indicated. Behind it, in a recess, and nearly illegible with mould, were the final thirteen cantos of the *Comedy*.

★

Can Grande, of course, published them. Dante, the embittered, disappointed exile, became the apogee of medieval
poetry. Although Boccaccio's story about the manuscript
recovered from beyond the grave has been doubted, dismissed
and even justified as a subconscious realization, a certain air
of precarious survival clings to the poem. As Thomas Carlyle
expressed it:

We will not complain of Dante's miseries: had all gone right
with him as he wished it, he might have been prior, podestà, or
whatsoever they call it, of Florence, well accepted among neigh-
bours – and the world had wanted one of the most notable works
ever spoken or sung.

Geoffrey Chaucer

(*c.*1343–1400)

Even though *The Canterbury Tales* is unfinished, it has an ending. After the Parson's Tale has concluded, there is the so-called 'Retraction': *Heere taketh the makere of this book his leve.* As if in response to the Parson's treatise on repentance and confession, Chaucer asks the reader 'for the mercy of God, that ye preye for me that Crist have mercy on me and foryeve me my giltes'. Specifically, he wishes pardon for having written 'many a song and many a leccherous lay', including his *Troilus and Criseyde*, the unfinished *Book of Fame*, the incomplete *XXV Ladies* (presumably *The Legend of Good Women*), *The Parlement of Fowls*, *The Book of the Duchess* and the mysterious *Book of the Leoun*, of which no copies survive. Likewise, we are exhorted to avoid the fragmentary *Canterbury Tales*, 'thilke that sownen into synne', and which the reader of the 'Retraction' is presumably holding.

Instead, we are directed to the translation of Boethius' *The Consolation of Philosophy*, as well as 'othere bookes of legendes of seintes, and omelies, and moralitee, and devocioun'. Presumably these included Chaucer's own translation of Origen's homily on Saint Mary Magdalene, and 'Of the Wreched

Engendryne of Mankynde', a translation of Pope Innocent III's *De Contemptu Mundi*, which are mentioned in the prologue to *The Legend of Good Women*. Although the former is lost completely, the Parson's Tale which the chastened reader has just finished contains material derived from that papal encyclical. More curiously, Chaucer also mentions a Life of St Cecilia in his list of ennobling works: surely this might be the self-same saint's life that is narrated by the Second Nun in *The Canterbury Tales*?

Another peculiarity about the 'Retraction' is its similarity in sentiment to the depiction, by the poet Thomas Gascoigne, of Chaucer's deathbed spiritual terrors. He is supposed to have cried out 'Woe is me! For I shall not now be able to revoke or destroy those things that I have wickedly written concerning the wicked and filthy love of men for women, and which shall now be passed down for ever from man to man, whether I wish it or not'. Did Gascoigne know the 'Retraction', and place similar words in Chaucer's mouth? Or is the 'Retraction' itself a later addition to *The Canterbury Tales*, that wrestles to conform the exuberant miscellany to the piety of the age?

Though *The Canterbury Tales* indeed contains moral exempla, saints' lives and religious treatises, they occur alongside scurrilous *fabliaux* and scatological farce. As John Dryden wrote: 'all human life is here'. The sincere Parson must ride alongside the hypocritical Pardoner, the 'verray parfit, gentil knight' and the inebriated Miller. Whatever Chaucer was planning for the Canterbury pilgrims, the imminence of death may have led him to hastily pen a disclaimer: in its incomplete form, it might well appear more irreverent than if it had been finished.

Like much medieval literature, *The Canterbury Tales* has a framing narrative. Opening at the Tabard Inn in Southwark, the Prologue introduces a group of characters on their way to the shrine of Saint Thomas à Becket in Canterbury. The innkeeper, Harry Bailly, suggests a story-telling competition to pass the time. Each pilgrim will tell two tales on the way to Canterbury, and two on the way back, with Harry Bailly acting as compère and arbiter. In the ten fragments we have, twenty-three of the pilgrims have told a story, and only one, the poet Geoffrey Chaucer, has told two. Some characters from the Prologue – the Yeoman, the Plowman, the five Guildsmen – have said nothing; and another pair, the alchemist Canon and his sly Yeoman, have joined the group, with the Canon's Yeoman offering a story about a mendacious Canon who is categorically *not* his master.

Simple arithmetic would suggest that there could have been as many as 132 Tales in the work. This neat scheme, however, quickly unravels. By drawing straws, Bailly suggests that the first story be told by the Knight, who duly entertains the company with a romance about the ill-fated rivalry between Palamon and Arcite for the love of Emily. At the end, Bailly congratulates the Knight and asks the Monk to begin his Tale: however, the drunken Miller decides that he can outdo the Knight, and launches into the notoriously bawdy tale of the Carpenter, his wife and a randy student. This aggravates the Reeve, who thinks he is being mocked, and who retorts with a similarly ribald offering about the cuckolding of a Miller's wife and daughter.

Not only are stories parried between the tellers, upsetting Bailly's notional ordering, they are also interrupted. When Chaucer himself is called upon, he narrates a 'drasty' old piece called 'The Tale of Sir Thopas'. The elegant English versifier, who has practically invented the iambic pentameter, surprises the audience with a clunking, naive, doggerel exercise. After 900 lines Bailly thunders 'Namoore of this, for Goddes dignitee', claiming that Chaucer's 'rymyng is nat worth a toord!' Humbled, Chaucer instead gives them a heavily allegorical prose homily, 'The Tale of Melibee'.

Because of the fragmentary nature of the text, we cannot

now tell if the unfinished 'Squire's Tale' and 'Cook's Tale' were cut short by the Host or another pilgrim or by Chaucer's own death. Some of the pilgrims prevaricate about their choice of story: the Monk tells a series of tragedies, though he also plans to tell the life of Saint Edward. The Man of Law eventually tells of Constance, a Roman princess betrothed to the Sultan of Syria, on the condition of his conversion; though he worries about choosing such a theme since Chaucer 'hath toold of loveris up and doun/Mo than Ovide made of mencioun', (despite the fact that the poet 'kan but lewedly / on metres and on rymyng craftily'). 'What sholde I tellen hem,' he wonders, 'syn they been told?'

The Canterbury Tales has, by some critics, been seen as a gallimaufry into which Chaucer could accommodate various works. 'The Knight's Tale', based on Boccaccio's epic *Teseida*, was composed before the Prologue; so too was 'The Tale of Melibee'. Had he lived, 'lost' works other than the complete *Canterbury Tales* might have survived, since Chaucer was happy to recycle older material into the rag-bag Tales. The Knight might have given us *The Book of the Leoun*, and the Wife of Bath might have stunned the misogynists with her version of Origen on Mary Magdalene.

It is not, however, the tales of the tellers, but the tellers' own tales that seem the most grievous loss. Though it is anachronistic to imagine a novelistic shape surrounding *The Canterbury Tales*, it is enticing. The characterization is immensely vivid. Moreover, this is revealed not just in the accumulation of detail – the wart on the Miller's nose, the 'gat-toothed' Wife of Bath – but in the pilgrims' words and inter-relationships. The Wife's tale, about the loathly lady and women's desire for 'sovereignty', tells us as much about her as her biographical prologue. She and the Clerk reach some accommodation between them, despite the opposing viewpoints of their tales.

Only the broadest outline of a shape for *The Canterbury*

Tales can be deduced. Harry Bailly promises a free meal for the winner of the story-telling competition: who would win, and how they were chosen, we cannot know. Although claims have been made for the Parson's Tale being an apposite ending, with the Celestial Jerusalem replacing the temporal Canterbury Cathedral, the circular structure implied by the rules of the story-telling suggest the true end is back at the Tabard Inn. Canterbury acts as a fulcrum in the narrative, and we can only speculate about whether or not any of the pilgrims radically changed their ways as a consequence of their pilgrimage.

Chaucer has supplied us with obvious villains – the hypocritical Pardoner, for example – as well as potential victims for their fraudulent deceits; such as the Wife of Bath with her five inheritances. The Pardoner himself may be a possible dupe for the mysterious Canon (whose Yeoman relates the story of how a Canon tricked venal priests). There are characters who represent earthly and heavenly justice in the Man of Law and the poor Parson. There is comic relief alongside chivalric splendour; bourgeois pretensions offset against unworldly meditation; sly misogynists trumped by an assertive widow. Chaucer has prepared all the elements of a plot, but we have none of the narration.

The poem was sufficiently new and popular that other writers exploited it after Chaucer's death. The 'Tale of Beryn' is included in some versions as the Merchant's Tale, and a popular, though anonymous, *Canterbury Interlude* told of the Pardoner's attempts to seduce a barmaid, Kit the Tapster, ending in his humiliation. The poet John Lydgate, in the fifteenth century, introduced his *Seige of Thebes* with a prologue telling how he met up with the Canterbury Pilgrims, who asked him to read his *magnum opus*. Neither Harry Bailly nor Geoffrey Chaucer interrupt the work.

What, then, is the significance of the 'Retraction'? How seriously should we take Chaucer's claim that he earnestly repented the lewd and profane elements in the Tales? It is not as if the reader goes unwarned about the bawdier moments in the Tales; or that the drunken tellers go uncriticized. Given the irony that pervades the whole of the poem, it is tempting to award it no more significance than the parody of Chaucer the pilgrim, stuttering out his mouldy tale. One might even point to the end of *Troilus and Criseyde* as evidence of a similar practice, where the poet bids envoi to his 'litel bok', praying that it is not misunderstood and that the folly of the pagan lovers is suitably noted.

The 'hale and hearty' bluff image of Chaucer that has accreted over the centuries would encourage the reader to dismiss the 'Retraction' as a final winking glimmer of irony. And yet, if we think of the author, stricken by who-knows-what disease or injury, certain in the knowledge of his imminent demise, is it really so unlikely that, at that pitch, he would have preferred to hear the Consolation of Philosophy rather than the rich evocation of the world he was about to leave? Or that, to save his own soul at the Pearly Gates, he might have suspected Saint Peter to be a rather harsh literary critic?

François Villon

(1431–c.1463)

Fugitive. Brawler. Thief. The man who stole 500 gold *écus* from the College of Navarre. The murderer of a priest. A condemned felon, thrice imprisoned, and once sentenced to death. Member of the criminal fraternity, the Brotherhood of the Coquille. Genius.

Other poets – Byron, Rimbaud and Swinburne, for example – have struck the bad-boy pose, and glorified in being 'accursed', 'bohemian' or 'rebellious'. François Villon was not carefully constructing an image or conforming to a literary stereotype. He really was a delinquent and a killer, a crook and a convict, who even wrote ballads in the secret language, *jobelins*, of the gangs. He was born François Montcorbier (or Des Loges: who he originally was is as slippery as his later identity is iconic), and, if we believe his self-descriptions in his most ambitious poem, *Le Testament*, his family had never had much money. When his father died he was placed under the guardianship of Guillaume de Villon, the chaplain of Benoît-le-Bétourné, and took his surname. What his bene-factor thought of this switched identity is not known. In *Le Lais*, a shorter version of *Le Testament* written five year beforehand, he dedicates his fame to Guillaume de Villoᵑ and, with the dark irony that typifies his work, refers to it as 'the honour of his name'.

Villon was sent to the University of Paris in 1449, and was made a master of arts in 1452. Three years later he was involved in a fight, in the cloisters of Saint-Benoît, that led to him running his sword through a priest. His friend's claim that he acted in self-defence led to his acquittal in 1456. In the same year, along with Guy Tabary and Colin de Cayeux, he burgled the College of Navarre. When Tabary confessed to the crime and implicated his co-conspirators, Villon went on the run, eventually drifting into the orbit of Charles d'Orléans. The Duke was sufficiently impressed by Villon's poetry during a competition that he had personal copies made. He could not, however, prevent him being imprisoned again, for the Navarre robbery, by the Bishop of Orléans. Villon was freed during the amnesty to celebrate the accession of Louis XI in 1461. He then was accused of affray against a papal notary, and was sentenced to be 'hanged and strangled': the sentence was again commuted, to exile, and after 1463 no more about him is heard. Rabelais claims that he travelled to England, though there is no evidence for this.

Villon's major work, *Le Testament*, is a mixture of spiritual autobiography and mordant bequests, a poetic will written humorously under conditions in which any other person might be considering doing the same thing seriously. As he asks for forgiveness, he conjures up the prostitutes and villains of his career. His pious imprecations are counterpoised with streetwise asides, his sincerity is laced with *double entendres*. Villon writes in the most exacting and complex ballade form, embedding acrostics at the beginning of the line with rigorous rhyme-schemes at the end. In such a formal framework, his wit nonetheless proves itself irrepressible, and his gruesome cadenzas on the corruption of flesh are bound in perfect cadences.

One looks in vain for a psychological unravelling, or an

apologia pro vita sua. When he revised, expanded and rewrote *Le Lais* as *Le Testament*, Villon changed his legacy to Guillaume de Villon: instead of his fame and name, he leaves his library. Only one item is specifically named, a poem by Villon called *The Romance of the Devil's Fart*, a work where the interest of the theme compensates for any stylistic infelicity. The poem is lost, but we know that Villon was involved in some undergraduate prank, involving the theft of a landmark door-sign from the ill-reputed house of one Mademoiselle de Bruyère, the so-called *Pet au Deable*, or Devil's Fart. If the poem were ever rediscovered, we might at least know the origins of his pathological dual career in rhyme and crime.

There is even the possibility that Villon knew the poem was lost when he left it to his guardian. In *Le Testament*, he mentions that Guy Tabary transcribed *The Romance of the Devil's Fart*, and one doubts that they were on particularly good terms during his spell in prison. Villon similarly bequeaths his sword to a friend, Ythier Marchant, while informing him it is currently in the pawn shop. Villon would hardly be nonplussed that his earliest work had not survived: throughout his works, the transitory sway of the world impresses frequently. As he put it in one of his most haunting lines, 'Mais où sont les neiges d'antan?' – 'But where are last year's snows?'

John Skelton

(1460–1529)

Erasmus called John Skelton 'that light and glory of English letters', the printer William Caxton praised his 'polysshed and ornate termes', and the Universities of Oxford, Cambridge and Louvain agreed, conferring on him the title of Poet Laureate. It is understandable that all these congratulatory encomia and admiring references went to his head.

In *A Ryght delectable tratyse upon a goodly Garlande or Chapelet of Laurell*, Skelton considers his literary accomplishment. He is welcomed into the Court of Fame by Gower, Lydgate and Chaucer. He modestly accepts their thanks for having made the renown of Britain 'encrese and amplyfy', even though it 'welny was loste when that we were gone'. The Queen of Fame assures him that 'by the preemynence/Of laureate triumphe, your place is here reservyd', and asks Occupation to tell them 'what Skelton hath compilid and wryton in dede' so that 'we wyll understande how ye have it deservyd'.

What follows is an extensive list of Skelton's poems, prose works and translations, which constitute the basis for his admission into the Court of Fame. Over thirty of them are lost, suggesting that his sense of his own importance to posterity might be somewhat elevated. His treatises on government – *The Book of Honourable Estate, Good Advysement* and *Sovereignty, a noble pamphlet* – presumably written when he was tutor to Prince Henry, have all perished. His play *Academios* and an interlude, *Virtue*, have vanished. We know little about his moral tracts – *How Men Should Flee Sin, The Book to Speak Well or be Still* – and less about his religious writings, such as *The False Faith* and the *Devout Prayer to Moses' Horns*. What *The Ballad of the Mustard Tart* or *The Epitome of the Miller and his Jolly Companion* or *The Pageants in the Joyous Garde* were about, we cannot know. His erotic *Repete of the Recule of Rosmundis bowre* has disappeared as completely, as has his *New Grammar*.

Nonetheless, his vision ends with:

> All orators and poetis, with other grete and smale,
> A thowsande, thowsande, I trow, to my dome,
> *Triumpha, triumpha!* They cryid all aboute.
> Of trumpettis and clariouns the noyse went to Rome.

Skelton gave his name to a verse-form, the Skeltonic, a hasty, tumbling metre used for comical poems. He describes it in *Collyn Clout*, saying

> For though my ryme be ragged,
> Tattered and jagged,
> Rudely rayne-beaten,
> Rusty and mothe-eaten,
> Yf ye take well therwith
> It had in it some pyth.

Several of the poems that have survived are in this slight and sprightly form. 'To make suche trifels it asketh sum konnyng', he averred in the *Garlande of Laurell*, granting even the least of his writings a modicum of wit and skill. That he should now be best known for them, rather than his mass of panegyrical, theological, political, theatrical, romantic and linguistic endeavour, would doubtless infuriate him.

Camillo Querno

(*fl.* 1513)

When Giovanni de' Medici became Pope Leo X in 1513, he established himself as a patron of the arts and literature. He also intended to leave an architectural legacy, and his sale of indulgences to finance the rebuilding of St Peter's precipitated Martin Luther's ninety-five theses, the foundation of the Reformation. His contribution to literary posterity was perhaps not as drastic, but was no less embroiled in bad judgement.

According to Paulus Jovius, who was made a knight by Leo as a token of respect for his history writing, one Camillo Querno had heard that the new Pope was an aficionado of poetry. Consequently, he set out from his native Apulia to present his verse to the pontiff. Accompanied by a harp, he recited the 20,000 verses of his execrable epic *The Alexias* to the Vicar of Rome, who promptly made him his poet laureate, in reward for his brass neck rather than his golden tongue. The poem perished, but the poet enjoyed a certain notoriety.

Alexander Pope, in his *Dunciad*, compared the election of Cibber as Poet Laureate to the ironic appointment:

Not with more glee, by hands pontific crowned,
With scarlet hats wide-waving circled round,
Rome in her capitol saw Querno sit,
Throned on seven hills, the antichrist of wit.

Querno's name was adopted at the end of the eighteenth century by an American Tory satirist, Jonathan Odell. Odell, who thought the American Revolution had been 'a sort of insane phrensy, produced by the wicked few in administering to their victims this potion of political necromancy . . . this hideous hell-broth made up of lies, sophistries, ambitions, hatreds, hallucinations', eventually emigrated to Nova Scotia and sunk into the same obscurity as his pseudonym.

The infrequency of surnames beginning with 'Q' offers Querno a mild afterlife in *Brewer's Dictionary of Phrase and Fable*, as an archetype of the untalented poet. We can surely be glad that if any book had to be lost, it was *The Alexias*.

Luis Vaz de Camões (Camoens)

(1524–80)

What did the gods have against Camoens? The question must have burrowed and writhed in his mind more than once as he sat in Mozambique, penniless, racked with tropical illnesses, stranded, frustrated in love, blinded in one eye, having been shipwrecked once, exiled in chains to Goa, imprisoned twice and recently robbed of his manuscripts to boot. That Ovid and Dante had suffered similar vicissitudes of fortune was hardly any compensation. It seemed as if nobody in his homeland of Portugal would ever realize he was their own, greatest epic poet.

Throughout his swashbuckling career, one factor remained constant: a poem called *Os Lusíadas*. In 1544, he was already being called the Lusitanian Virgil, on account of an episode he had written about the medieval Inês de Castro. Few suspected then that this was merely a part of a much grander conception. An unfortunate love affair with the Queen's lady-in-waiting led to temporary exile from Lisbon, and Camoens signed up as a soldier. The depredations of war rendered him quick-tempered and imprudent, and a brawl in 1552 led to his imprisonment. He was pardoned by the King, with the proviso that he leave for India and the colonial service.

In 1553, on the *São Bento*, bound for India under the command of Alvares Cabral, he safely rounded the Cape of Good Hope. These storms and tempests would eventually be integrated into his epic poem. The Cape, he imagined, was not just the Cape, but the Giant Adamastor, who forbade vessels to pass. He had left with the words of Scipio Africanus stinging on his lips – 'Ungrateful fatherland, you will not be allowed to hold my bones' – but was already understanding that the real heroism of the Portuguese was not in archaic glories and half-fictitious founders lost in the mists of time, but in the explorers and navigators who triumphed over the all-too-actual weathers of the present. He was sailing into the realms that Vasco da Gama had opened less than fifty years beforehand.

His trading prospered in the Orient, though his temper still caused grievances. In 1559, however, events took a turn for the worse. The boat that had been transporting him back to India from China sank at the mouth of the Mekong river, and he did not save the papers necessary for his impending trial (for threatening the settlers in Macau), nor the wealth he had accumulated. What he did rescue was *The Lusiads* to date: seven complete cantos. A sheaf of dampening paper and bleeding ink, and it survived.

He decided to return to Portugal, but soldiers had to pay their own fare back. In 1567 Captain Pedro Barreto took the poet as far as Mozambique, but with no more money, refused to take him further. With no means to pay another captain, he spent three years marooned on land, impecunious and frequently ill. He wrote a work called *The Parnassus of Camoens*, described by the historian Diogo do Couto, who knew and supported Camoens there, which was stolen. It was, apparently, 'of much learning, doctrine and philosophy'. But the thieves did not find *The Lusiads*.

Camoens eventually escaped from the African coast, and returned to Lisbon; typically, during a plague. *The Lusiads* was published: an epic, not about fabled origins and distant triumphs, but of the present. It was not arms and the man, but trade and the empire: a poem in which the gods of Greece vainly attempted to confound the destiny of Vasco da Gama. Bacchus and Cupid and Jupiter were merely personifications who either helped or hindered the manifest destiny of the world-spanning, Catholic Portuguese. Dionysus, Neptune and the classical pantheon were deployed only to fail in obstructing the determined prow of the now. It was the last attempt to use the gods of Greece and Rome as if they were actual beings.

It was praised by the poet Tasso, who sent a sonnet in congratulation; but Camoens died in poverty anyway. He had ended the poem with a vision of the harmony of the spheres, where Portugal, at the edge of Europe but nonetheless at the centre of the universe, was the pivot of reality. He bitterly remarked of the governance he found on returning, that he was so patriotic he would not only die in his country, but with it.

Copernicus had already levered the earth from the centre of the universe. Cervantes was about to inject irony into chivalry, nobility and heroism. Shakespeare was hesitating towards his first, faltering attempts at drama. As Camoens died, a world died with him. Had the old classical gods, crumbling in the face of modernity, preserved the last poem to invoke them in all their power and grandeur? If so, they would be disappointed by the result. Camoens, the bard of spice routes and treaties, of an emerging capitalist era, had ultimately shown them up as the tattered stage props they were: broken, unlikely, fallen and absolutely irrelevant to destiny. *The Parnassus of Camoens* was lost in Africa, but *The Lusiads* guaranteed Camoens' place in the actual Parnassus of geniuses.

Torquato Tasso

(1544–95)

It is hard to understand the ebullience of Charles Lamb, who, on acquiring a copy of the 1600 translation of Tasso's epic poem *Jerusalem Delivered*, or *Gerusalemme Liberata*, scribbled to Coleridge, 'I have lit upon Fairfax's *Godfrey of Bullen*, for half-a-crown. Rejoice with me.' The poem, which recounts the Crusaders' siege of the Holy City under the leadership of Godfrey of Boulogne, was ranked alongside *The Iliad* and *The Aeneid* by no less a poet than Milton. Dryden thought Tasso was 'the most excellent of modern poets . . . whom I reverence next to Virgil'. He was translated by Richard Carew, Edward Fairfax, and even more minor writers (Henry Layng, Philip Doyne, John Hoole, J. H. Wiffen, J. R. Broadhead and a plethora of vicars with nothing better to do) who now languish in similar obscurity. One looks in vain for a smart paperback of Tasso in any airy, coffee-scented modern bookshop.

Torquato was born in Sorrento, near Naples, in 1544, the son of Bernardo Tasso, a noted poet of his day, and, at the time, the secretary to the Prince of Salerno. The vacillating alliances and shifting allegiances of the period were hardly conducive to domestic tranquillity: by the time he was twenty-one, the young Tasso had been shunted between Rome, Ravenna, Venice, Bologna, Mantua and Padua. His legal studies at Padua were punctuated with amorous attachments, scurrilous verses, bar-room brawls and the study of Aristotle's *Poetics*. He left in 1565, adamant he would not practise law, to join the household of a family that would have a dramatic, and not always beneficial, impact on his future: the d'Estes of Ferrara.

The political turmoil of Renaissance Italy took its toll on his father's writing, in a manner that would be echoed in his own literary career. Poetry was a potent tool of diplomacy, a courtly arena where panegyric could lead to patronage. As a teenager, Torquato had helped his father transcribe revisions to his epic poem *Amadigi*, based on the romance of *Amadís de Gaula*. He would have been made clearly aware of the value of flattery in his father's shift of emphasis in the subtle contemporary allusions away from the French and on to the Spanish, who were allied to Bernardo's benefactors.

There were aesthetic as well as pragmatic changes to consider as well. The most lauded modern poem was Ludovico Ariosto's *Orlando Furioso*, a mammoth entertainment of chivalrous knights, magical steeds and anthropophagous ogres. Published in 1516, it continued the story of Orlando and Angelica which had been so successful for Boiardo in his unfinished *Orlando Innamorato*. Even after Ariosto's death, the poem continued to grow in popularity, and size, enlarged from forty to forty-six cantos in 1532, and gaining another five cantos after that. It was irregular, ironic and cautiously irreverent.

With the resurgence of interest in Aristotle's lectures on poetics, however, literary critics were now seeking a different kind of epic: a single hero and a single action, a poem of elevating moral principles. Ideally, it should express the very quality which Ariosto had become celebrated for shunning: serious virtue.

Bernardo Tasso was torn between these models; the Aristotelian seriousness and Ariostan jollity. All previous attempts at the high heroic style had been greeted with indifference. Even the classical *Amadigi* required 'the variety which pleases', he capitulated. Torquato claimed his father had written at least part of an epic following the Aristotelian strictures: at a public reading, it emptied the hall. The text in question is lost.

Torquato Tasso's ambition was to succeed where his father had failed, to unite the charm of Ariosto's work among readers with the rigorous classicism demanded by the critics of his day. Throughout his life, the fear of public failure, anxieties about critical dismissal and political expediency blighted Tasso's well-being. He was prone to paranoia and quick to take offence. While still studying at Padua he had drafted a work on the Crusades under the title *Rinaldo*. He abandoned his creative work, resuming instead his study of the theoretical principles of epic poetry. But his aim was now fixed: he would write an epic. Well, to be honest, like most young men he wanted fame, acclaim and money; and uniting classical and modern traditions in one work seemed a feasible way to acquire them.

In 1579, fourteen years after entering the service of the d'Estes, the 'madman' Torquato Tasso was in their dungeon. Tradition has it that the reason for his incarceration was an imprudent *amour* with Duke Alfonso's older sister, Leonora. Although the image of the shackled, lovelorn poet was to inspire Byron and Goethe, it is pure fabrication, a fantasy of later biographers, and makes little sense given the nature of court life. Suppose Tasso were having an affair. He would most likely have ended up like Count Ercole Contrari, strangled on Alfonso's orders for his dalliance with Leonora's sister Lucrezia.

Tasso had been on good terms with both the sisters, and read parts of the embryonic poem – then called *Gotifredo* – to them. According to Milton, Tasso offered several different topics for the epic treatment to Alfonso; luckily, the Duke chose the very one on which Tasso had already been work-ing: the *Rinaldo* abandoned during student days. He had also written a pastoral drama for the d'Este sisters, entitled *Aminta*, and undertaken a diplomatic journey to the court of Charles IX in Paris, with the Duke's brother, Cardinal Luigi d'Este. So why was he kept chained, in solitary confinement, in the 'hospital' of St Anna, for seven years?

Call it a surfeit of melancholic humour or an imbalance of endorphins; call him bipolar or possessed: whatever caused it, something was wrong with Torquato Tasso. His letters are full of imagined slights and malicious conspiracies. The doctor is trying to poison him. The servants are untrustworthy. Nobody appreciates his genius. He has no genius.

Other courtiers were more than concerned by his habit of surrendering himself up to the Inquisition. It was as if he gained some momentary equilibrium, after he unburdened his anxieties about heresy and catalogued the sins he might have committed, and the priest, scrying into the corners of his soul, pronounced him forgiven. Like a caricatured contemporary novelist, he relied on the closest thing in the sixteenth century to a shrink. But in the gossipy, secretive world of a Renaissance court, Tasso's compulsion to con-fession was a dangerous liability.

This need for perpetual reassurance can be seen in his manner of composition. As he wrote each of the cantos of the poem now called *Gerusalemme Liberata*, they were sent to his friend Scipione Gonzaga, a prelate in Rome. He then circulated the manuscript amongst a coterie of trusted advisers: Pier Angelio da Barga, the Latin poet; Flamminio de' Nobili, a scholar of Greek and philosopher; Silvio Antoniano, Pro-fessor of Eloquence; and Sperone Speroni, the renowned literary critic. They wrote back with comments on the polish of the verse, how well the poem followed the various *dicta* of Aristotle and other critics of antiquity, and whether the epic was in line with the teachings of the church.

They provided orthodox precedents for the use of guardian angels and demons to replace the gods of Homer and Virgil, and made notes on the allegory, the moral and scriptural interpretations of the poem. They offered advice on how best to blend the contemporary chivalric love elements with the martial splendour of *The Iliad*. From the theology of the efficacy of prayer to the most minuscule points of probability, the elite group of critics suggested alterations. Tasso made numerous changes, then burned every scrap of the copious correspondence from the poem's intellectual regulators. When the poem did appear in print, it would be unimpeachable.

Tasso's behaviour became markedly more erratic in 1576. It is tempting to think that the trigger, if not the cause, was the publication of a pirated edition of the poem; a breach of trust that must have seemed like confirmation of his worst paranoid delusions. By the summer of 1577, Alfonso had him under house arrest, under the care of a physician and a priest. Tasso escaped, and travelled in disguise to his sister in Sorrento. He left behind the manuscript of the poem.

The d'Estes would not have him return to court; nor would they return the manuscript of *Gerusalemme Liberata*. Over the next two years, Tasso drifted to his old haunts in Mantua and Padua. He attempted to sell his services to the unimpressed Medicis in Venice. He even trawled round the minor courts in Pesaro and Turin. Eventually, on condition that he display some restraint, the d'Estes allowed him to return. He had barely arrived when he flew into another temper at some supposed snub, and was dragged to St Anna. Fearful that he might destroy the manuscript, Alfonso d'Este refused to allow him to work on the poem.

In the age before copyright, the author's intellectual property was never too nicely observed anyway. When the author was a certified maniac in a prison, pirated editions appeared apace. Despite the fact that the copies were riddled with errors and set from uncorrected manuscripts, the *Gerusalemme Liberata* was an immediate success.

It was such an indisputable cultural phenomenon that it soon evolved into a full-blown contretemps, with critics divided between Tasso's supporters, the so-called *Tassisti*, and the *Cruscanti*, who took their name from the Accademia della Crusca, and preferred Ariosto. From St Anna, a torrent of letters carried complaints about his involuntary and unjustified imprisonment and his cheating and slapdash publishers, to anyone who listened.

In 1586, Tasso was released into the care of the Duke of Mantua. If the Duke was expecting to set himself up as a patron of the arts, however, he must have been sorely disappointed. Tasso dredged up and completed his bombastic tragedy, *Il Re Torrismondo*, failed to appear at his scheduled lectures on Aristotle and left for Rome, fulminating against the d'Estes.

The rest of his life was a melancholy transit from court to court, and patron to patron. He wrote panegyrics for Pope Gregory XIV and genealogies for the Gonzago faction. He died in Rome in 1595, before he could complete an encomium on his latest doctor.

Before he died, Tasso tried again to recapture his lost book: the poem in his head, which had only been manifested in debased, erroneous and misbegotten versions. *Gerusalemme Conquistata* (1593) incorporated many of the revisions he had originally been sent by his clique of collaborators. It expanded the poem's length by four books and renamed many of the principal characters. It is, by any reasonable definition, a different poem. The public, and the critics, preferred the earlier version.

Undeterred, Tasso wrote two books justifying his later version, in terms of its historical accuracy and allegorical import (a further book on its technical and stylistic superiority was advertised, but never appeared). The poem also altered any subtexts complimenting the d'Estes; and transferred his affections to his new patron, the Prince of Conca.

Even after the publication of *Gerusalemme Conquistata*, Tasso wrote to his friends about corrections, improvements and alterations which he believed were necessary. In the end, because of the endless revisions and changes, there can be no 'definitive' version of the poem. Given Tasso's psychological instability, it is unlikely that any rewrites could have finally fixed his aesthetic intentions.

In a late letter to Barezzo Barizzi, dated 15 May 1591, Tasso suggested that the extant epic is, in fact, only half of his projected work. He hinted at a sequel, which would stand in relation to *Gerusalemme Liberata* or *Conquistata* as *The Odyssey* did to *The Iliad*. Certain episodes from the original version were to be cut from the revised version (such as the love plot between Sophronia and Olindo, on the grounds that they were 'too romantic'). Could they be reintegrated into a more picaresque successor?

Would the sequel, like *The Odyssey*, describe the home-coming of the heroes? Not for Godfrey of Boulogne, the central character, who died of the plague in Jerusalem. In several letters in that month, Tasso asked friends to send copies of Dionysus of Halicarnassus' *History of Rome*, and Lucian's satirical novellas. Was he collecting material for a new poem, or establishing facts for his self-justificatory prose work?

'Everyone, we suppose, who reads at all, reads Tasso; has contemplated with delight the immortal productions of his Muse . . .' said the *Eclectic Review* in 1810. The sentiment seems immeasurably distant two centuries later. All we do know for certain about Tasso's never-written sequel is that, even if he had had the chance to write it, very few would now bother to read it.

Miguel de Cervantes Saavedra

(1547–1616)

At the beginning of the first part of Cervantes' most famous novel, *Don Quixote*, just after the rationally mad and beautifully deluded knight has returned from his first, abortive adventure, his niece, the Barber and the Priest discuss what to do with the volumes of old romances which have coloured his fantastical imagination. They decide to burn them. *The Exploits of Esplandian, Florismarte of Hyrcania* and armfuls of other tales of derring-do are consigned to the flames, while the judicious priest makes exception for the occasional volume. After the romances are thoroughly purged, they turn to the books of poetry, in case they instigate a new form of mania in Quixote. As they pass judgement on Spanish poetry of the sixteenth century, they come across a well-known tome:

> 'But what is that book next to it?'
> 'The *Galatea* of Miguel de Cervantes,' said the Barber.
> 'That Cervantes has been a great friend of mine for many years, and I know he is better acquainted with reverses rather than verses. His book has some clever ideas; but it sets out to do something and concludes nothing. We must wait for the second part he

promises, and perhaps with amendment he will win our clemency now denied him. In the meantime, neighbour, until we see, keep him as a recluse in your room.'

Galatea had been Cervantes' first success, and the Priest and Barber were doomed to be disappointed about its sequel. At the end of the prologue to Part II of *Don Quixote* Cervantes plugs his forthcoming *Persiles and Sigismunda*, 'which I am just finishing', and, 'the second part of *Galatea*'. He had announced in the preface to *Persiles* that he was preparing a new play (*Fooled with Open Eyes*), a romance (*The Famous Bernardo*), a collection of novellas (*Weeks in the Garden*) and, as expected, the second part of his pastoral drama *Galatea*. The *Persiles* was published posthumously. None of the other works ever appeared.

Cervantes spent half a lifetime not getting round to completing *Galatea*. Given the replete nature of that life, this is hardly surprising; and given his exquisite gift for irony, the permanent deferral of the conclusion to the book that made his name might well be taken as a sly self-referential aside.

Cervantes was not just an author. He had been a soldier at the naval battle of Lepanto in 1571, where an alliance of Christian countries defeated the Ottoman Empire, and where he himself lost the use of an arm. He had been captured in 1575 by Barbary corsairs and sold into captivity in Algiers. For five years he remained the prisoner of the notorious Hassan Pasha, and, despite four failed attempts at escape, he was ransomed and returned to Spain. Within a few years he was starting to attract attention: not, at first, for *Galatea*, but as a playwright. His captivity inspired *Life in Algiers*, a melodramatic comedy rediscovered in the eighteenth century. No doubt his military service inspired *The Naval Battle*, a play as yet undiscovered, and more than likely lost perpetually.

Nonetheless we know that Cervantes was proud of the plays – if the postscript to *The Return from Parnassus* is trustworthy, there are ten or more other titles that are lost to us. Cervantes makes great claims for his dramatic career: he, he says, was the first to reduce the five-act structure to three acts, and the first to introduce the 'soul's imaginings and hidden thoughts' through allegorical figures. Nobody, he insists, threw any cucumbers, and the plays completed their runs without hissing or booing.

At this time he met, or at least made the acquaintance of, a man twenty years his junior who would prove to be a grievous thorn in his side. Lope Félix de Vega Carpio was merely the gentleman caller to the daughter of the famous actor for whose wife Cervantes had served as witness to a promissory note. Lope de Vega's 2,000 plays (a quarter of which survive), his friendship, and his feud with Cervantes were still in the future. As were Lope's scurrilous satires on his ex-mistress once he and the actor's daughter parted company. Lope de Vega, sentenced to exile, declared he would join the Armada. Miguel de Cervantes was occupied in the more mundane business of requisitioning grain for the troops.

By the turn of the century, Lope de Vega, having survived the Armada (if he was ever in it), was known as the Phoenix, the foremost literary man of the period, and stellar centre of a constellation of authors, as much at home with printers as with princes. Indeed, for the marriage of Philip III, he even staged a play called *Captives in Algiers*, mostly derived from the play Cervantes drew from painful experience.

We do not know what Cervantes was doing. The few facts we do know include that he acted as executor for his brother's will, and was godfather to a friend of a friend's daughter. What is clear is that somehow he fell out grievously with Lope de Vega: in 1604 Vega made it known that he thought his former friend had been slandering his aesthetic ability. In hindsight, we can at least imagine what Cervantes was doing, because in 1605 the first part of *Don Quixote* appeared.

That Cervantes knew *Don Quixote* was a new kind of

literature is clear in his prologue. 'Many times I took up my pen . . . and many times put it down, not knowing what to say.' This book rehashes nothing, it is so original that the author 'does not even know what authors he is following in it; and so . . . cannot set their names at the beginning in alphabetical order . . . starting with Aristotle and ending with Xenophon – and Zoilus or Zeuxis, though one of them was a libeller and the other a painter'.

It is the story of an old man, obsessed with tales of chivalry, who, suddenly, even heroically, erodes the flimsy film between life and reading. He and his bemused squire, Sancho Panza, set out on a quest and are diverted at every turn. Don Quixote, who has never seen a windmill, thinks that windmills are probably giants, and that his conquering of them (eyes screwed shut all the while) is proven by the fact they are now mere wooden edifices. The Knight of the Woeful Countenance, as Don Quixote styled himself, is every reader who thought that generosity of spirit was a fiction and shabbiness the norm. Characters can be noble; people are irredeemably self-centred. Don Quixote's quest, more than his search for the lovely Dulcinea, is to prove the cynics wrong.

Even though the King himself gave a jacket-quote anecdote – 'Either that student laughing out loud there is a madman, or he's reading *Don Quixote*' – Lope de Vega hated it. A sonnet appeared, either from Lope himself or an eager acolyte, contrasting the Apollo, Vega, with the *Quixote*, which it predicted, would circle the world, 'arse to arse', as toilet paper, or be used only to wrap second-rate saffron.

Not content with scatological poetry, Lope de Vega certainly conspired with the author of a continuation to *Don Quixote* by 'Avellaneda'; he may even have been the pseudonymous author whose identity has never been unravelled. At the end of Part I of Cervantes' *Don Quixote*, the knight has been brought to his home, insensible, and the supposed

compiler of the story, Cide Hamete Benengeli, tells the
readers that he is unable to find any accurate sources
for the further adventures, though they were known to
include the jousts at Saragossa.

Avellaneda's *Part II* appeared in 1614 and opens with the
Don and Sancho on their way to Saragossa. Cervantes retorted
in 1615 with his own continuation, setting aside the *Galatea*
yet again. The gross imposture becomes embroiled in the
book itself. *Part II* of *Don Quixote* is a form of lost book:
whatever Cervantes wanted to write, or planned to write,
had to be set aside in order to counter the claims of the
spurious sequel.

In chapter LIX of *Part II*, Don Quixote and Sancho Panza
are introduced to someone who demands the innkeeper
listens to the latest episode of *Don Quixote*. The Knight and
Squire are nonplussed, and demand to see the work in question. It is the Avellaneda *Part II*. Don Quixote is furious that
he is depicted as being out of love with Dulcinea; and Sancho
is equally irate that his wife's name seems to have changed.
They study the book, and conclude that the author writes in
the Aragonese dialect, as well as being a traducer, libeller and
mendacious historian. They resolve not to go to Saragossa at
all, since the false author had depicted them there as mere
fools, and strike out for Barcelona instead. Even there, they
find the book on sale, even though Quixote 'thought it had
been burned by now'.

But if Cervantes ever intended to take them to Saragossa,
a more melancholy end now awaited the Knight. To short-
circuit any future impostures, and to give a truly meaningful
end to their adventures, the Don goes home. There they
meet Don Tarfe, from the spurious *Part II*, who does not
recognize them; and the real Quixote, shaken, is oppressed
by omens of his death. He becomes lucid, and forgives even
Avellaneda, before returning to being Alonso Quixano the
Good. Cide Hamete Benengeli hangs up his pen and curses

anyone who would dare intrude on the relationship between creator and character: 'for me alone Don Quixote was born, and I for him'.

Cervantes did continue to write. The *Persiles and Sigismunda* still attracts the occasional, apologetic enthusiast; but it is clear that the work he shone in most was now extinguished. No doubt, Cervantes could have written countless escapades for his characters, but they had to be perfected. We only have an intact Don Quixote because Cervantes knew that unfinished works attract a swarm of maggoty continuers, and the Don was so perfect he would only be safe if he was dead. *Don Quixote*, as we have it, is a supreme act of authorial self-sacrifice.

Edmund Spenser

(?1552–99)

Only sixty years after his death, rumours were circulating, in the highest echelons of academia, about the lost books of Edmund Spenser, an author so esteemed he was called the 'Prince of Poets' and was buried next to Chaucer in Westminster Abbey. Dr John Worthington, the Master of Jesus College, Cambridge, wrote thus to Milton's friend Samuel Hartlib:

Sir, Yours I receiv'd last week; which exprest a great desire of the catalogue of those pieces of the renowned Spenser, which are only mentioned, but were never yet printed. This I now give you, as it was collected out of the scatter'd intimations of them in his printed works.

1. A Translation of Ecclesiastes
2. A Translation of Canticum Cantorum
3. The Dying Pelican
4. The Hours of the Lord
5. The Sacrifice of a Sinner
6. The 7 Psalms
7. His Dreams
8. His English Poet

9. His Legends
10. Court of Cupid
11. His Purgatory
12. The Hell of Lovers
13. A Sennights Slumber
14. His Pageants

Of these, Dr Worthington most regrets not having *The English Poet*, supposedly a prose disquisition on prosody, and the religious poems. Although he mentions that there are 'besides many others in the hands of noble persons, and his friends', the doctor omits several other titles quoted in Spenser's correspondence and postscripts: the *Stemmata Dudleiana*, a genealogical poem presumably for Robert Dudley, the influential Earl of Leicester, of which Spenser said 'more aduisement must be had'; a poem on the marriage of the river Thames; and a sequence of nine comedies, one for each of the Muses, which his friend Gabriel Harvey much preferred to the master-work on which Spenser's fame now rests, *The Faerie Queene*.

'But the greatest want is of the other six books of that incomparable poem, the Faery Queen,' laments Worthington. The first three books of the poem were published in 1590, with Books IV to VI appearing six years later. A letter from Spenser to Sir Walter Raleigh accompanied the initial publication, in which he outlined the structure of the poem.

The beginning therefore of my history, if it were to be told by an Historiographer, should be the twelfth book, which is the last, where I deuise that the Faery Queene kept her Annuall feaste xii dayes, upon which xii seuerall dayes, the occasions of the xii seuerall aduentures hapned, which being undertaken by xii seuerall knights, are in these xii books seuerally handled and discoursed.

Each book, therefore, contained the exploits of a knight, in twelve cantos, and each knight, Spenser intimates, is an exemplar of one of Aristotle's twelve moral virtues. In addition, the hero of the poem, Prince Arthur, betrothed to the Fairy Queen, appears in each book representing 'Magnificence', the perfect realization of the dozen characteristics of the others.

Book I introduces the Redcrosse Knight, emblematic of Holinesse, and his quest to defeat the Dragon of Sin. Book II has as its hero Sir Guyon, the paragon of temperance, who seeks to capture the enchantress Acrasia, whose witchcraft robs humans of their capacity for self-control, and unfetters them to succumb to their passions. Britomart, a female knight, is the heroine of Book III, where the principal virtue is chastity and the enemy to be vanquished is the lustful sorcerer Busyrane, who has imprisoned the virtuous maiden Amoret. A similar pattern occurs in Books IV to VI: Friendship, as demonstrated by Cambel and Triamond, takes up Book IV; Sir Artegall embodies justice in Book V, and Sir Calidore in Book VI is the template of courtesy, struggling against the Blatant Beast.

The narratives are not wholly confined to the individual books, and, especially in Books III and IV, stories are interlaced and interconnected. Britomart is destined to marry Sir Artegall, and duly comes to his rescue in Book V when he is captured by Amazons. Arthur tends to provide essential help in canto VIII of each book: he rescues Redcrosse from Orgoglio, the Giant of Pride; assists Guyon in fending off Pyrocles and Cymocles; and joins forces with Artegall to liberate Princess Belge from her oppressors.

Each book also has set-piece descriptions of palaces, pageants and masques. Britomart witnessed the Masque of Cupid in Busyrane's abode (perhaps this was the 'Court of Cupid' poem mentioned by Worthington?); Book IV concludes with the marriage of Thames and Medway (again, a lost book absorbed into the great work?).

Given the almost programmatic nature of Spenser's poem,

even though we have only half of the projected complete work, one would have thought that it would be easy enough to speculate about the contents of the missing books. For example, in Book II, canto 11, stanza 6, Arthur praises Guyon by proclaiming him potentially the equal of Gloriana the Fairy Queen's two staunchest knights, Sir Artegall and Sir Sophy. The reader meets Artegall and learns much of his temperament and character. This is, however, the sole reference to Sophy, who, it is implied, is of equal stature. His name derives from the Greek word *sophia*, meaning wisdom: one can imagine a lost book in which the Knight of Wisdom is pitted against the Ogre of Ignorance, the Basilisk of Heresy or the Kobold of Ultracrepitudinarianism.

Similarly, there are strong hints about the final conclusion of the poem. Redcrosse's epic battle with the dragon is awe-inspiring, but is as nothing compared to a conflict between the Fairy Queen and the 'Paynim' (or pagan) king; a struggle to which Redcrosse plights his troth after successfully dispatching his particular nemesis.

So what would have been the subjects of Books VII to XII? An obvious starting point would be Spenser's claim that each knight represented one of Aristotle's virtues. Immediately, the picture becomes more complex. Of Aristotle's virtues, Spenser has only dealt with two, temperance and civility. Holiness, chastity, justice and friendship are not in Aristotle's list. Plato proposed four cardinal virtues – justice, temperance, wisdom and courage, which provide a philosophical framework for Artegall, Guyon, potentially Sir Sophy and possibly an unnamed Knight of Courage (though shouldn't *all* knights be courageous?).

Two cantos and two stanzas of what appears to be another book of the *Faerie Queene* were added in to the third edition in 1609, after Spenser's death. They are written in the stanza-form Spenser used for the poem, and, the publisher suggested, formed part of the Legend of Constancy. Whether the

publisher or Spenser or some other hand decided that these
lines, about the Titaness Mutability attempting to storm
Heaven, comprised cantos 6 and 7, we cannot know. They
are wonderful poetry, but what is evident is that they lack
one thing present in all the other books: they have no hero.

Ralph Knevett (1600–1661), the Rector of Lyng in Nor-
folk, unacademically attempted to supplement Spenser's
poem by writing three further books, introducing Sir Albanio,
the Knight of Prudence, Sir Callimachus, the Knight of Forti-
tude (which might double up as Courage) and Sir Belcoeur,
the Knight of Liberality. Knevett's intention was 'to make this
Zodiacke perfect', which introduces a further complication.

Elizabethan poets were accustomed to building astrological
meanings into their poetry. In Spenser's own *Epithalamion*,
the 24 stanzas and 365 long lines allow the reader to calculate
the very date of the marriage the poem celebrates. *The Faerie
Queene* is no less nuanced. As Alastair Fowler says in his study,
Spenser and the Numbers of Time,

we find numerological significance in line-, stanza-, canto-, and
book-totals; in the location of these units; and even in the number
of characters mentioned in each episode. Pythagorean number
symbolism, astronomical symbolism based on orbital period figures
and on Ptolemaic star catalogue totals, medieval theological number
symbolism: all these strands, and more besides, are worked together
into what – in this respect at least – must be one of the more
intricate poetic structures ever devised.

To take some simple examples: Book I has as its heroine Una
(One, unity, wholeness) and as its villainess Duessa (Two,
doubled, duplicity). Book I, canto 1 has 55 stanzas; Book III,
canto 1 has 67; the book between, which insists on temperance as the medium between extremes, has 55+67, divided
by 2: 61 stanzas. The evidence is incremental, and what may
appear as coincidence in isolation occurs too frequently to be

discounted. Astrologically, for example, the end of Book II features 8 major and 17 minor characters; 8 stars make up the constellation of Libra and 17 stars are used to locate the constellation in Ptolemy's star-charts. Libra, the scales, is an apposite symbol of the balance that typifies the book.

It is difficult, at times, to decide exactly which numbers are significant. What are we to make, for example, of the Blatant Beast, who appears in Book V, canto 12, boasting a hundred tongues, only to reappear in Book VI, canto 1 with the number increased tenfold? Does this conceal an arcane meaning, or an authorial slip?

The Romantic poets lauded Spenser as a dreamy, somnambulant poet: could the converse be the case? Is *The Faerie Queene* a mathematical puzzle, an undeciphered code? Researching this, I tried to borrow Dr Fowler's study from Edinburgh City Library, but, I was informed, their copy had vanished in the 1980s. Walking home, slightly miffed at having to use the National Library's copy instead, I pondered the possible motives of the volume's purloiner.

Was there someone, somewhere in this city, elaborately uncovering the algebraic structure of *The Faerie Queene*? And if so, to what end? Just suppose the unknown monomaniac succeeded, and cracked the fundamental form of the poem . . . if Book II was governed by Libra, Book I, with Una the Virgin, would be under the auspices of Virgo . . . and Book XII would then have had to be Leo, a symbol for Majesty and Magnificence. The rest might click like the wheels of a Leibnitz calculating machine. Was someone writing the rest of *The Faerie Queene*? Or rather, could the poem now be actually writing itself?

More than likely, not. Moreover, the layered dimensions of *The Faerie Queene* are not restricted to astrological and philosophical concepts. Political and historical matters are shadowed by the other-worldly figures. Elizabeth herself is variously Gloriana, Una, Belphoebe and Britomart; Duessa, conversely, is Mary Queen of Scots. Sir Philip Sidney is hinted at in Sir Calidore and Lord Grey's career in Ireland is paralleled in Artegall. Our monomaniac would need a time machine as well as a genius for abstruse trigonometries to recapture fully the subtleties of the poem.

Did the other six books of *The Faerie Queene* ever exist? Some contemporary critics believe that the poem is, in its way, complete; that Spenser changed his plans to curtail the twelve-book structure. His initial letter to Raleigh was more akin to a proposal than a prospectus; and, indeed, Spenser does suggest he might contribute a further twelve books on the political, rather than personal, virtues, should the first twelve find favour. Satisfying though the idea is that the poem is complete, Spenser seemed intent on finishing it. In his sequence of sonnets, the *Amoretti*, written at the same time, he asks for 'leaue to rest me being halfe fordonne' after having compiled six books.

John Dryden, at the end of the seventeenth century, claimed Spenser had intended to flatter Sidney and Elizabeth by ending the poem with their marriage, but Sidney, 'dying before him, depriv'd the Poet, both of the Means and Spirit, to accomplish his Design'. Sir James Ware, in 1633, claimed that in Ireland, Spenser 'finished the later part of that excellent poem of his *Faery Queene*, which was soon afterwards unfortunately lost by the disorder and abuse of his servant'.

Spenser, who was Lord Grey's secretary in Ireland, had had to flee back to England in 1598 after his property at Kincolman was attacked and burned by rebels. The earliest biographical notice, by William Camden, only claims that he was forced out and his goods were despoiled: no mention of the missing manuscript and cack-handed servant. The inveterate compiler of oddments and anecdotes John Aubrey maintained that playing-cards, with stanzas of *The Faerie Queene*, were found in the wainscot of a chamber in Sir Erasmus Dryden's house, where Spenser had stayed. Aubrey does not mention if these cards contained stanzas not present in the extant books.

John Worthington, in his letter on the lost works, suggested that manuscripts 'may perhaps lie hid in some libraries or closets'. 'He lived heretofore in the north of England, and in the south, viz., Kent,' he adds, narrowing down the search. And indeed, they may lie there still. Countless undergraduates fervently hope they lie there for a long, long time.

William Shakespeare

(1564–1616)

Imagine yourself sitting on a bench in a garden at dusk, with a house behind you and the view in front. The hill slopes gently towards a river, the night-scented stock is beginning to bloom, and the pale summer light fades. Wisps of mist seem caught like sheep's fleece on the branches of the trees lining the river; gradually, it thickens and coalesces, inching up the fields, billowing, solidifying, obliterating the trees it seemed to hang on, creeping, silently, towards where you are sitting. You think – I will wait, and see if it reaches me. It swirls and chills as the sun sets: a fence, running down the hill, lets you measure its progress up the field as the stobs are one by one enveloped, erased. It stops. You wait. Wait. The wall of cloud does not move; exactly the same number of fence-posts remain, the last one barely visible. It gets slightly colder, and slightly darker, but the obstinate haze has halted. You stand up, stretch, and turn around, only to see the lighted windows of the house shimmering and blurred by the mist you are in. You pause, and realize: it was never the edge of the mist you were watching, but the limits of your own vision. You saw only the distance that your eye could pierce, rather than the periphery of inexorable mist. That moment of realization is like thinking about Shakespeare, as he disappears behind Shackespere, Shakeshafte, Shakspere, Shagspere, Shxpr.

There is a large number of documents relating to Shakespeare's life – baptismal registers, marriage licences, loan agreements, satirical swipes, enthusiastic praises: but no letters, no memoirs, no autobiography. In the absence of incontrovertible evidence, countless scholars have chased will-o'-the-wisps through the plays, looking for allusions, disappointments and the settling of scores. Did Shakespeare get his own back on Sir Thomas Lucy by depicting him as Justice Shallow in *The Merry Wives of Windsor*? Is fellow playwright Christopher Marlowe the dead shepherd in *As You Like It*, and does the 'great reckoning in a little room' refer to his death? What connects the performance of *Hamlet, Prince of Denmark* in 1601 and the death by drowning of Hamnet Shakespeare, William's son, in 1596? What triggered the great, late plays, which undo and mend the tragedies of the previous decade? Who is the Dark Lady of the Sonnets? What happened in the 'Lost Years' between 1585 and 1592, or in the final years between the performance of *The Two Noble Kinsmen* in 1613 and his death three years later?

That way madness lies: and the history of Shakespeare criticism is littered with fantastical theories, dogmatic speculation and lunatic conspiracy. Let us leave biography along with its awful ghost: those reams of obsession that, discomfited by Shakespeare's lack of self-presentation, presume instead that John Donne, Edmund Spenser, Christopher Marlowe, the Earl of Oxford, Francis Bacon, Sir Philip Sidney's sister and Shakespeare's own wife must have written his work. Let us begin with what isn't: *Love's Labour's Won*, *Pericles* and *Cardenio*.

In 1598, Francis Meres wrote in his *Palladis Tamia, Wit's Treasury*, the first panegyric on Shakespeare:

As Plautus and Seneca are accounted the best for comedy and tragedy among the Latins, so Shakespeare among the English is the most excellent in both kinds for the stage. For comedy witness his *Gentlemen of Verona*, his *Errors*, his *Love's Labour's Lost*, his *Love's Labour's Won*, his *Midsummer Night's Dream*, and his *Merchant of Venice*; for tragedy, his *Richard the 2.*, *Richard the 3.*, Henry the 4., *King John*, *Titus Andronicus* and his *Romeo and Juliet*.

The only plays written before 1597 which Meres omits are the trilogy on *Henry VI* and *The Taming of the Shrew*. This led to the supposition that the mysterious *Love's Labour's Won* was an alternative title for *The Taming of the Shrew*; and, one could argue, Petruchio wins his love, albeit aggressively, in that play. The chance discovery, in 1953, of a scrap from a bookseller's list bound into a later volume demolishes that theory.

The fragment seems to be a list of volumes sold in August 1603: it includes 'marchant of vennis', 'taming of a shrew', 'loves labor lost' and 'loves labor won'. Since it mentions both works, it precludes them being one and the same text. It does, however, raise further problems; since it would seem to imply that *Love's Labour's Won* was actually printed.

Nineteen of Shakespeare's plays – called quarto editions – were printed individually. In 1623, seven years after Shakespeare's death, his friends John Heminges and Henry Condell edited his manuscripts or 'foul papers' and published the Folio edition of thirty-six plays (which does not include *Love's Labour's Won*). The chimera nevertheless persisted that *Love's Labour's Won* was an alternative title for another play by Shakespeare. The title might be thought to fit the plot of *Much Ado About Nothing*, which was performed in 1598, but published in 1600 under its own name. *As You Like It* or *All's Well that Ends Well* could have been the subtitle for *Love's Labour's Won*, in the same fashion as *Twelfth Night* is subtitled *What You Will*: neither exists as a quarto. By interpreting

'labour's won' as 'suffering deserved', it has even been proposed that the *Troilus and Cressida* was the mysterious lost
play. The idea of actually having lost a play by Shakespeare
seems too much to bear, and these alternative ascriptions belie
a desperation *not* to have lost anything.

But the other possibility is that *Love's Labour's Won* is, in
fact, *Love's Labour's Won*. Since it appears to have been
printed, over 1,000 copies might have existed in Elizabethan
London. That Heminges and Condell did not include it in
the Folio does not mean that it had disappeared by 1623.
They do not include *Pericles* or *The Two Noble Kinsmen*, and
analysis of the composition and printing of the Folio has
established that *Timon of Athens* was only added at a later stage,
and that *Troilus and Cressida* was nearly left out altogether. The
Folio is a Collected Works of Shakespeare, not a Complete
Works.

The quarto of *Titus Andronicus* was only discovered in the
first decade of the twentieth century; so the chance that *Love's
Labour's Won* is bound, somewhere, in an anonymous bundle
of old plays is not outside the realms of possibility. But the
likelihood diminishes with every passing year. *Love's Labour's
Lost* ends on a bittersweet note: 'The words of Mercury are
harsh after the songs of Apollo. You, that way: we, this way.'
While *Love's Labour's Lost* is left secure in the canon, its
putative sequel exits into a darker, more obscure off-stage
future.

Pericles, Prince of Tyre, as mentioned above, is not in the Folio.
The play was printed in quarto in 1609, though to justify its
presence in this book requires a further distinction: the good
and bad quartos. If the Folio is the album, and the quartos are
singles, then the bad quartos are bootleg copies. Many of
them were constructed by jobbing actors who memorized as
much as possible, and then cashed in on the play's success.
What makes *Pericles* a lost work is that all we have is the

version seen through a glass darkly: an unofficial, clandestinely created simulacrum of the real play.

How do you spot a bad quarto? Thankfully, we have two quartos of *Hamlet* to compare, Q1 and Q2, printed only a year apart. It looks suspiciously as if the second was a retort to the plagiarized first version. There are some obvious corkers in Q1, particularly in soliloquies when 'Hamlet' could not be overheard by his eavesdropping fellow actor. 'To be, or not be, I there's the point,' reads one famous line; and 'O what a rogue and peasant slave am I!' is oddly rendered as 'Why what a dunghill idiot slave am I!', let alone the wonderfully problematic fact that Polonius, in Q1, is called Corambis. The evidence for how the bad quartos came about is equally persuasive: in Q1 Horatio does not 'season', but 'ceasen' his admiration; Fortinbras' bedridden uncle is 'impudent' rather than 'impotent', and the play that 'pleased not the million, 'twas caviare to the general' instead 'pleased not the vulgar, 'twas caviary to the million'. Slips and mishearings, presumptions and anticipations typify the hastily assembled bad quarto.

So with *Pericles*, all we can read is an image thus disfigured. Despite its mangled and mutilated state *Pericles* retains features that seem classically Shakespearean. Like the other late plays, *The Winter's Tale*, *Cymbeline* and *The Tempest*, it involves a parent reconciled with the child they thought they had lost. Just as the apothecary in *Cymbeline* reversed the tragic accident in *Romeo and Juliet*, or the insane jealousy of Othello is redeemed in Leontes' penitence in *The Winter's Tale*, or the irascible Lear is forgiven in Prospero's own contrition, *Pericles* enacts a startling transformation of the potentially monstrous into an unexpected atonement.

It opens in horror, with Pericles, looking for a wife, and realizing the incestuous relationship between his prospective father-in-law and his intended. He leaves in disgust and, endangered, is shipwrecked, married and shipwrecked again. He thinks he has lost both his own wife and his own daughter, since he put one overboard, dead to the world, and left the other behind on his travels, and is reduced over the years to madness and misery. Then he glimpses his wife in his miraculously returned daughter (who has escaped, unharmed, from a brothel) and allows her to lead him to an epiphanic reunion with his similarly restored wife. Paternal devotion and daughterly love emancipate him, and counter the perversion of those attributes at the play's beginning.

There are flashes of Shakespeare's language: when Pericles' wife, Thaisa, regains consciousness in her coffin, the onlooker says, 'Her eyelids . . . begin to part their fringes of bright gold.' Prospero similarly addresses Miranda, saying, 'The fringèd curtain of thine eye advance.' The dialogue of the fishermen and the brothel frequenters has some recognizable brio. In his elegiac laments, Pericles occasionally reaches an almost familiar grandeur:

> A terrible childbed hast thou had, my dear;
> No light, no fire: the unfriendly elements
> Forgot thee utterly; nor have I time
> To give thee hallow'd to thy grave, but straight
> Must cast thee, scarcely coffin'd, in the ooze;
> Where, for a monument upon thy bones,
> The aye-remaining lamps, the belching whale
> And humming water, must o'erwhelm thy corse,
> Lying with simple shells.

But in other places, the verse is clunking and bloated.

> Few love to hear the sins they love to act
> 'Twould 'braid yourself too near for me to tell it.

In Ben Jonson's *Ode to Myself*, he derided *Pericles* as a 'mouldy tale', 'stale/as the shrieve's crust, and nasty as his fish'. He could not have known just how corrupted and corroded our version of it would be. It is tempting to imagine a perfect *Pericles* that would rank alongside *The Tempest*; although, since Shakespeare reworked these notions of redemption and absolution in his subsequent plays, it might suggest that he too was somewhat dissatisfied with *Pericles*.

Prospero, adjuring his magic and consigning his staff to the bottom of the sea at the end of *The Tempest*, has become romanticized into Shakespeare's own farewell to the stage. It's a lovely image, even if it is utterly wrong. Far from renouncing the theatre in 1611, Shakespeare continued, in collaboration with the up-and-coming John Fletcher on *Henry VIII, or All is True*, *The Two Noble Kinsmen* (based on Chaucer's 'Knight's Tale') and the enigmatic *Cardenio*. John Heminges, leader of the King's Men, was paid by the Privy Council for presenting 'Cardenno' or 'Cardenna' in May and June of 1613; and the Stationer's Register for 1653 attributes *The History of Cardenio* to 'Mr Fletcher and Shakespeare'. Even if it was not entirely written by Shakespeare, it nonetheless raises some intriguing possibilities.

The name 'Cardenio' comes from Cervantes' *Don Quixote, Part I*, which appeared in English in 1612, and in which we learn his story intermittently from chapter XXIII onwards. Don Quixote and Sancho Panza meet Cardenio, a man driven mad by the duplicity of his erstwhile friend, Don Ferdinand, who has connived Cardenio's beloved Lucinda into marriage and abandoned the farmer's daughter, Dorothea, whom he had seduced. By a series of lucky coincidences, chance meetings and the timely intervention of Don Quixote, the lovers are reunited, the wicked Ferdinand repents and Cardenio is cured. Even this brief outline indicates that many of the elements are consistent with Shakespeare's concerns in his last plays.

Did Shakespeare read Cervantes in the original, or in the translation? Or did Fletcher summarize the plot and allow the elder dramatist to freely adapt the material? More importantly, did *Cardenio* keep Don Quixote, or dispense with the romance-obsessed knight entirely? Francis Beaumont, another collaborator of Fletcher's, had staged a play called *The Knight of the Burning Pestle* in 1607, which featured an apprentice called Ralph, who harboured chivalric delusions, and was clearly modelled on Don Quixote. It is not impossible, though it is unlikely, that *Cardenio* contained the first appearance of Don Quixote on a British stage; and, in a manner as romantic and mythic as the identification of Prospero with Shakespeare, it is a pleasant conceit that the old playwright found in the gentle knight with the jangled mind another redemptive self-image.

Cardenio had a curious afterlife. In 1727, Lewis Theobald, the Shakespeare editor whom Pope bitterly attacked in the first version of *The Dunciad*, presented a tragicomedy at Drury Lane entitled *Double Falsehood, or The Distrest Lovers*, which he claimed was adapted from *Cardenio*, 'written originally by W. Shakespeare'. Theobald maintained he was working from the manuscript prompt-copy, not a quarto version, of the play.

The plot has broad similarities: Cardenio is renamed Julio, and again he spies on the wedding of his fiancée and his one-time confidante. He goes mad, and with the help of Dorothea (now called Violante), brings Henriquez/Ferdinand to justice. There is no Knight of the Doleful Countenance, or his waggish squire. Perhaps the only strikingly Shakespearean device is that Violante disguises herself as a shepherd. How much of the 'real' *Cardenio* was present in the later version is problematic: this was the age that gave us Tate's *King Lear*, complete with happy ending, and Dryden's *The Enchanted Isle*, which added a female monster and a man who has never seen a woman to *The Tempest*. Theobald would not have thought it disrespectful to radically rewrite Shakespeare. It is more difficult to explain why Theobald did not ever print the original. After his death in 1744, the precious copy lingered on, according to a newspaper advertisement, in the Museum of Covent Garden Playhouse. The building, including its library, burned down in 1808.

Shakespeare's collaboration with other writers provides our final, tantalizing proximity to expanding his oeuvre. The only manuscript of Shakespeare's creative work is a censor's copy of *The Booke of Sir Thomas More*: the so-called 'Hand D' is presumed to be Shakespeare's by comparison to other examples of his handwriting. 'Hand D' provides a longish speech for the protagonist. As a professional man of the theatre, Shakespeare might well have had a hand in countless works. Later copies of the Folio included other plays – *Arden of Feversham, Edward III, The Yorkshire Tragedy, Sir John Oldcastle, The Merry Devil of Edmonton, The London Prodigal, The Birth of Merlin, The Tragedy of Locrine, The Puritan* and the like – and, though little of the 'Shakespeare Apocrypha' has found favour with critics, the ghost of a chance exists that Shakespeare's words are scattered throughout a far wider corpus. Shakespeare is like language itself, diffuse, ever-present, in constant flux, and we might read far more by him, if only our eyes were sharp enough to see words for what they are.

John Donne

(1572–1631)

'Antes muerto que mudado' ran the legend across John
Donne's earliest portrait: 'sooner dead than changed'. At the
time, Donne was a self-assured, intelligent eighteen-year-old
Catholic; a precarious enough position in persecutory Protestant England, where suspected priest-harbourers were publicly executed. It was even more perilous if your uncle
happened to be the head of a crack team of covert Jesuits; so
hazardous, in fact, that emblazoning your miniature with a
quotation in the language of the recently defeated Spanish
Armada would seem reckless, if not suicidal.

Although the young Donne could hardly have scryed into
the future, even he might have been surprised to see himself
as a law student, MP, acclaimed poet, eloping lover, naval
adventurer and Anglican convert. It might have raised the
teenager's eyebrow, archly, to know that at forty he would
publish a withering satire on the Jesuits and their founder,
entitled *Ignatius His Conclave*, where the Jesuit leader applied
for the position of second-in-command to the Devil. He might
even have blanched to see himself, at fifty, as the Dean of

St Paul's Cathedral, an impassioned and inspiring preacher. It
may have been some comfort for him to know that he would
at least have the self-clarity to write, in his Holy Sonnet XIX:

> Oh, to vex me contraries meet in one:
> Inconstancy unnaturally hath begot
> A constant habit.

Of all the poets of the Renaissance, Donne remains the
one we know – or think we know – best; not in terms of a
compendious memorization of his verse and sermons, but as a
once-living human being, who loved, thought, ate and argued.
Whether as Jack Donne, the bawdy, sophisticated, pirouetting
poet of *Songs and Sonnets*, or as Dr Donne, the grave, tortured,
unflinching author of such lines as 'Ask not for whom the
bell tolls', Donne is a palpable presence. In fact, it appears
that the very riven-ness of him is what appeals. How did one
transform into the other? How did he hold the contradictory
and centrifugal aspects of his identity together? And, as always,
he shimmers just ahead of the reader, pre-empting questions
and preventing answers. In a sermon preached on New Year's
Day 1625, he says, 'It is an execrable and damnable monosyllable, *Why*; it exasperates God, it ruins us.'

Donne's poetry is as slippery as his motivations. Even in a
relatively straightforward piece, such as Holy Sonnet X, it is
impossible to distil out of the words a singular, intact meaning.
At first sight, it seems clear enough: 'Death be not proud,
though some have called thee / Mighty and dreadful, for,
thou art not so.' Donne catalogues the weaknesses and limitations of supposedly almighty Death; he whittles away the
Grim Reaper to a pathetic skeleton, triumphantly concluding:
'And death shall be no more, Death thou shalt die.' But that
final paradigmatic paradox rankles in its bald simplicity. If
Death is such a slight, inconsequential entity, why deploy
such formidable rhetorical powers to argue us out of our fear?

Writing a poem ostensibly to dispel the terror of death, Donne simultaneously manages to evoke that very horror.

In the early decades of the twentieth century, when T. S. Eliot was looking for a new kind of poetic voice, it was to Donne's ironic, elusive register he turned. What is more remarkable is that if it had not been for a gruesome incident, we would have had to strain just to catch even a few echoes of it.

John Donne Jnr was expected to follow his now-respectable father into the church. He had a middling gift for poetry, and his father's ability to weather the storms of political upheaval: he managed to live through the Commonwealth and into the Restoration with scant personal disturbance. He was also implicated in a murder. In 1634, he and a university chum were horse-riding in Oxford when a little boy called Humphrey Dunt inadvertently gave their steeds a start. John Donne Jnr, aggravated by the whelp's carelessness, thrashed him with a whip around the head. The child died a few days later. John Jnr was tried, and though several doctors testified that the walloping had done nothing directly attributable to the child's demise, he found his career path distinctly hampered.

Dr Donne had died in 1631, three years before, and his literary remains were in the hands of his friend Henry King. Somehow – and there have been imputations of outright theft – John Donne Jnr obtained the manuscripts, and for the next thirty years brought out publication after publication of his father's essays, poetry and sermons.

His father had published little during his lifetime. He was, moreover, disinclined to publish at all. This was not merely a case of Dr Donne disregarding the antic verses of his earlier incarnation Jack; as early as 1600, Donne wrote to a friend, including a copy of his *Paradoxes*, with the following plea:

Yet, Sir, though I know their low price, except I receive by your next letter an assurance upon the religion of your friendship that no copy shall be taken for any respect of these or any other of my compositions sent to you, I shall sin against my conscience if I send you any more.

Amongst Donne's papers were works such as the controversial and perhaps tongue-in-cheek *Biathanatos*, which argued that suicide was not a sin: Dr Donne would certainly not have approved of its appearance in the booksellers.

Much of Donne might have been lost. One major project, however, remains regrettably incomplete: *Metempsychosis* – though Donne himself was probably glad in later years he abandoned the poem subtitled 'The Progresse of the Soule'. Ben Jonson, the poet and dramatist, probably in his cups and possibly unaware his conversation was being eagerly noted by his friend William Drummond, gave a brief précis of the work:

The conceit of Donne's transformation or μετεμψυχοσις, was that he sought the soul of the Apple which Eve pulled, and thereafter made it the soule of a Bitch, then of a she-wolf, and so of a woman. His general purpose was to have brought in all the bodies of the Heretics from the soul of Cain and at last left it in the body of Calvin. Of this he wrote but one sheet, and now since he was made a Doctor he repenteth highly and seeketh to destroy all his poems.

The doctrine of metempsychosis, where an individual soul is reincarnated in different bodies, was controversial enough. To write a biography of the soul of persistent wickedness was even more dangerous.

Jonson is not wholly accurate. Donne actually wrote 520 lines, and his son published them in 1635. He begins:

> I sing the progress of a deathless soul,
> Whom Fate, which God made, but doth not control,
> Placed in most shapes;

The poem continues to find homes for the soul. It would animate Luther and Muhammad, and work its way through a mandrake root, a sparrow, a fish, a whale, a mouse, a wolf and a 'toyful ape' with certain unhealthy impulses towards human females.

What would be the final vessel of this diabolical psyche? The opening epistle promises to 'seriously deliver' the reader 'from her first making when she was that apple which Eve eat, to this time when she is he, whose life you shall find at the end of this book'. Calvin, advanced Jonson. Later critics, such as Edward Gosse, thought it would be Queen Elizabeth herself – the poem is written before 1601, so the still-Catholic Donne might have relished demonizing the head of the state that had killed his uncle and brother. Such an identification is abetted by the fact that some manuscripts have 'this time when she is she', rather than he. Moreover, the seventh stanza drops some heavy hints:

> For the great soul which here amongst us now
> Doth dwell, and moves that hand, and tongue, and brow,
> Which as the moon the sea, moves us, to hear
> Whose story, with long patience you will long;
> (For 'tis the crown, and last strain of my song).

If the reference to the crown were not enough, Elizabeth was frequently depicted as Cynthia, the moon, by Raleigh, Jonson and others. One can imagine the headlines if this happened today: Dean of Westminster claims Queen is Reincarnation of Devil. The passing of time blunts much, but not the deeply controversial nature of this poem. No wonder Donne attempted to lose his own work.

Ben Jonson

(1572–1637)

Considering that the author was so besotted with posterity, it is ironic that Ben Jonson's first and last works are lost. As early as 1616, his voluminous writings were issued as *Works*, not merely *Plays*, nor just *Poems*, not even *Prose and Other Writings*. He had his own coterie devoted to his kind of literature: the 'Tribe of Ben'. He was the sort-of Poet Laureate, enjoying the royally approved pension but not the title; the *de facto* not *de ipso* leading author of the day. His masques had been performed with monarchs, queens and favourites in the leading roles. As a writer of epigrams, tragedies, satires, odes, comedies, lyrics, epistles and elegies, he was the spin-doctor and jester of the court, as well as the toast of the underlings. He had even been Shakespeare's drinking buddy, antagonist and commemorator.

It had started somewhat differently. The adopted son of a bricklayer, he was apprenticed into that trade, even though he had attended the prestigious Westminster school and studied under the antiquary and scholar William Camden. He tired of 'having a *trowell* in his hand, [and] a *book* in his pocket', and enlisted in the army. If we are to take him at his word, he fought in the Netherlands and defeated a Spanish champion in single combat. Perhaps by way of playing roles in a touring company, Jonson drifted into the theatre. Even at the height of his career, his lower-class background provided plenty of ammunition for his enemies: he was a 'whoreson poore lyme- and hayre-rascal', 'the wittiest fellow of a Bricklayer in England'.

Jonson was originally attached to Philip Henslowe's theatrical company, and from Henslowe's diaries we learn that Jonson was paid for such plays as *Robert II of Scotland*, *Page of Plymouth*, *Richard Crookback* and *Hot Anger Soon Cold*. None of these has survived. Jonson, however, fares slightly better than his enemy and sometime co-author Thomas Dekker – Henslowe records forty titles of Dekker's works that have vanished. Francis Meres, the Elizabethan literary critic, ranked Jonson as among 'our best in tragedy'; nonetheless, we have none of the plays by which Meres came to his judgement.

The first play, however, with which Jonson was involved was not lost through chance or carelessness, but active suppression. In 1597 he acted in and wrote part of a satirical comedy entitled *The Isle of Dogs*, in collaboration with the pamphleteer Thomas Nashe. The Privy Council ruled that the work contained 'very seditious and slanderous matter'. Jonson, along with two other actors, was arrested; Nashe, whose quarters were searched, left London, and hid out in Great Yarmouth. All copies of the play were to be burned. All theatres in London were closed, as a precautionary measure.

What had riled the authorities in *The Isle of Dogs*? Nashe, in his prose work *Lenten Stuff*, recalls the affair:

The strange turning of *The Isle of Dogs* from a comedy to a tragedy two summers past, with the troublesome stir which happened about it, is a general rumour that hath filled all England, and such a heavy cross laid upon me as had well near confounded me.

Although he claimed only to have written the first act, Nashe was never to return to London, and was cut off from lucrative sources of patronage. He rails against the miserly aristocrats, and compares his fate to that of Homer, a wandering minstrel reliant on occasional generosities. Nashe hopes that 'those greybeard huddle-duddles and crusty cum-twangs' would be 'struck with such stinging remorse of their miserable euclionism and snudgery'. All the reader learns about the lost play is that Nashe found it difficult to write.

The Isle of Dogs . . . breeding unto me such bitter throws in the teeming as it did, and the tempests that arose at his birth so astonishing outrageous and violent as if my brain had been conceived of another Hercules, I was so terrified with my own increase, like a woman long travailing to be delivered of a monster.

Whatever *The Isle of Dogs* contained, it was clearly so sensitive that no one dared even to record the nature of the misdemeanour. Ben Jonson was imprisoned again in 1605 for his part in a play called *Eastward Hoe!*. In that instance, it seems that the King was offended by a seven-line attack on the Scots in act III, scene III (ironically, the play ends with the villains washed up on the Isle of Dogs). So *The Isle of Dogs* may have had but a few lines that offended, or the whole plot of the piece could have been treasonable.

Jonson could barely keep out of trouble. Just a year after the brouhaha about *The Isle of Dogs*, he was back in prison, charged with murdering a fellow actor, Gabriel Spenser, who had been imprisoned alongside him during the investigations into the 'lewd play'. Jonson, being literate, pleaded benefit of clergy, and was branded on the thumb rather than hanged by the neck. During the late 1590s and early 1600s, he was an active protagonist in the 'War of the Theatres', attacking rival playwrights John Marston and Thomas Dekker (though their subsequent collaboration suggests that the whole affair may have been subtly stage-managed). Even Shakespeare was not spared his barbed asides; Jonson's *Bartholomew Fair* begins with a dig at 'those that beget tales, tempests, and such-like drolleries'.

The testy, hot-tempered playwright would enjoy major successes with *Volpone*, *The Alchemist* (said by Coleridge to be one of the three perfect plots in existence), *Bartholomew Fair* and *Epicoene*, as well as playing a significant role in the Jacobean court with his masques and entertainments (though, typically, he fell out with the stage designer Inigo Jones on the subject of correct classical imagery).

It seems that Jonson sickened of the theatrical life. In his *Ode to Himself*, he erupts,

> Come leave the loathèd stage,
> And the more loathsome age,
> Where pride and impudence in faction knot,
> Usurp the chair of wit:
> Indicting and arraigning every day,
> Something they call a play.
> Let their fastidious, vain
> Commission of the brain
> Run on, and rage, sweat, censure, and condemn:
> They were not made for thee, less thou for them.

Jonson did not live to complete his final play, *The Sad Shepherd.* The play was obviously advanced in conception: nearly half is extant, as well as the dedicatory preface. *The Sad Shepherd* is a new direction and thus especially unfortunate in its incomplete state. Jonson finally tries his hand at pastoral.

The pastoral tragicomedy was not a new genre: the double-act stars of the stage, Francis Beaumont and John Fletcher, had already produced such works as *Philaster* and *The Faithful Shepherd*. As early as 1618, Jonson had confided in William Drummond that he 'had in hand' a pastoral called *The May Lord* about which nothing else is known. In *The Sad Shepherd* Jonson does not use the rococo caricatures of the Italian pastoral, but grafts into this form authentic English mythology: his work features Robin Hood, Friar Tuck, Little John, Maid Marian and Maudlin, the Witch of Paplewick. His strengths had always been in realizing indigenous English characters; from the thinly disguised portraits of contemporaries in *The Poetaster* to the quacks, conmen, puppeteers, Puritans and popinjays of *Bartholomew Fair*. Even the title of *The Isle of Dogs* hints at a particular local significance. Throughout his career, it was the vibrant chaos of the streets, as much as the sonorous splendour of the classics, that informed his writing.

The Sad Shepherd opens with a prologue in which Jonson looks back, and forward:

> He that hath feasted you these forty years,
> And fitted fables for your finer ears,
> Although at first he scarce could hit the bore;
> Yet you, with patience, harkening more and more,
> At length have grown up to him, and made known
> The working of his pen is now your own:
> He prays you would vouchsafe, for your own sake,
> To hear him this once more, but sit awake . . .
> His scene is Sherwood, and his play a Tale,
> Of Robin Hood . . .

Had he completed *The Sad Shepherd*, the English stage might well have benefited from an injection of new idioms and traditional legends. As it was, the Civil War was looming, and the theatres would soon be silent for a generation.

John Milton

(1608–74)

In the seventeenth century, every poet knew that the deepest honours and highest praises were reserved for the writer capable of producing an epic. Such an endeavour was, in the words of the poet laureate John Dryden, 'undoubtedly the greatest work the soul of man is capable to perform', and, as such, very few examples of it existed. Homer's *Odyssey* and *Iliad* were the source and fount; Virgil's *Aeneid* and Tasso's *Gerusalemme Liberata* the chief tributaries. Although Spenser's *Faerie Queene* had the scope and length of an epic, it had drifted and meandered too far from the classical precedents to be considered a successor, or a success. The 'heroic poem' to use the language of the time was, at the beginning of the century, an unclaimed prize.

John Milton had the ambition, and knew he had the ability, to write an epic. At the age of just seventeen, in his first year at Cambridge, he started a poem entitled *in quintum novembris*, which attempted to recast the events of Guy Fawkes' Gunpowder Plot in terms of Virgilian grandeur. Demonic and supernatural figures intervene in contemporary history. Satan himself suggests the treasonous conspiracy to the Pope, and the youthful poet, already a committed Protestant, daringly pries into the pontiff's bedroom ('neque enim secretus adulter / producit steriles molli sine pellice noctes', 'for the secret libertine spends no chilly nights without a supple concubine'). Although it begins with invention and flourish, it ends in an oddly off-hand manner, with hasty arrests and clichéd celebration. Young Milton could hit, but not hold, the notes.

In his twenties, Milton described himself as an epic poet more often than he attempted to compose an epic poem. To his university friend Charles Diodati he sent jesting verses about how he was not cut out for amatory lyrics, maintaining instead he was one who would 'tell . . . of wars, and of heaven . . . of pious leaders and god-like heroes, who sings now of the solemn decrees of the gods above, now of the infernal kingdoms'. In lines written to his father after leaving university, he justified his vocation, writing 'do not scorn the work of the poet, divine song'. His father seemed to accept the demand, allowing Milton to enjoy five uninterrupted years of leisurely study. But there was still no epic poem.

The portrait of the man that emerges from the early verse persists. He is committed to Protestantism, to the divine right of people to choose, to sombre, sober consideration rather than fashion or rash action. He is uncompromising, even if, as yet, he is also unfulfilled.

Milton travelled to Europe in 1638, and sought out Count Manso, the Italian aristocrat who had supported Torquato Tasso. In a Latin poetic epistle, Milton flattered Manso, insisting that 'if only Fate would grant me such a friend' he would 'call back into verse our native kings'. He had, it seems, found an appropriate topic – 'the great hearted heroes united in the unbreakable friendship of the Round Table'. The following year, Milton made his most unambiguous statement about his intentions. In an elegy for Charles Diodati, Milton vowed to write a poem describing Uther Pendragon, Merlin and King Arthur. Moreover, the poem would 'sound out a

British theme in its native strains'; an epic about England, written in English.

The Arthurian epic haunted the British literary imagination. Edmund Spenser had used some of the legends in his *Faerie Queene*; but his Arthur was in the dream-world of Fairyland, not on British soil. Instead of Lancelot, Guinevere and Mordred, he described Artegall, Amoret and Archimago. Eighteen years after Milton's death, Dryden was considering an epic poem about Arthur, and in the preface to his translations of Juvenal and Persius, he outlined the project to the Right Honourable Charles, Earl of Dorset and Middlesex:

Thus, my lord, I have, as briefly as I could, given your lordship and by you the world, a rude draught of what I have been long labouring in my imagination . . . a work which would have taken up my life in the performance of it. This, too, I had intended chiefly for the honour of my native country, to which a poet is particularly obliged. Of two subjects, both relating to it, I was doubtful – whether I should choose that of King Arthur conquering the Saxons (which, being farther distant in time, gives the greater scope to my invention), or that of Edward the Black Prince in subduing Spain . . . (wherein, after Virgil and Spenser, I would have taken occasion to represent my living friends and patrons of the noblest families) . . . my salary ill paid, and no prospects of a future subsistence, I was then discouraged in the beginning of my attempt.

Dryden even described how he would introduce supernatural 'machines', such as guardian angels, evil spirits and individual countries' Geniuses, to dignify his narrative and provide a contemporary counterpart to the pagan deities of Homer and Virgil.

While Dryden was peddling obsequies to his potential patron, one Richard Blackmore was not reading poetry, and, in his own words, had not even written a hundred verses. The Arthur idea must have struck him as potentially lucrative, and within three years his epic 'Prince Arthur' was published. It was so successful, he brought out another, 'King Arthur', two years later. Dryden seethed at this hack who had popped between the election and his hopes, and fulminated in the preface to his *Fables* (1700). 'I will only say,' he began, 'that it was not for this noble knight' − Blackmore had bagged a Sir for his verses − 'that I drew the plan of an epic poem on King Arthur . . . yet from that preface he plainly took his hint.' An amateur Arthur seemed worse than no epic at all.

Alexander Pope, Dryden's self-appointed successor, planned his own 'British' epic, but chose instead the even more mythical Brutus, so as not to disturb the shade of his elected ancestor. Sir Walter Scott tested the waters with an anonymous poem said to be in the style of Sir Walter Scott, *The Inferno of Altisidora*, which dealt with Arthurian legends, but switched to novels soon thereafter. Finally, Tennyson produced his *Idylls of the King*, by which stage the power of the epic, eroded by the novel, minimized by politics and travestied by domesticity, seemed profoundly irrelevant.

Milton never wrote his *Arthuriad* either. In 1639, he heard of the brewing discontent between the King and the Parliament, and, fired with a sense of mission, returned to support the rights of the people. In the storms of the approaching Civil War he would sign a king's death warrant, become a notorious pamphleteer in defence of liberty, reformation and the press, and even lend his name to a dissenting cult of 'Miltonists or Divorcers', according to the Rev. Thomas' encyclopedia of heretics. Of course, he would also eventually write an epic.

Why did he forgo Arthur? In his *History of Britain*, written many years later, Milton gives a chink into his misgivings: 'But who *Arthur* was, and whether ever any such reign'd in *Britain*, hath bin doubted heretofore, and may again with good reason . . . We may well perceave to have known no more of this *Arthur* 500 years past, nor of his doeings, than we now living.' Every element of Milton's character demanded that the epic would have to be true, not fabled.

Sixteen hundred and forty: the year Oliver Cromwell demands that Parliament must be recalled annually, that the hated Archbishop Laud is arrested, and Milton is writing a list in his spare time. Not only has he dispensed with the idea of an Arthurian work, it seems that even epic is off the agenda. He notes ninety-nine possible topics for a tragedy, ranging from the seduction of Adam and Eve to one described as a 'strange story of witchcraft, & murder discover'd, and reveng'd. Scotch story' (although this may sound familiar, it is worth noting that three items later, Milton is also considering a tragedy on Macbeth).

Most of the topics are taken from the Bible. The first glimmers of Milton's last work, the drama *Samson Agonistes*, are here; 'Dagonalia: Judges 16' contains the material he will adapt. Many of the scenarios will eventually be written by others, though none of them knew about the manuscript: Jean Racine takes no. 46 'Athaliah'; Abraham Cowley is already discarding his version of King David, nos. 28 and 29; Dryden will pick up on Achitophel (no. 31) for his satirical mock epic and even Oscar Wilde will provide a particular take on no. 54, Salome and John the Baptist. Countless schoolchildren will fulfil idea 55, which reads, simply, 'Christ born'.

As well as looking for biblical themes, Milton is looking for biblical forms. He believed that the Bible contained exemplars of literary genres: the Song of Songs is a pastoral drama (like his own *Comus*), the Book of Job is a short epic and the Book of Revelations is a 'high and stately tragedy'. The Bible was not, however, written in the style of Homer, and, for the time being, Milton's wavers between epic and tragedy. In the handful of topics drawn from English history, the epic is still raised as a possibility: 'An Heroicall Poem may be founded somewhere in Alfreds reigne. especially at his issuing out of Edelingsey on the Danes. Whose actions are wel like those of Ulysses.'

There is, however, one possible story that Milton outlines in some detail. Four different drafts appear in the manuscript for a drama founded on the opening of the Book of Genesis, sketches for a tragedy called *Adam Unparadiz'd*. Milton's daughter, Mrs Susannah Clarke, told Voltaire in 1727 that her father had actually written nearly two acts of the work; but it was set aside and somehow lost.

The Civil War delayed and deferred Milton's creative ambitions. Throughout the Commonwealth period, he engaged in polemical controversies, wrote political tracts and diplomatic documents. He served the state, advanced the Puritan cause, but his calling erupts, occasionally, in his prose. In the *Reason of Church Government urged against Prelacy* (1642), he interrupts himself to inform the reader he is no mere pamphleteer.

Time serves not now, and perhaps I might seem too profuse to give any certain account of what the mind at home, in the spacious circuits of her musing, hath liberty to propose to herself, though of highest hope and hardest attempting: whether the epic form . . . or whether the rules of Aristotle [i.e. tragedy] are strictly to be kept . . . and lastly, what king or knight before the conquest might be chosen in whom to lay the pattern of a Christian hero.

Politician or poet? Epic or drama? Saxons or Israelites? He is drawn to origins: even when defending the freedom of the press, that most modern of estates, his mind snags on the oldest story. 'It was from the rind of one apple tasted, that the knowledge of good and evil, as two twins cleaving together, leaped forth into the world,' he wrote in the *Areopagitica*, desperate to denounce the 'mere artificial Adam' of his pro-censorship opponents. If there is a way out of the chaos of the present, it is in first principles: wisdom older than Virgil, Homer and Moses. If there is to be a heroic poem he knows it must be true, needs it to be holy, and is adamant it must be absolute.

Sixteen sixty: he is blind. The Commonwealth has collapsed and the King sits again upon the throne. The Civil War was won, but by the enemy, now engaged in dismantling the project. Milton, the great justifier of regicide, who only just avoids the gallows, is without influence, income, hope and sight. But he does, at least and last, have time, and his daughters, who can copy down his words. Whatever he had scribbled and drafted beforehand, *Paradise Lost* is begun in his isolation. No one knows exactly when he started, or with which line, or word. But the finished production includes his own long path to the poem:

> Since first this subject for heroic song
> Pleased me long choosing, and beginning late;
> Not sedulous by nature to indite
> Wars, hitherto the only argument
> Heroic deemed, chief mast'ry to dissect
> With long and tedious havoc fabled knights
> In battles feigned (the better fortitude
> Of patience and heroic martyrdom
> Unsung), or to describe races and games
> Or tilting furniture, emblazoned shields,
> Impresses quaint, caparisons and steeds
> Bases and tinsel trappings, gorgeous knights
> At joust or tournament; then marshaled feast
> Served up in halls with sewers and seneschals;
> The skill or artifice or office mean,
> Not that which justly gives heroic name
> To person or to poem.

'I know thee not, old man,' Milton whispers to Spenser. The only remnant of his dreams of an *Arthuriad* is a denunciation of the whole juvenile idea. The planned dramas remain skewered in the blank verse like a skelf under the skin: Milton's self-dramatized, self-deluded, soliloquizing Satan is the son of Shakespeare's tragic heroes, and the father of the novel's self-knowing villains.

After so many fits and starts, in internal, eternal exile, the ways of God will be justified to man. The English will get their epic.

Paradise Lost very nearly never appeared at all. It was published in 1667, the year after the Great Fire of London. Many printers' and booksellers' premises around St Paul's had suffered particularly badly – indeed, the manuscript and every printed copy of John Ogilby's epic poem *The Carolies* were now so much ash. Milton's work survived the conflagration.

Its afterlife makes even *Paradise Lost* a curiously lost work in itself. The literary world wanted it to, well, go away.

John Dryden huffily acknowledged its greatness, but denied it the laurels on a technicality.

As for Mr Milton, whom we all admire with so much justice, his subject is not that of an heroic poem, properly so called. His design is the losing of our happiness; his event is not prosperous, like that of all other epic works; his heavenly machines are many, and his human persons are but two.

Moreover, in an almost petulant exercise in dumbing-down, Dryden turned it into a stage opera, entitled *The State of Innocence and the Fall of Man*. Dryden rewrote the blank verse as rhyming couplets, though he did ask Milton's permission. 'You may tag my verses' is all that remains of an exceptionally curious literary meeting.

Richard Bentley (1662–1742) was a formidable scholar of

Latin and Greek, most renowned for conclusively ending the debate about whether the *Epistles of Phalaris* were genuine (they weren't). He decided to turn his copious erudition to *Paradise Lost*, and became convinced that the true work had been mangled by Milton's soft-witted daughters' attempts at taking dictation, and the slapdash carelessness of his editors. After all, a blind poet cannot check his proofs. Take, for example, the closing lines:

> They hand in hand, with wand'ring steps and slow,
> Through Eden made their solitary way.

Ridiculous! How could *two* people be solitary? What Milton meant to say was:

> Then hand in hand, with social steps their way
> Through Eden took with heav'nly comfort cheer'd.

Even if Bentley hadn't managed to annoy Alexander Pope, by slighting his abilities as a translator of Homer, he was destined, just for this small editing job alone, for a place in the expanded edition of Pope's *Dunciad*.

William Lauder, who died in 1771, was at the opposite end of the social spectrum, but in a similar line of work to Mr Bentley. A one-legged Scottish classics tutor, he also possessed a monomaniacal hatred of *Paradise Lost*. In *An Essay into Milton's Use and Abuse of the Moderns* of 1750, he sensationally showed how Milton had plagiarized from Taubmann, Staphorstius, Masenius and other little-known contemporary Latinists. In fact, Lauder had translated *Paradise Lost* into Latin and then inserted his lines into the works of the said authors. He also included an advert for his services as a tutor. Once the forgery was revealed, the publishers decided that 'we shall for the future sell his book ONLY as a masterpiece of fraud, which the public may be supplied with at 1s6d stitched'.

Even Samuel Johnson managed to lard his biography of Milton with caveats. 'The original deficience cannot be supplied,' he argued, continuing with damning short sentences: 'The want of human interest is always felt. *Paradise Lost* is one of the books the reader admires and lays down, and forgets to take up again. None ever wished it longer than it is. Its perusal is a duty rather than a pleasure.'

And perhaps even Milton felt some resentment to his poem. Despite the fact that he had written the English epic, when the countless other attempts – the risible *Alfred* and *Eliza* of Blackmore, the countless *Wellingtoniads* and *Alexandriads* – moulder on shelves; perhaps he would have preferred power to poetry. If the Devil had taken up John Milton unto an high place, and offered, on the one hand, the laurel of posterity, and on the other, the chance for his Commonwealth to continue beyond Cromwell's death, the extirpation of monarchy, the collapse of Catholicism and England transformed into a global beacon for his ideals – what would the old Iconoclast have chosen?

Sir Thomas Urquhart

(1611–60)

Soldier, gentleman, traveller, mathematician, genealogist, poet, translator, linguistic philosopher and, possibly, madman: Sir Thomas Urquhart had many talents, but by far the greatest was for hyperbole.

Thomas was the eldest son of the impecunious Laird of Cromarty. He studied at King's College, Aberdeen, and then embarked on a Grand Tour of Europe, where he was conspicuous for defending the honour of Scotland and acquiring books for his library, a collection which he later called 'a complete nosegay of flowers which in my travels I have gathered out of the gardens of above sixteen several kingdoms'. On his return, apart from unsuccessful attempts to alleviate the debts and placate the creditors of his father, he travelled to London, to the court of Charles I. Urquhart began to fashion himself as a Cavalier wit, writing 1,103 epigrams entitled *Apollo and the Muses* in thirteen weeks in 1640, and publishing a further 134 *Epigrams: Divine and Moral.* He was knighted in 1641, and returned to Scotland after the death of his father, barely having time to dash off his impenetrable treatise applying Napier's Logarithms to trigonometry. Among the more extravagant claims of the *Trissotetras, or a most exquisite table for resolving triangles* was that a student could, using Urquhart's method, learn a year's worth of mathematical formulae in the space of seven weeks.

With the outbreak of the Civil War and the execution of Charles I, Urquhart rallied troops for a Royalist counter-offensive. He had already earned the enmity of the Protestant Covenanters after a skirmish at Turriff, purportedly the first blood to be shed in the defence of the Solemn League and Covenant. He was cautioned by the General Assembly for his 'dangerous opinions', but nonetheless hastened to Charles II, and joined his army that was attempting an invasion of Cromwell's England in 1651.

After the defeat of the Royalists at the Battle of Worcester, Urquhart was taken to the Tower of London as a traitor, but seems to have enjoyed some degree of liberty. While in prison he petitioned Cromwell's government with various claims, including that he had a secret 'advantageous to the nation', which he would make known on his release. He translated Rabelais, and compiled three fantastical books – the *Pantochronochanon*, the *Ekskubalauron* and the *Logopandecteision* – before being exiled around 1655. He died, in 1660, on hearing the news of the Restoration of Charles II, 'in a fit of excessive laughter'.

So what were these strange tomes? The *Ekskubalauron*, also known as *The Jewel*, contains material from the *Pantochronochanon*, Urquhart's genealogy of himself from Adam, and the *Logopandecteision*, his proposal for a Universal Language, as well as including a panegyric on Scotland in the character of a polymathic soldier and scholar, the Admirable Crichton. In his translation of Rabelais, Urquhart indulges in copious expansions and erudite exaggerations: for example, when Rabelais gives nine examples of onomatopoeic animal noises, Urquhart extends this to seventy-one. His version is 70,000 words longer than the original. Stylistically, his sentences stretch like two mirrors facing each other, warping to incorporate classical neologisms, demotic asides and a plethora of quirks and curiosities. To call it 'Shandy-esque', 'Carlyle-ish' or 'Joycean' is to obscure Urquhart's originality, and underplay his peculiar grandiloquence. As the Rev. John Willock wrote, 'only a mind like his own could trace the maze of its windings and turnings, and fathom the depth of its eccentricity'.

The *Pantochronochanon* shows how influential the Urquharts have always been. Tracing their descent from Adam's third son, Seth, rather than through Cain, Urquhart's forebears have an uncanny knack for being tangentially involved in world history. His great × 109 grandmother, Termuth, found Moses in the rushes. Uthork, his great × 66 grandfather, was the general for the mythic Fergus I of Scotland. He can, he claims, 'produce testimonies of Arabic, Greek and Latin', which will be as disprovable as the Elements of Euclid.

Similarly, in the *Logopandecteision*, he outlines his Universal Language, but withholds the grammar and vocabulary which he has already developed. The language creates a one-to-one correspondence between words and things, as in Leibnitz's scheme, and each word, being built up from syllables, contains in itself its location in the scheme of things: as if the scientific Latin name of an organism, containing its phylum, genus and species, could be compressed into a word of no more than seven syllables. Urquhart's image is of a map,

so many cities which are subdivided into streets, they againe into lanes, those into houses, these into stories wherof each room standeth for a word; and all these so methodically, that whoso observeth my precepts thereanent shall at the first hearing of a word know to what city it belongeth and . . . after a most exact prying into all its letters, finding the street, lane, house, story and room thereby denoted, he punctually hit upon the very proper thing it represents by its most specifical signification.

Not only can everything be named; every sound the mouth can make is made meaningful.

Precision is not the least of the virtues of Urquhartese. Each word 'hath at least ten several *synonymas*' and the language has 'a wonderful facility . . . in making of anagrams'. In his true, hyperbolic style, his Language outdoes every other tongue, having eleven genders, seven moods, ten cases and 'four voices, although it was never heard that ever any other language had above three'. The names of soldiers express their exact rank, and the names of stars contain their latitude and longitude, in degrees and minutes. Urquhart could, if let free, single-handedly rebuild Babel.

Before he is written off as a harmless lunatic, it is worth mentioning that Urquhart does express some linguistic truths. He understands that translation is, by its nature, impossible, and that 'were . . . languages stript of what is not originally their own, we should not be able . . . to purchase so much as our breakfast in market'. Though it is highly speculative, and possibly satirical, it is not the work of an unversed charlatan.

Why were the proofs of a Universal History and the primer of the Universal Language denied to the world? Partly, of course, because they were never written. The whole phantasmagoria is an elaborate charade designed to win him his freedom and announce his fame. But he did lose a large number of manuscripts after the Battle of Worcester. Even if they did not contain the Elixir of Eternal Life and the Specifications for an Engine to Travel to the Stars, they would have been shot through with his own quintessenced and cup-shotten mokes, his serpegiar bliteri and heteroclite idiosyncrasy, as he himself would say. It seems appropriate to let the good knight tell his own tale of misfortune, when, after the rout of the regal party at Worcester, two swindlers and plunderers in Master Spilsbury's house find nothing . . .

but manuscripts in folio to the quantity of sixscore and eight quires and a half, divided into six hundred fourty and two quinternions and upwards . . . they in a trice carried all whatever els was in the room away save those papers, which they then threw down on the floor as unfit for their use. Yet immediately thereafter, when upon carts the aforesaid baggage was put to be transported to the country, and that by the example of many hundreds of both horse and foot whom they had loaded with spoil, they, . . . apprehending how useful the paper might be unto them, went back for it and bore it straight away; which done, to every one of those their camards whom they met with in the streets, they gave as much thereof for packeting up of raisins, figs, dates, almonds, caraway and other such like dry confections and other ware as was requisite; who, doing the same themselves, did together with others kindle pipes of tobacco with a great part thereof and threw all the remainder upon the streets save so much as they deemed necessary for inferiour employments and posteriour uses.

Of those dispersedly-rejected bundles of paper, some were gathered up by grocers, druggists, chandlers, pie-makers or such as stood in need of any cartapaciatory utensil and put in present service to the utter undoing of all the writing thereof both in its matter and order.

Abraham Cowley

(1618–67)

Like many a child prodigy, Abraham Cowley found his middle age to be fraught with the dark memories of dashed hopes. The seventh son of a posthumous father, he had certainly flourished quickly. Before the age of ten he had found, and read, a copy of Spenser's *Faerie Queene* in his mother's chamber, a fortuitous discovery, since the bulk of her books were theological treatises. Enthusiasm soon turned to imitation, and by the age of eleven he had composed and published two poems. By 1633, he had written sufficient verses for them to be collected together as *Poetical Blossoms*. The teenage writer went on to produce a pastoral play, *Love's Riddle*, and a Latin comedy, *Naufragium Joculare*, while at Cambridge. The stage seemed set for his erudition, wit and gentle amiability to secure for him the position of foremost writer of the age.

The Civil War, however, intervened. With his 'heart set wholly upon letters, I went to the university, but was soon torn from thence by that violent public storm, which would suffer nothing to stand where it did, but rooted up every plant, even from the princely cedar to me, the hyssop'. As an adherent to the monarchy and Charles I, Cowley moved from Parliamentarian Cambridge to Royalist Oxford, dashing off a satire on the King's foes entitled *The Puritan and the Papist*. But, as he would later recollect in biting understatement, 'a warlike, various and a tragical age is the best to *write of* but the worst to *write in*'.

Between 1644 and 1654, Cowley was based on the Continent, predominantly in the service of Lord Jermyn, the secretary to Henrietta Maria, the wife of Charles I. He continued to publish, with *The Mistress* in 1647 and another comedy, *The Guardian*, in 1650; most of his time, however, was taken up with coding and deciphering documents for his master and correspondence between Henrietta Maria and Charles, as the pitched battles on English soil were superseded by espionage and intrigue. Between continents, Cowley undertook several undercover missions, to the Netherlands, Jersey and Scotland. In 1655, he returned to England, apparently to live in semi-retirement and discreetly provide occasional reports on the state of the nation to the exiled court. He was arrested as a Royalist spy, in London, and released on bail of £1,000.

It has been suspected that Cowley struck a deal with the establishment of the day. Antony à Wood, the seventeenth-century academic gossip, maintained there was an encomium by Cowley on Cromwell, though these lines have never surfaced. What is certain is that Cowley did retire, eventually to Kent, where he seems to have been held in slight suspicion after the Restoration of Charles II (despite an enthusiastic ode welcoming the King back). He became a doctor of physic, and spent the last years of his life composing a Latin poem in six books on herbs, flowers and fruit trees: from poetical blossoms to botany.

What caused Cowley's change, from debonair poet at the heart of the political system, to secluded naturalist? A snapshot of his state of mind can be found in the remarkable *Preface* to his *Collected Works* of 1656, published the year after his release from prison.

'My desire has been for some years past,' he wrote, '. . . to retire my self to some of our *American Plantations*'. A comprehensible enough inclination for a man slung in jail the instant he stepped back on the native soil which had been soaked with his King's and colleagues' blood. But throughout the *Preface*, Cowley's stance towards himself as a poet, and towards poetry in general, is almost pathological. What happened in the past was over and never to be repeated or explored. His *Collected Works* was, he claimed, 'a little *Tomb* of *Marble*'. 'To make my self absolutely dead in a *Poetical* capacity, my resolution at present, is never to exercise any more that faculty,' he wrote and, when asking his critics to look kindly on his efforts, maintained, 'I may make a just claim to the undoubted priviledge of *Deceased* Poets.'

This literary death-wish, this 'encourage[ment] to learn the Art of Oblivion' is not without its psycho-sexual undertones. He was 'made a poet as irremediably as a child is made a eunuch'. Moreover, 'as the marriage of infants do but rarely prosper, so no man ought to wonder at the diminution or decay of my affection to Poesy, to which I had contracted myself so much under age'. The poem 'Destiny' offers another, bizarre image: the Muse

> circumcised my tender soul, and thus she spake:
>> 'Thou of my church shall be;
>> Hate and renounce' said she
>> 'Wealth, honour, pleasures, all the world for me.
>> Thou neither great at court, nor in the war,
>>> Nor at th'Exchange shalt be, nor at the wrangling Bar.
>>> Content thyself with this small, barren praise
>>> That neglected verse does raise'.

Cowley's description of the poetical life here sounds more like an undesirable designation than a restful and expected tapering. 'I can no longer write' was an adequate cover-story for 'I will not longer write'.

He included, in the 1656 *Collected Poems*, four books of an epic poem which he had 'neither *Leisure* hitherto, nor . . . *Appetite* at present to finish'; and though he may have subsequently had time, desire did not return over the last eleven years of his life. He described his abandoning of the poem with characteristic sly self-deprecation: 'men commonly play not out the game, when it is evident that they can win it, but lay down their cards and take up what they have won'. Nonetheless, he included an analysis of his intentions that would have a significant impact on English poetry.

The Davideis was to be an epic poem on the life of the biblical King David. He 'designed [it] into *Twelve Books* . . . after the *pattern* of our Master *Virgil*'. Fidelity to his model even led Cowley to include hemistichs, or half-lines, since such lines appear in *The Aeneid*: he seems not to have realized that they are evidence that Virgil's poem too is unfinished, or at least unperfected. Cowley clearly had the poem plotted out in no small detail. It would encompass

many noble and fertile Arguments behind; as, the barbarous cruelty of *Saul* to the *Priests* at *Nob*, the several flights and escapes of *David*, with the manner of his living in the *Wilderness*, the *Funeral* of *Samuel*, the love of *Abigail*, the sacking of *Ziglag*, the loss and recovery of *David's* wives from the Amalekites, the *Witch* of *Endor*, the war with *Philistia*, and the *Battel* of *Gilboa*; all of which I meant to interweave upon several occasions, with most of the illustrious *Stories* of the *Old Testament*, and to embellish with the most remarkable *Antiquities* of the *Jews*.

The poem would end, not with David's anointment as King of Israel, but with his 'most Poetical and excellent *Elegie* . . . on the death of *Saul* and *Jonathan*'.

Poetry, Cowley argued, in the ungodly time of Cromwell as much as in the pagan past, had been usurped by the Devil, and needed to be redeemed. 'Why will not the actions of *Sampson* afford as plentiful matter as the *Labors* of *Hercules*? . . . Does not the passage of *Moses* and the *Israelites* into the *Holy Land*, yield incomparably more Poetical variety, than the voyages of *Ulysses* or *Aeneas*?'

In an astonishing moment of clarity, Cowley bows away from his poem, and nods to the future simultaneously. 'I shall be ambitious of no other fruit from this weak and imperfect attempt of mine, but the opening of a way to the courage and industry of some other persons, who may be better able to perform it thoroughly and successfully.' Step forward, John Milton.

Cowley resembles a poetic mutant, a hopeful monster in the evolution of English poetry: he developed new sensitivities, better strategies; he adapted himself towards an obvious niche that, unfortunately, did not yet exist. He was the new, right kind of poet, in the wrong old place, time and uniform.

His *Collected Poems* is a pruning of his output. 'I have cast away all such pieces as I wrote during the time of the late troubles . . . as among others, *Three Books* of *The Civil War* it self.' Book I of this appeared in 1679, the other two were discovered in the mid-1980s. The poem was an attempt to narrate the conflict between Roundheads and Cavaliers as if it were an epic already, and with the epic's foregone conclusion that the good would triumph. God blessed the King, and the Devil inspired Cromwell. Life, however, took a different turn from literary precedent. Cowley dismissed his political epic brusquely, saying, 'it is folly to weave laurels for the conquered'.

One wonders if Milton realized the irony: that the epic would always be written in political exile. His *Paradise Lost* was composed under the autocratic rule of Charles II, not the government of Cromwell. John Dryden would only translate the *Aeneid* after James II was forced to cede the British throne to William III. Alexander Pope put *The Iliad* into English at a time when the King couldn't even speak the language. James McPherson's forged epic poem *Fingal, by Ossian* was launched after Culloden, when the Gaelic it was supposedly written in was being actively suppressed. Epic, for the British poet, is always tinged with elegy.

Molière (Jean-Baptiste Poquelin)

(1622–73)

'Manuscripts don't burn,' wrote Mikhail Bulgakov in his greatest work, *The Master and Margarita*, even though, as a biographer of Molière, he knew that the letters and unpublished works of his hero, including the final masterpiece, *L'Homme du cour*, had been consigned to the flames. But Bulgakov does not mention in *The Life of Monsieur de Molière* another work we know to be lost: though whether or not it is truly lost is problematic.

Despite many of the events of his life, Molière was the luckiest and sanest of comedians. When his stammering on the stage elicited cat-calls and well-aimed vegetables, he turned into a writer, and a writer of genius at that. When his company was thrown out on the street, he bounced back into opulent surroundings. When his daring works caused outrage, he was safely under the patronage of the duc d'Orléans. When an outraged theatre-goer stood up during a performance of *Sganarelle, ou le cocu imaginaire*, and loudly declared he was being libelled, the audience laughed twice as hard that anyone would willingly claim they were the model for an avaricious, jealous, bourgeois fool. Fortune's vacillations and vicissitudes always ended up as opportunities, and every brick-bat became a laurel. Even the rumour that he had married his own daughter barely scratched his public standing; though his former mistress's offspring made his life a misery nonetheless.

Molière's comedy proceeded from a sense that vices were follies. It was not just the gulling of the miserly Harpagon in *L'Avare* that was funny; it was the intrinsically ludicrous nature of thinking that hoarding one's wealth was a feasible scheme. Intellectual pretension in *Les Précieuses ridicules*, the fear of death in *Le Malade imaginaire*, hypocrisy in *Tartuffe*, cynicism in *Le Misanthrope*, lust in countless disguises: every atrocious kink in human psychology, whereby the inevitable was pointlessly avoided, was the source of gloriously unaffected glee.

But from what secure vision of the world did Molière's iron-hard ironic castigation stem? As a boy he had been taught, like countless other young men, to read the work of the Latin philosopher Lucretius. In *De Rerum Natura*, Lucretius advocated an Epicurean world-view: the gods were unnecessary, error was its own punishment, and, as individuals from St Paul to Samuel Johnson found, there was no use kicking against the pricks of a cosmos that cared nothing about the vanity of human wishes. Happiness was the product of avoiding pain: so, syllogistically, the person who not only provided pleasure, but also highlighted the unprofitability of mankind's habitual sloppy thinking and silly desires, would be nothing less than a mundane saint in a heavenless universe.

In one instance, Molière outdid his mentor. Lucretius, to prevent the future sufferings he would no doubt have to endure, committed suicide. Molière, on finding his friends so lachrymose in drink that they were intent on drowning themselves, agreed with them, but cautioned that such a philosophically relevant protest at the conditions of existence would no doubt be undermined if it transpired they performed the action when flushed with wine. The suicide would take place the next day, after breakfast, when, of course, it didn't.

Molière wrote a translation of Lucretius. The Abbé de
Marolles had mentioned in 1661 that Molière intended to
publish the work, the year before his first major success with
L'Ecole des femmes. It never appeared. Since we have Lucretius
himself, the loss of a French version might seem a minor
affair. To an extent, this is true. Just as the orbit of Uranus,
strained out of kilter by the presence of Neptune, allowed
Verrier to predict the existence of another planet without
having seen it, so Molière's debt to Lucretius can be fathomed
in the elliptical circuit of his thinking, even though the actual
homage has perished, save for a speech on the blindness of
lovers derived from Lucretius in *Le Misanthrope*.

To hear him, with his own elegance, express the futility
of striving and the fiction of the divine, would have been
invigorating. But – as he might well have chosen to translate
the title of *De Rerum Natura* – *c'est la vie*.

Jean Racine

(1639–99)

In Eric Linklater's satirical novel *Magnus Merriman* (1934), the eponymous hero and his friend Meiklejohn end up spending the night in the cells of Edinburgh's Central Police Station after an argument gets out of hand. The dispute was occasioned by Merriman's assertion that Shakespeare is 'the greatest poet of all time'. When asked to 'name a better poet', Meiklejohn had retorted 'Racine'. Magnus responds:

That dull, pedantical schoolroom exercise! That prosy, plodding, weary, unimaginative padding for a deserted library! That's not poetry: that's route marching to Parnassus with a full pack and a sergeant alongside to see that you keep step.

Though they did not use this as their defence the next morning, their *contretemps* enacted cultural assumptions that stretched back 150 years. Praising Shakespeare over Racine was a convenient short-hand for any number of political or aesthetic debates. Johann Gottfried Herder thundered, 'Woe betide the frivolous Frenchman who arrives in time for Shakespeare's fifth act, expecting it will provide him with the quintessence of the play's touching sentiment.' William

Hazlitt denounced the 'didactic' Racine, saying, 'tragedy is human nature tried in the crucible of affliction, not exhibited in the vague theorems of speculation'.

An easy method of extolling the northern, natural, passion of Shakespeare was to set it in invidious comparison with the perceived courtly *froideur* of Racine. For example, Pyrrhus in Racine's *Andromaque* (1667) attempts to force the reluctant Andromache (whose husband has been murdered by Pyrrhus' late father) into marriage by threatening to kill her son; he does so nonetheless in tones of stifling *politesse*.

> Well, then, my lady, you must be obeyed.
> I must forget, or rather hate you. Yes
> My passion's violence has gone too far
> Ever to halt in mere indifference.

The original French elegantly rhymes *leur violence* with *l'indifférence*.

Moreover, as the influential critical theorist Roland Barthes observed, Racine's plays rely upon stylized chains of romantic disappointment. Orestes loves Hermione, who loves Pyrrhus, who loves Andromache. Amurat is married to Roxane, who falls for Bajazet, who loves Atalide. Theseus is married to Phaedra, who lusts after Hippolytus, who is forbidden to love Aricie.

It is, however, a mistake to suppose Racine was merely the 'literature which appealed to our great-grandfathers', as Stendhal claimed in *Racine et Shakespeare*. In his day, he was the very archetype of the rebellious avant-garde.

Jean Racine was born in 1639, in the backwater village of La Ferté-Milon, to a family of minor bureaucrats. He was orphaned at the age of four and subsequently brought up by his grandparents. When his grandfather died in 1649, his grandmother decided to retire to Port-Royal, a centre of religious seclusion inextricably associated with the movement known as Jansenism. Cornelius Otto Jansen, the Bishop of Ypres, developed his theology after studying the works of St Augustine. Pope Urban VIII condemned the Jansenist movement in the 1641 Papal Bull *In Eminenti*. Jansenism, however, had a secure foothold in France, and included amongst its adherents the philosopher Blaise Pascal.

Jansenism taught of an immeasurably distant God, whose grace alone could redeem man from a state of ingrained and perpetual sinfulness. It was outspoken about the moral laxity of the age, dismissive of the carnivals and gallantries of Louis XIV and positively puritanical about the theatre.

We do not know exactly when Racine became dissatisfied with the piety of his guardians, nor do we know when he first entertained thoughts of a dramatic career. He was, however, a truculent pupil. He was taught Greek by the sacristan Claude Lancelot, and it was undoubtedly from him he first learned of the works of the Athenian playwrights. According to one anecdote, he was caught reading a less than ennobling Greek romance called the *Aethiopica*, attributed to Heliodorus of Emesa. Lancelot threw the book in the fire. Racine, undeterred, found another copy, read it through, and gave it to the sacristan, saying, 'You can burn this one now as well.' A boast about his memory or a judgement on the literary merit of the tale? The *Aethiopica* resurfaced during Racine's faltering steps towards theatrical acclaim.

After schooling, Racine went to Paris to study philosophy. With his distant, and dissolute, cousin, the fable-writer La Fontaine, he was 'un loup avec les loups' – running with the wolves. He wrote eulogies for Cardinal Mazarin, Louis XIV's chief minister and an implacable opponent of the Jansenists, and received 100 *louis d'or* from the King for a poem on the Nymph of the Seine. He frequented the court, where showmanship and elegance glossed over *realpolitik*.

Racine's first attempt at a dramatic composition was entitled *Amasie*. Apart from the title, all we know is that the

Marais Theatre accepted it in 1660, but never performed it. The title itself adds nothing more: it may, perhaps, have been about the Egyptian ruler Amasis, and offer an early indication of Racine's interest in exotic locales.

In 1661, the Hôtel de Bourgogne turned down a tragedy, now lost, called *Les Amours d'Ovide*. The Roman poet Ovid, who was exiled to Tomis for an unspecified indiscretion, had appeared on the stage before: he is the hero of Ben Jonson's comedy *The Poetaster*. Racine obviously took some care in the plot construction, and, in a letter, he described how writing the well-turned verse was an easy matter once he had streamlined the actions, choices and consequences. Drama was plot, not poetry.

The tragedy lingered in Racine's mind, and, when he wrote to his friend L'Abbé le Vasseur from the small town of Uzès, where he was studying theology with his uncle, in late 1661, he compared himself to Ovid, the 'si gallant homme', languishing with the barbarous Scythians.

The next year, after he returned to Paris, Racine's third attempt at theatrical success was offered to the company of the comic playwright Molière. It was based on his childhood reading of the *Aethiopica*, and took its name from the hero and heroine, *Théagène et Chariclée*. Chariclea is the daughter of King Hydaspes of Ethiopia. Her mother, Queen Perside, unfortunately looked at a marble statue during her pregnancy, with the unforeseen outcome that the girl is born with white skin. Terrified that Hydaspes will think she has been unfaithful, she secretly sends the child to Delphi, to become a priestess. Theagenes, the Prince of Thessaly, falls in love with her, and the two elope. After various shenanigans involving pirates, disguises and the like, all the characters converge on Meroe, where, through another series of improbabilities, Hydaspes is going to sacrifice Chariclea. As luck would have it, all the convolutions and contortions of the plot are resolved in the nick of time.

Although the plot may seem artificial and melodramatic, it was not without appeal to earlier writers. Torquato Tasso based the early life of Clorinda in his epic *Gerusalemme Liberata* on the story, and Miguel de Cervantes wrote the first part of a version of it in *Persiles and Sigismunda*. The climactic scene, with the father preparing to sacrifice his daughter, would be reprised in Racine's *Iphigénie* (1674).

Although the play was not performed, it did provide Racine with his début. The Parisian theatres were engaged in serious rivalries, and were not averse to a little oneupmanship. The Hôtel de Bourgogne was rumoured to be rehearsing a play called *La Thébaïde*, by Boyer, and Molière asked Racine to adapt the story for them. Jean Racine's *La Thébaïde* was performed on 20 June 1664.

Racine did not repay Molière's kindness with loyalty. His next play, *Alexandre le Grand*, was to be performed in 1665, by Molière's company. After the success of *La Thébaïde*, Molière had invested in elaborate sets for the new play, depicting the shores of Hydaspe (an odd echo of the lost *Théagène et Chariclée*) and the first instance of the shore-side setting of many of Racine's tragedies: Racine, incidentally, never saw the sea.

Secretly, and perhaps as some form of insurance, Racine had the manuscript sent to Molière's rivals at the Hôtel de Bourgogne. He also persuaded one of the actresses, Mlle Duparc, to transfer with him; not wholly because of her acting ability. She would later become Racine's mistress. In an unprecedented move, *Alexandre le Grand* played in both theatres on 18 December. Molière was livid, and never spoke to Racine again.

Was it ambition, or arrogance, or some real or imagined slight that led Racine to double-cross Molière? Racine's son, in his biography of his father, claims the split was due to Racine's frustration at the lacklustre delivery and diction of Molière's players. His next play, *Andromaque* (1667), with Mlle Duparc in the lead role, certainly drew some comments about the hyperbolic acting style. In a satirical snipe at Racine, a poem called *Le Parnasse réformé*, the renowned actor Montfleury, who played Orestes and died in 1668, is made to say, 'If anyone . . . should wish to know what I died of, let him not ask whether it was of fever, dropsy or gout, but let him know that it was of *Andromaque*.'

The rivalry between Racine and Molière simmered on for years, and, not content with one enemy, Racine also took up against Corneille, the leading tragedian of the age, who had made some rather dismissive remarks about *Alexandre le Grand* with the effect of cementing a relationship between his antagonists. Racine and Corneille competed with versions of the Emperor Titus' relinquishment of love for duty, with *Bérénice* by Racine being premiered the week before Corneille's *Tite et Bérénice* (at Molière's theatre) in 1670. Racine regularly sniped at Corneille in the prefaces to the printed editions of his plays, referring to 'a certain malicious old poet'. Racine's plays had the more modern edge: they presented amoral heroes who would sacrifice their honour for their desire, unscrupulous admissions of expediency, overwhelming urges that stripped their sufferers of each shred of self-control, and each vestige of self-interest.

That year, Mlle Duparc having died in 1688, Racine also obtained a new mistress, Mlle Champmeslé. According to the rumours of Mme de Sévigné, the actress enjoyed 'diableries', or orgies, with Racine and the poet-critic Nicolas Boileau. The boy educated by Jansenists seemed determined to conform to every cliché of the degraded stage.

By 1677, Paris was enthralled by *Phèdre*, a drama about the tragic love of a stepmother for her stepson. Unfortunately for Racine, the plaudits were for a protégé of Cardinal Mazarin's niece, Nicolas Pradon, who wrote a work of the same name as the play that many still regard as Racine's masterpiece. His response has been a puzzle for biographers ever since: Racine did not write for the theatre again for twelve years.

Instead, he married a rich, childbearing woman whom he did not love, was appointed Royal Historiographer, and was reconciled with his Jansenist past to the extent that his children were brought up in its strictest devotions. Mme de Sévigné wryly observed that Racine now loved God as much as he once had his mistresses. The *enfant terrible* became a stolid, churchgoing, academic historian.

At the behest of Mme de Maintenon, whom Louis XIV had secretly married, Racine wrote two final works: biblical dramas that were performed by the schoolgirls of Madame's charitable foundation, Saint-Cyr. *Athalie*, the final work, is imbued with Jansenist theology. The pagan queen Athaliah is crushed by a God as unrelenting as a juggernaut. Imprecations cannot alter His Inevitable Plan. No pity, tears or change of conscience can stay the executioner's hand. To Voltaire it was 'the work which closest approaches perfection by a mortal man'.

No doubt many scholars would dearly love to pore over the pages of a rediscovered *Amasie*, or *Les Amours d'Ovide*, or *Théagène et Chariclée*. Interesting and salient material about Racine's versification, narrative dynamics or conceptions of heroism would certainly be forthcoming. But a glimpse into the twelve-year silence would outbalance all three. Was it professional pique, age, a handsome salary or a profound change of belief that made him reject the theatre? Had he come to agree with his Jansenist inheritance about the luxury and worthlessness of the stage, or merely retired, a comfortable bourgeois with no inclination to muddy his hands with greasepaint and fripperies? Behind the wig, thin lips and hooded eyes, Racine is frustratingly, confrontationally silent, as silent as the God in whom he came to believe.

Ihara Saikaku

(1642–93)

Apart from Murasaki Shikibu's *The Tale of Genji*, the most widely admired and painstakingly reproduced novels in classical Japanese are those of Ihara Saikaku. With works such as *The Life of an Amorous Man, Five Women Who Loved Love* and *The Eternal Storehouse of Japan, or The Millionaire's Gospel, Revised Version* he revolutionized the form, breaking with tradition in a wholehearted embrace of modernity. Although he tried his hand at writing samurai classics, it was the depiction of the *chōnin* class – the merchants – that typified his work. During the Tokugawa Shogunate under which he was writing, the government's strongly isolationist policy and ruthless enforcement ensured the longest period of uninterrupted peace in Japan's history. It also encouraged the movement away from feudalism towards a more commercial society. Divorced from contact with other cultures, the old Buddhist ideal of the *ukiyo*, or 'sad world', was metamorphosing into its homophone, the more distinctively Japanese vision of 'the floating world' of erotic abandon, eased by riches.

Saikaku did not purvey stale melancholy and world-weary acquiescence, but a vivid bustle of getting, losing, cheating, pleasing and changing. Bordering on the pornographic, replete with humour, cynicism, charm and ribaldry, he had, as the saying went, 'not one Chinese character in his stomach'. Widowed at thirty-four, he launched himself into society with vigour, and not without causing some offence. A notable criticism of his work was entitled *Saikaku in Hell*.

Before his career as a novelist, Saikaku was renowned as a poet. He, and the Danrin School, opposed the pre-eminent haiku writer of the day, Matsunaga Teitoku. Teitoku, influenced by Chinese aesthetics, emphasized concentration, the honing and whittling of seventeen syllables into their most perfect balance. Saikaku, on the other hand, wanted spontaneity, brilliance and improvisation. His formidable skill can be seen in the accounts of *yakazu*, or poetry marathons, in which he competed.

In 1671, he astonished his contemporaries by extemporaneously composing 1,600 haiku in 'a day and a night'. Nine years later, he notched up the almost fantastic rate of 4,000 in twenty-four hours. It was, however, in 1684 that he set his record: a phenomenal 23,500 haiku in the lifespan of a mayfly – slightly less than seventeen sets of seventeen syllables per minute. It is no wonder he was nicknamed 'The 20,000 poet'. Ephemerality was the quintessence of his genius: it is equally unsurprising that not all his work survived. He would not, one imagines, even have wanted it to.

Saikaku's method did have its detractors. His younger rival Bashō, who became the most popular and renowned haiku-writer, developed his own distinctive style of epiphanic compactness only after declaring himself dissatisfied with both Teitoku and the Danrin School. Others, disconcerted by the frequent oddness and impenetrability of Saikaku's off-the-cuff cadenzas, referred to him with an epithet that was synonymous with everything extravagant, far-flung and downright peculiar: Saikaku, they declared, must be Dutch.

Gottfried Wilhelm von Leibniz

(1646–1716)

Of all the infinite, hypothetical Gottfried Wilhelm von Leibnizs, God chose to actualize the one that was born in Leipzig, on Sunday 1 July 1646 to the Professor of Moral Philosophy at Leipzig University and his third wife. This was the Leibniz who, since this is the best of all possible worlds, would develop differential calculus independently of Sir Isaac Newton, write the equation for a cycloid in parametric form (which, although he did not realize it, governs the destruction of matter in a black hole) and advance the System of Pre-established Harmony and the Principle of the Identity of Indiscernibles. He would, moreover, be paid for most of his life to write a book which he would never quite get round to, while researching a book which could never logically be written at all.

Though Leibniz has often been described as an Enlightenment thinker, or, at least, a precursor to the Rationalist eighteenth century, his diversity of interests and lifelong concern with synthesizing those interests seem more akin to the role of the Renaissance man. Leibniz was, in short, a polymath of prodigious proportions. In addition to mathematics, theology, philosophy and physics, he wrote on Chinese religion and the I-Ching, silk production, fountain design, public health reforms, phantom-limb sensations and inefficient heat-loss in chimneys. He was also an alchemist and librarian, who spent years trying to drain the mines at Harz, and undertook the kind of diplomacy that edged into espionage.

In 1668, during the Polish Succession crisis, he used a geometric proof to promote the claims of the candidate favoured by the House of Brunswick, his employers. To strengthen the claim, he had it printed under the pseudonym of Georgius Ulicovius Lithuanus, with a fake title page asserting it was produced in Vilnius in 1659, adding the mystery of prophecy to the indisputability of mathematics.

After a spell in the service of Baron von Boineburg, Leibniz became Court Councillor to Duke Johann Friedrich of Hanover in 1676 (although it took a full year and several stern injunctions before he physically presented himself at court). He would remain with the family until his death, fulfilling a similar position for Duke Ernst August and George Ludwig (later George I), as well as being an intimate correspondent with the Electress Sophia and Queen Sophie Charlotte of Prussia.

In 1685, Duke Ernst August suggested that, as well as Leibniz's supervision of the library and various political duties, he might write a History of the House of Brunswick, partially to codify their dynastic claims and partially, one suspects, out of vanity. The Brunswicks could trace themselves back to a semi-mythical family called the Guelfs: the d'Estes, another branch, claimed to be able to go back as far as their Roman ancestors. The courts of Hanover, Brunswick-Wolfenbüttel and Celle were all contributing to the project and making available their archives. Ernst August's commission seemed clear: an account of their family from the earliest times.

Had the Duke been more fully apprised of Leibniz's mathematical interests, especially the differential calculus that provided the limit of an infinite series, he might have substituted 'since 825 CE' or 'since the Birth of Christ' rather than 'from the earliest times'. Between 1698 and 1711, Leibniz published nine volumes of edited archival papers, as a framework and reference source for the *History of the Brunswicks*. He drafted a preliminary essay for the book, the *Protogaea*, about geology and fossil formation, and a second work on the movement of early European tribes as inferred from the etymology of place names (during the course of which, incidentally, he proved conclusively that Swedish was not the oldest known language). One can understand the frustration of the various Dukes, whose thirty-year investment looked increasingly unlikely to produce a neat précis of their grandparents' achievements.

A mild air of fiasco, or a charming whiff of foible, surrounds the *History of the Brunswicks* in its display of Leibniz's characteristic drive towards completeness. The same could be said about his proposed work on religion. His *Discourse on Metaphysics* was to be the first part of a massive disquisition that would encompass (after the proof for the existence of God through Natural Religion) a volume on Revealed Religion and a volume which explained and delimited the relative authorities of church and state. Leibniz's estimation of the effect of the treatise was as ambitious, and as hopelessly optimistic, as the work itself: it would reconcile the Roman Catholic and Lutheran churches. He even, through his notion of a 'substantial connector', claimed to be able to find common ground between Catholics, Lutherans and Calvinists on the question of transubstantiation.

The *Demonstrationes Catholicae* never came about. Leibniz's major lost work, however, was not misplaced, or destroyed, or even really conceived: it was impossible. His schemes for integrating all the fields of knowledge, 'harmonizing the philosophers' as he put it, crystallized into the idea of the *Universal Encyclopedia*.

If we are to believe his own version of the facts, the idea

first wormed into his brain at the age of thirteen. Having read all the poetry, history and rhetoric in his father's library, he started on philosophy, and specifically Aristotelian logical syllogisms: 'All men are mortal, Socrates is a man, therefore Socrates is mortal.' In its capacity to provide definitions, and to verify or falsify propositions, the syllogism seemed to him to be 'the official roll call of all the things in the world'.

Complex ideas, he concluded, were made up of combinations of simpler ideas, just as words were made up of letters. Using the medieval technique of division, whereby a characteristic was identified as something certain objects possessed and others did not, concepts could be taxonomized: 'everything' was made up of the 'material' and the 'immaterial', the 'material' could be divided into the 'animate' and the 'inanimate', the 'animate' into the 'sensible' – or animals – and the 'insensible' – plants and so forth.

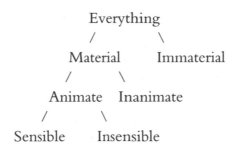

Leibniz argued that the definition of the 'species' always contained the 'genus': for example, the definition of 'gold' included that of its genus, 'metal'. By replacing a term with its definition, propositions could be tested; e.g.:

All gold is metal.

Replace gold with its definition:

All 'yellow metal' is metal.

Since the same term appears on both sides, it is taken to be proven. This method of ratiocination was described by Leibniz as 'an alphabet of human thought'.

This method had captured Leibniz's interest earlier in his life. His doctoral mathematical thesis, *De Arte Combinatoria*, had been a (not wholly successful) attempt to apply mathematical exactitude to the 256 'moods' of logical syllogisms. At stake was the possibility of a purely mechanical form of reasoning. Leibniz believed it was fundamentally possible to create a machine that, with the correct input, could imitate human reason.

Such projects were satirized by Jonathan Swift in *Gulliver's Travels*. On the island of Balnibarbi, Lemuel Gulliver encounters the Professors of the Academy, one of whom has a similar machine.

He then led me to the frame, about the sides whereof all his pupils stood in ranks. It was twenty foot square, placed in the middle of the room. The superficies were composed of several bits of wood, about the bigness of a die, but some larger than others. They were all linked together by slender wires. These bits of wood were covered on every square with papers pasted on them, and on the papers were written all the words of their language in their several moods, tenses and declensions, but without any order. The professor then desired me to observe, for he was going to set his engine at work. The pupils at his command took each of them hold of an iron handle, whereof there were forty fixed round the edges of the frame, and giving them a sudden turn, the whole disposition of the words had entirely changed. He then commanded six and thirty of the lads to read the several lines softly as they appeared upon the frame; and where they found three or four words together that might make a sentence, they dictated to the four remaining boys who were scribes . . . Six hours a day the young students were employed in this labour, and the professor showed me several volumes in large folio already collected, of broken sentences, which he intended to piece together, and out of those rich materials to give the world a complete body of all arts and sciences . . .

Leibniz had already realized that the fundamental utility of any such machine was only as good as the quality of the data used in it. What was needed was a volume that contained accurate definitions of all possible axioms and individuals, with which the computer could set its dials. What differentiated each individual from every other individual, and their relative places within their genus, was the substance of the *Universal Encyclopedia*.

Leibniz's various attempts to systematize human knowledge were never met with anything other than confused boredom or irascible impatience: they paid 'no more attention than if I had related a dream', carped Leibniz to the duc d'Orléans. He was even expressly forbidden to rearrange the library according to his principles. In Leibniz's correspondence, he resorts to specifying a book he needs by its position in the library relative to the window, or door, or its size, or colour. His attempts to found and sustain academies, the published proceedings of which would contribute to the encyclopedia, were hampered and disappointed.

But he persisted. As early as 1676, stranded at Sheerness awaiting a boat back to the Continent, he had considered (since he could not understand the sailors) that the *Universal Encyclopedia* required a Universal Language. Chinese ideograms interested him, in their capacity to include in the word itself a sense of its definition. He also considered binary numbers, he had invented previously. In a moment of hubris he had even grandiloquently imagined a medal in his honour being made proclaiming: 'The Model of Creation discovered by G.W.L.: One is Enough to derive Everything from Nothing'.

There is an irony here, in that Leibniz's conception that the Universal Language had to be digital makes him seem

shockingly modern: machines, logic, the primacy of binary –
all he needed was an inkling of electricity to imagine the
possibility of a computer. Leibniz's vision of the *Universal
Encyclopedia* relies on his microcosmic understanding of
knowledge itself, where each part contains the whole. 'In the
least of substances, eyes as piercing as those of God could read
the whole course of things in the Universe,' he wrote. This
is where the *Universal Encyclopedia* implodes.

Imagine all the atoms in the universe. To record the current
position of each of them, let alone their past or future, requires
an equal number of entities that can signify that position. If
any particular atom is recording the position of another,
where is its own position recorded? The total amount of
information about the Universe is greater than the total
number of entities in it. A *Universal Encyclopedia* can never be
written because there is not enough matter on which it could
be transcribed.

Most of Leibniz's ideas are known to us, not through his
published works, but through correspondence with other
thinkers, memos to the dukes and a mass of unedited notes.
'He knows me not who knows me only through my publications', was one of his aphorisms. He is known now, mostly,
because of one particular published work, *Theodicy*, and a
satirist's indignation at its explanation for the existence of evil
in a perfect universe.

Voltaire thought that Leibniz's formulation – that everything is ordained for the best, and that our perception of
things as 'evil' or even 'unfortunate' is merely an indication
of our limitations – was ludicrous. As the ever-optimistic
Dr Pangloss in *Candide*, Voltaire immortalized an aspect of
Leibniz. Yet the caricature contains a grain of truth.

With his Universal Language, *Universal Encyclopedia* and
occasional recourse to the infallible machines, Leibniz
believed that humanity might evolve to the extent that 'correct reasoning, given time for thought, will be no more

praiseworthy than calculating large numbers without any error'.

Leibniz lived on the cusp when the dream that everything might be known was fading; yet the thought that everything might be amicably and incontrovertibly resolved still seemed feasible. His optimism, caricatured as the wilful negligence of Dr Pangloss, now seems almost touching.

Alexander Pope

(1688–1744)

Alexander Pope died in 1682, at the age of three. His mother had died in childbirth and his father, unable or unwilling to take on a nurse, had sent him to stay with his late wife's sister in Pangbourne, Berkshire, safely away – or so he surmised – from the pestilential and unwholesome air of London. His father remarried and, in 1688, named his new son after the lost half-brother. It was a common enough practice (indeed, Pope Snr was named Alexander as well). Although it would be rash to impute any lingering psychological shadow on the young poet from his literal and nominal predecessor, it would be fair to say that his birth was attended with a little more unspoken hopefulness than was usually the case.

The child seemed to be of a hale and sound constitution. The earliest portrait, painted when he was seven, shows a suave, poised boy. He had a 'sweetness of disposition' and a voice so melodious he was nicknamed 'the Little Nightingale'. He was, admittedly, slightly frail, but, one supposes, his parents may have been particularly sensitive to any signs of illness.

Even during these tender years, the young Alexander Pope displayed an astonishing felicity in composing verses, a remarkable fluency he described in retrospect, saying, 'I lisped in numbers, for the numbers came.'

Then the beautiful, precocious child hit puberty.

The best contemporary diagnosis is that Pope suffered from Pott's Disease, a tubercular infection of the bones. It may have been transmitted through his wet-nurse's milk, or through unpasteurized cow's milk (cows appear to have had a malign effect on the young Pope's health in general: at the dangerous age of three, his elder half-sister recollected, he had been trampled by a wild cow).

The effect, as he began to grow, was immediate. His spine twisted like a question mark, his legs were bandied like a pair of brackets. The pain of his grinding vertebrae contorted his features into an ampersand. He was stunted, never to grow much higher than four and a half feet, constantly afflicted with cramps and seizures. As his literary star rose, his detractors took every opportunity to belittle him further: he was a hunchbacked toad, a poisonous spider, an incontinent ape.

The 'mildness of mind' was gone. Wrung out by his own body, exacerbated by the unashamed cruelty of his invidious opponents, Pope became the stiletto-sharp satirist of his age. The child that had lisped quickly learned to hiss.

Any writer as formidably gifted as Pope will probably produce a great deal of juvenilia; the truly great will have the sense to destroy it. According to a later letter, Pope was expelled from Twyford School after only a year, on account of a satire he had written on one of the teachers. Alongside this propensity for mischievous, or even malicious, lampooning, the young Pope showed a deep fascination with the works of Homer. He recast scenes from *The Iliad* as a play, co-opting his school-fellows and the master's gardener to play roles.

By the age of fourteen, Pope's poetic enthusiasm was in spate. Samuel Johnson's *Life of Pope* records that he had already written panegyrics on all the crowned heads of Europe, as well as a comedy, a tragedy and an epic poem.

'Of the comedy there is no account,' says Johnson.

The tragedy was based on the life of St Genevieve. The more famous saint who bears that name, St Genevieve of Paris, whose prayers saved the city from Attila the Hun, hardly seems a model for that kind of play: indeed, she died at the ripe old age of ninety-five, much loved and already venerated. A more likely candidate is St Genevieve of Brabant, who was accused of infidelity by her husband and executed. Unbeknownst to him, she in fact escaped to the forest, where, with the assistance of a kindly disposed deer, she lived on fruits and shoots. The couple were reconciled just in time to die, thus offering a suitably tear-jerking tragic denouement. Why she was canonized as a saint is much less clear.

The epic was called *Alcander*. Pope, so he says, 'endeavoured . . . to collect all the beauties of the great epic writers into one piece. There was Milton's style in one part and Cowley's in another, here the style of Spenser imitated and there Statius, here Homer and Virgil, and there Ovid and Claudius.'

The name 'Alcander' crops up occasionally in Greek mythology. Homer and Ovid give the name to a Lycian whom Odysseus kills at Troy, and Virgil adopts the name for one of Aeneas' companions: again, he is slain in battle but this time by Turnus. If Pope had read the *Metamorphoses* of Antoninus Liberalis as well as Ovid's better-known poem of that name, he would have known that Alcander was also a seer from Molossus, turned into a bird by Zeus, who was upset that some bandits had torched the prophet's house. None of these seems particularly rich material for a budding epic writer.

Pope may have come across the name in a historical text, Plutarch's *Life of Lycurgus*. Lycurgus, the Spartan founder of democracy, was assaulted by a gang of aristocratic thugs, one of whom was called Alcander. Alcander, who blinded Lycurgus in one eye during the attack, was also the only assailant brought to account for it. Rather than demanding retribution, the noble and ascetic Lycurgus took on the wayward youth as a companion and taught him the meaning of virtue, and Alcander became one of his strongest supporters.

This tale seems to fit with Pope's description of one of the 'incidents' in *Alcander*, a side-plot about a Scythian prince who thought even a pillow made of snow was excessively luxurious. On the other hand, Pope may have just liked the name and invented his own story, as fourteen-year-olds are wont to do.

Johnson informs us that *Alcander* was burned at the suggestion of Francis Atterbury, the Dean of Westminster and Bishop of Rochester, who was later arrested and exiled for treason in supporting the deposed Stuart monarchy. Pope had become close to Atterbury some time before 1718. That Atterbury had read *Alcander* at all means that Pope had kept the manuscript for sixteen years after its creation. This retention argues that its author had some attachment to the work greater than his later wry recollection might otherwise suggest.

Atterbury's negative advice is typically regarded as an aesthetic verdict, but in the fractious theatre of eighteenth-century politics, this may be an underestimation. Although it is highly improbable that *Alcander* was openly seditious, the concentration of plot and character on an earlier, less corrupted version of government could be read as a rebuke, at the very least, to the ruling administration. Pope was already well known for his friendship with Bolingbroke, who had fled to the Continent to support the Stuart pretender James III, and who had been vocal about the dishonest electioneering tactics of the Walpole government. *Alcander* might have furnished his detractors with copious examples of Pope's party loyalties, dangerous political principles and juvenile verse, had the manuscript become publicly available.

The idea of creating the Great English Epic was to haunt Pope's career. Five years later, aged nineteen, he planned another long poem, on the immediately inspiring topic of Gaius Gracchus' agrarian reforms. Timoleon, the Corinthian prince who assassinated his brother rather than let him turn the state into a tyranny, was another potential subject, which withered to a passing mention in his poem *The Temple of Fame*.

The Dunciad (1728, expanded 1729 and revised 1742) united Pope's neoclassical urge to write an epic with his talent for excoriation. He bolstered the authority of his mock-epic by referring to Homer's lost comedy the *Margites* and by comparing his position to that of the satyr play which came after the classical dramatic trilogy. After the epic triumvirate of Homer's *Iliad*, Virgil's *Aeneid* and Milton's *Paradise Lost*: the sneering farce of Pope's *Dunciad*. Despite his ingenious attempts to intellectually justify the mammoth satire, and to place it in a tradition of epic poetry, Pope seems to have had qualms about it. We have Jonathan Swift to thank that *The Dunciad* exists: he snatched the first draft from the fire and persuaded Pope to continue.

Instead of the heroic protagonists of Homer and Virgil, Pope's epic is peopled by every hack, scribbler, poetaster and publisher that ever attacked him. It was not Troy, but Grub Street, that would burn. Pope had assiduously kept copies of all the pamphlets and broadsheets that mocked him, the endless vituperative polemics by Cibber and Theobald; *The Dunciad* would become a mausoleum in which Pope would inter his enemies. The perfectly modulated rhyming couplets belie the furious seething of this apocalyptic vision.

The apotheosis of Dullness at the end of book IV describes a universe where every book is a lost book: the utter extinction of all culture.

She comes! She comes! The sable throne behold
Of Night primeval and of Chaos old!
Before her, fancy's gilded clouds decay,
And all its varying rainbows die away . . .
Thus at her felt approach, and secret might,
Art after art goes out, and all is night . . .
Lo! Thy dread empire, Chaos! is restored;
Light dies before thy uncreating word;
Thy hand, great Anarch! lets the curtain fall,
And universal darkness buries all.

The Dunciad was as much a personal revenge against innumerable acts of *ad hominem* animus as it was a global castigation of his contemporary culture, which Pope believed could no longer either inspire or appreciate the epic.

And yet, despite his pessimism, illness and thwarted political hopes, at the end of his life Pope once again attempted an epic. It would form part of his *Opus Magnum*, along with his philosophical *Essay on Man* and the studies of character he had been assembling as moral and satirical epistles. The epic would recast his ideas about personal and state morality as a narrative. In 1738, Pope told the poet and editor Joseph Spence that it would be 'wholly on civil and ecclesiastical government'. It was to be called *Brutus*.

Amongst his manuscripts, Pope left detailed notes on the substance of the poem. Set sixty-six years after the fall of Troy, the eponymous hero, Brutus, was either the grandson or great-grandson of Aeneas. 'Benevolence ye first Principle & Predominant in Brutus,' he wrote. 'Then a strong Desire to redeem ye Remains of his Countrymen (ye descendts frō Troy) now captives in Greece: & to establish their freedom and felicity in a Just Form of Governmt.'

The Trojans, vanquished in Homer's *Iliad* and refugees in Virgil's *Aeneid*, were to become the moral victors of Pope's epic. The enslaved Trojans, scattered through Greece and Italy, would also have valuable experience of the different forms of government. Dismayed that there was nowhere in the known world that had implemented his Utopian vision, Brutus consults an Egyptian Oracle. He is told that there is a 'Savage people yet uncorrupted in their manners, and only wanting Arts and Government, worthy to be made happy', and that their land lies in the Atlantic. This place, 'mark'd out by some circumstances to be Britain', has 'a climate equally free from ye Effeminacy & Softness of ye Southern Clymes & ye Ferocity & Savageness of ye North'.

Book I of the poem opens with Brutus and his entourage approaching the Straits of Calpe (modern Gibraltar, and known as the Pillars of Hercules). In a scene derived from the debate of the fallen angels in Milton's *Paradise Lost*, there is dissension among his Trojan followers about how to proceed. Brutus knows he must cross through the Pillars into the Unknown Ocean; however, some of his lieutenants demur, saying that not even the divine Hercules had dared go so far. Brutus counters their charges of presumption, saying that superior Virtue means they 'w^d be as much as Gods'. Leaving any cowards behind, he presses onwards. His choice is sanctioned by the appearance of Hercules in a dream, who recounts his own decision to follow the hard road of Virtue rather than the easy path to Vice.

In Book II, the heroes reach the Fortunate Islands, an uninhabited paradise where they want for nothing. Many of his companions recommend settling there: Brutus, however, knows that their mission is not only to seek their own comfort, but to bring the benefits of civilization to a benighted people. They continue their quest, leaving behind the elderly and those unfit for active service, turning Tenerife into the first retirement home.

They are subsequently blown to Lisbon, then known as Ulyssport. There, they meet the son of a Trojan captured by the cunning Ulysses, who recounts the founding of their city. Ulysses had sought to govern through Superstition and Wickedness, and had enslaved the population. They rose up against him, and, although they murdered the Tyrant, they now lack leadership. Brutus 'leaves one of his own people to govern 'em, and abolish ye new Gods introduced by Ulysses'.

Book III brings the Trojans to Britain. Landing in Torbay, Brutus encounters the Druids. They are monotheists, as he was led to believe, and worship the sun, offering fruits and flowers on an altar made of turf. 'No bloody sacrifices,' Pope notes.

The idyllic existence of these noble savages is under threat. In the east and north, there are Giants, most notably Gogma-gog and Corinaeus, whose castles are protected by thunder and lightning. Brutus resolves to defeat these monsters, and, it seems, he would show how their supposedly supernatural powers are founded on deceits and priestly superstitions. Their magical storms would be revealed as gunpowder.

Pope sketched out some of the other characters: an 'old cautious counsellor', 'a soldier seeking only Plunder' and 'a bloody cruel hero, always for violent Measures'. Aside from the tyrannical giants scenes were planned in which Brutus would face difficulties in his own camp, especially from 'The Achilles, Alexander, Rinaldo' character. In contrast to the wise and judicious Brutus, this figure was impetuous, 'fierce, ambitious, brave to excess'. Instead of co-operating with the Druids, this intemperate young blade would prefer to conquer by force, and even cause a rebellion by kidnapping a local princess betrothed to another.

Although the Giants would pass off their technological superiority as supernatural powers, there would have been bona fide supernatural entities in the poem. These guardian angels and demonic adversaries were authorized by scripture and literature, and Pope planned to use the names of Milton's devils for his 'spiritual machinery'.

Towards the end of the poem, Brutus would receive another oracle from an aged Druid. The prophecy would remedy the poem's major narrative problem: if Brutus was successful in establishing a society based on Virtue and Truth, why did the Romans discover an island controlled by Picts and Pagans four hundred years later? 'The Britons shou'd Degener over an Age of Two, and Relapse into a degree of Barbarism, but that they shou'd be Redeemed again by a Descendant of his [Brutus'] family out of Italy, Julius Caesar, under whose successes they shou'd be Repolished & that the love of Liberty he had introduced, the Martial Spirit & other Moral Virtues shou'd never be lost. With observations upon the Impossibility of any Institution being Perpetuall.'

Pope succumbed to his illness in May 1744. He was delirious for a week, and claimed to see an arm coming through the wall. Had he lived, *Brutus* would have been a major literary event. It would, no doubt, still be read today, even if its dogmatic insistence on certain theories of government had somewhat tarnished its appeal. Benjamin Martin, a minor eighteenth-century playwright, who had heard of the proposed poem, thought it would be 'a performance equal to the Iliad or the Aeneid'. Samuel Johnson rather huffily referred to it as 'a ridiculous fiction' and castigated Pope for being 'thoughtless enough to model the names of his heroes with terminations not consistent with the time or country in which he places them'. Johnson decided it had been abandoned 'without much loss to mankind'.

Pope wrote the opening eight lines of the *Brutus*.

> The Patient Chief, who lab'ring long arriv'd
> On Britain's shores and brought with fav'ring Gods
> Arts Arms & Honour to her Ancient sons:
> Daughter of Memory! from elder Time
> Recall; and me with Britains Glory fir'd

Me far from meaner Care or meaner Song,
Snatch to the Holy Hill of spotless Bay,
My Countrys Poet, to record her Fame.

Unexceptional, by any standard, except for one curious difference to the rest of his oeuvre. The lines from *Brutus* are in blank verse, rather than rhyming couplets. At the end, Pope forgoes the form he perfected, and squares up to his only English rival: Milton.

Dr Samuel Johnson

(1709–84)

The Great Cham, moralist and manic depressive, succumbed in his last years to the desire to pre-empt posterity. As his assiduous and exasperating biographer James Boswell (the blubbing Stan to Sam's impatient Ollie) records:

The consideration of the numerous papers of which he was possessed, seems to have struck Johnson's mind with a sudden anxiety, and as they were in great confusion, it is much to be lamented that he had not entrusted some faithful and discreet person with the care and selection of them; instead of which, he, in a precipitate manner, burnt large masses of them, with little regard, as I apprehend, to discrimination.

Which 'faithful and discreet' individual did Boswell have in mind? A few moments earlier he had informed the reader that Johnson had been working on a journal concerning his sickness – at the time, he was suffering from racking attacks of asthma and dropsy, as well as his perpetual struggle with melancholy – and that the *Aegri Ephemeris*, as it was called, was now in Boswell's careful hands.

Boswell's wistful reminiscence of the literary conflagration is further compromised. Why the passive voice – 'of which he was possessed'? Was Johnson bewitched by his own productions, unwilling host to his own words? Given his rash and incendiary urges, were the papers alone in confusion?

The story layers itself further. Among the burned papers, Boswell remembers, were 'two quarto volumes, containing a full, fair, and most particular account of his own life, from his earliest recollection'. Exactly the kind of manuscript, one is tempted to speculate, which, if published, would seriously stimie interest in any forthcoming biography. Boswell admits to Johnson that he, poor soul, simply could not help himself but sneak a little peek – or, as he says, 'read a great deal in them'. Johnson, magnanimously, concurs that Boswell could not have helped himself. But more: the penitent future biographer confesses that, for the first time in his life, the idea seized him to actually steal the two volumes, and abscond, never to see Johnson again. In a pitch of considerateness, he asks his breathless and bloated mentor how this would have made him feel. 'Sir, (said he,) I believe I should have gone mad.'

Mad for loss of the friend or for the loss of the manuscript? In fact, Boswell's competitor, Sir John Hawkins, had stolen one of the volumes. It was returned when Johnson confronted Hawkins in surprisingly similar terms: his excuse had been to keep them out of the hands of another prospective biographer, George Steevens, who would 'make ill use of them'. What had both men read in the Doctor's self-diagnosis? 'There is something noble in publishing truth, though it condemns one's self,' pronounced Johnson, or at least so Boswell recalled him once saying.

The Scotsman drops dark hints that Johnson's 'amorous inclinations were uncommonly strong' and that, when younger, he was 'not so strictly virtuous'. He had 'take[n] women of the town to taverns, and hear[d] them relate their

histories'. Even on Coll in the Hebrides, Boswell had witnessed the lion of literary London bouncing a Scots lassie on
his knee, a moment unmentioned by Cham in his narrative.
Turning his gaze upon his own tics and black dogs, his
uncontrollable outbursts and fearsome prickings of the flesh,
did the high-minded Dr Johnson pen a confession?

So *The Erotic Autobiography of Dr Samuel Johnson* crumbles
into ash, and *The Life of Samuel Johnson LLD comprehending an
account of his studies and numerous works, in chronological order; a
series of his epistolary correspondence and conversations with many
eminent persons; and various original pieces of his composition never
before published; the whole exhibiting a view of literature and literary
men in Great-Britain, for near half a century, during which he
flourished* goes on to be hailed as the best biography ever.

The Rev. Laurence Sterne

(1713–68)

On the face of it, Laurence Sterne's *A Sentimental Journey through France and Italy* is quite clearly a lost book. The title does not correspond to the tale: the narrator, Parson Yorick, has not yet set foot in Italy when the second volume ends. It concludes with one of the most famous curtailed moments and unfinished sentences in the history of literature: 'So that when I stretch'd out my hand, I caught hold of the Fille de Chambre's – '. Sterne died in the same year as *A Sentimental Journey* was published; but to presume that it was the mere inconvenience of personal mortality that prevented Yorick getting to Rome or the reader discovering exactly what noun of the Fille de Chambre's was to agree with his extended grasp is to misunderstand the nature of Sterne's fiction entirely.

The first two volumes of Sterne's masterpiece, *The Life and Opinions of Tristram Shandy*, appeared in 1759. At the time, he was the vicar of a country-living in Yorkshire whose only previous sallies into print had been satirical squibs during a controversy about ecclesiastical courts, most copies of which had been promptly burned by the authorities. His marriage was marred by his own juvenile crushes and lustings, as well as his wife's nervous disorders and her propensity for 'quarrels and prabbles'; he lacked any close circle of like-minded peers, and was frequently isolated because of the weather and house-bound because of his weak lungs.

Tristram Shandy's idiosyncratic style has been considered the result of its author's seclusion: he could, whether he wished to or not, do whatsoever he wanted, indulge each whimsical notion and vivisect each passing fancy. But the genius of *Tristram Shandy* cannot be reduced to a by-product of circumstance. Moreover, he not only threw an early draft into the fire when the neighbour to whom he was reading it dozed off (it was, however, rescued, slightly charred), he toned down satirical allusions to the Yorkshire clergy at the behest of the publisher Robert Dodsley: 'all locality is taken out of the book,' he wrote. For all the manifest queerness of his book, Sterne was an author who intended to have, and keep, an audience.

What would a reader of 1759 have been confronted with, on opening *The Life and Opinions of Tristram Shandy*? It be-gins with the conception of Tristram, whose spurt into exist-ence is precipitated by his mother questioning his father about whether or not the clock had been wound up at a crucial moment. The narrator informs us he will not stick by Horace's rules – contrary to the Latin poet's advice, he even begins his story literally *ab ovo*, 'from the egg', though for the father, at least, it seems to have been *in media res*, 'in the middle of things'. Nor will he stick 'to any man's rules that ever lived'. There are hobby-horses and asides to the pub-lisher, typographical switches and whole pages blacked out, the fact he should be called Trismegistus, except, as always, there was a mistake, footnotes, asterisks, pshawing, a sermon: and yet by the end of volume II, the narrator is yet to be born. To those who expected a novel to involve a linear progression from 'In the beginning' to 'world without end', Sterne offered a series of graphical symbols for his own particular manner of plotting:

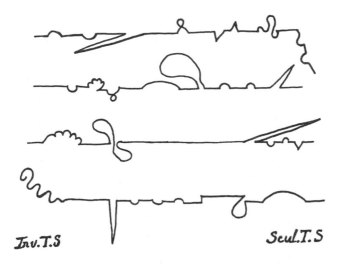

Inv.T.S | *Scul.T.S*

Dr Johnson, in perhaps his most famous critical error, years later declared, 'Nothing odd will do long – *Tristram Shandy* did not last.' The *Monthly Review* was, at the time, more enthusiastic: Sterne's novel might feasibly 'afford him matter enough to write about, tho' he should live to the age of Methusalem'. It might even have been this very review that inspired Sterne into a customary digression on the differences between writing, reading, being and living in volume IV, when it came out the following year:

I am this month one whole year older than I was at this time twelve-month; and having got, as you perceive, almost into the middle of my fourth volume – and no further than to my first day's life –'tis demonstrative that I have now three hundred and sixty four days more life to write just now, than when I first set out . . . at this rate I should just live 364 times faster than I should write – it must follow, an' please your worships, that the more I write, the more I shall have to write – and consequently, the more your worships read, the more your worships will have to read.

Eventually, and chronologically, Tristram must come to be the age he is when he started to write, whereupon he must tell us what it was that he was then writing, and in that chapter must narrate the chapter we have just read as well as his other observations on and during writing it (the fly on the mantelpiece, the figure in the carpet, the weasel behind the cocktail cabinet). It is a recursive paradox, a hitch in time that spares none: Tristram can never write the end of his life, since, when his heart clenched, or lungs erupted, or brain clotted, he would not be able to pen that ultimate ●, let alone the penultimate phrase that explained what it had all been about. *Tristram Shandy* was staggeringly different from all novels before, and most after: but it was still clearly a novel. At one point, the narrator imagines a glass pane set in every human being's breast, so that one could see 'the soul stark nak'd; – observ'd all her motions, – her machinations; – traced all her maggots from their first engendering to their crawling forth; – watched her loose in her frisks, her gambols, her capricios'. It might stand as a metaphor for Sterne's novelistic method. He makes visible all the artificial devices and plot dynamics which the conventional novel uses to simulate reality: counter-intuitively, the Russian critic Viktor Shklovsky referred to this eccentric production as 'the most typical novel in world literature'. He was right. All novels feign, and engage the reader in a contract of disbelief. The difference is that Sterne shows how the trick is done.

If it were only an elaborate debunking of the novel's hidden scaffolding, it would have been as insubstantial as Johnson believed it to be. Sterne's immortality lies in doing the same to the story we call our lives as he did to the narrative we expect in our fictions. In the depictions of Tristram's pedantic father, bemused mother and gently war-obsessed Uncle Toby, Sterne created vivid characters, who nonetheless retained an ineffable privacy from the reader. 'We live,' he says in volume IV, 'amongst riddles and mysteries, the most obvious things, which come in our way, have dark sides . . . tho' we cannot reason upon it, – yet we find the good of it.'

The deeply humanistic vision of the author was so comprehensive that he would not allow even fictional humans to be reduced to soulless automata. In Dickens, Joyce and Perec we find this same investment in the independence of the characters. Only amateur novelists treat their creations like chess-pieces.

Sterne wrote nine volumes of *Tristram Shandy*, ending the ninth with a statement which might well be a judgement on the whole:

L—d! said my mother, what is all this story about? –

A COCK and a BULL, said Yorick – And one of the best of its kind, I ever heard

THE END

Sterne had written to his friend William Combe that a volume X was, at one point, in preparation, but it 'miscarried', due to another bout of tuberculosis. Another learned that after a different, four-volume work, presumably *A Sentimental Journey*, he would resume *Tristram Shandy*. But the two words at the end of volume IX seem definitive. For the man who made 'Once upon a time' a dubious and controversial beginning, there could be no 'Happily ever after'; and having eluded the snares of his own conclusion so long, the ending that is not an ending might be seen as the final wriggling out of the constraints of convention. One suspects that Sterne himself, like his possibly unfinished, certainly terminated, all-too-human and divinely comic works, reached out to try and grasp an intangible, always-just-beyond-reach, celestial Fille de Chambre's –

Edward Gibbon

(1737–94)

Looking back over his career in his *Memoirs of my Life and Writing*, Edward Gibbon asserted that, despite his friend Dr Johnson's denial of 'any natural propensity of the mind to one art or science rather than another', his intellectual inclinations were formed practically in the womb. 'I *know*, by experience,' he wrote, 'that from my early youth I aspired to the character of an historian.' But 'of what' remained a moot question.

As a child, he amassed a 'stock of erudition that might have puzzled a doctor, and a degree of ignorance of which a schoolboy would have been ashamed'. His reading was haphazard and exotic; 'the Arabs and Persians, the Tartars and Turks' were all devoured, and 'the dynasties of Assyria and Egypt were [his] top and cricket-ball'. At the age of fifteen, he embarked on his first attempt at writing: a *Life of Sesostris*.

The Greek historian Herodotus mentioned Sesostris as an Egyptian pharaoh whose agricultural reforms led to the introduction of geometry. He conquered Asia; erecting pillars marking his glorious victories over the tribes who attempted to withstand him, and monuments over the peoples who meekly submitted, calling them 'a nation of women'. Gibbon's youthful plan was to reconcile the various Egyptian, classical and biblical chronologies. It was 'wisely relinquished', although only destroyed during a 'general clear of papers' in 1772. However, one of Gibbon's strategies for making sense of the disparate sequences was sufficiently relevant to his later career for him to remember it when writing the *Memoirs*.

During his time as a captain in the Hampshire Militia, Gibbon read equally voraciously and comprehensively, still in search of a subject. Beginning with the expedition of Charles VIII, which he judged as rather too 'preliminary' a topic, he 'successively chose and rejected the crusade of Richard I, the barons' wars against John and Henry III, the history of Edward the Black Prince, the lives and comparisons of Henry V and the Emperor Titus, the life of Sir Philip Sidney, of the Marquis of Montrose'. He thought he had eventually found a suitable hero in Sir Walter Raleigh, and assiduously researched the available biographies, histories of the period and state papers, before reluctantly concluding that he had nothing to add. Although Oldys had 'read everything relative to his subject' for the *Life of Sir Walter Raleigh*, he had turned out 'a very poor performance'. Moreover, having lived on the Continent for nearly five years, Gibbon was aware that Raleigh's fame was 'confined to the narrow limits of our language and our island'. He may not have found a central figure, or even a broad period, but he already had an enviably ambitious aim.

Finally, he hit upon a subject equal to his aspirations and intelligence: *The History of the Liberty of the Swiss*. Having immersed himself in Schilling, Tschudi, Lauffer and Leu, he read the first chapters, written in French, to a literary society in London. Whatever caveats and criticisms they made, they were taken to heart. Gibbon 'delivered [his] imperfect sheets to the flames, and for ever renounced a design in which some expense, much labour, and more time had been so vainly consumed'.

On a visit to Italy in 1764, while sitting in the ruins of the

Roman Capitol, listening to the friars singing vespers, he had fleetingly entertained 'the idea of writing the decline and fall of the city'. At the time, the project extended only to the actual city, not the Empire it governed, and was dismissed in favour of his laborious study of Helvetican politics. In 1776, the first volume of the work which made him famous, *The History of the Decline and Fall of the Roman Empire*, appeared. Over the next twelve years, this mammoth achievement covered thirteen centuries, from the Antonine emperors to the Fall of Constantinople, and the rise of the religions of Christ and Muhammed.

The end of volume I, on the earliest forms and spread of Christianity, made Gibbon notorious. In his juvenile *History of Sesostris*, he had explained the Egyptian priest Manetho's claim that the Pharaoh was the brother of the Greek king Danaus, who lived 1,500 years before Christ, in terms of his allegiance to the Ptolemies, who claimed a mythic descent through Danaus and Hercules. This piece of propaganda skewed the chronology by half a millennium. 'Flattery is the prolific parent of falsehood,' he wrote in the *Memoirs*, 'and falsehood, I will now add, is not incompatible with the sacerdotal.' His unwillingness to take ecclesiastical pronouncements at face value was already active in childhood and blossomed in *The Decline and Fall*.

His approach was characterized by a slyly ironic style, a nod at orthodoxy followed by a plethora of polite qualifications. Why had Christianity taken root in the Roman Empire? Because it was divine Truth. But, Gibbon averred, the world is not overly partial to the unvarnished truth, as the crucifixion itself demonstrates (though he wonders why the Roman authors never mentioned the three hours of darkness which accompanied it).

Why else, then, did it flourish? 'So urgent on the vulgar is the necessity of believing that the fall of any system of mythology will most probably be succeeded by the introduction of some other mode of superstition,' he wrote, then congratulated the Creator for his wisdom in intervening in history at just the point when paganism was eroding.

Gibbon not only addressed the simplistic level of history – the mere chronology of what happened, like his early synthesis of dynasties – but, as a rational eighteenth-century thinker, sought causes and consequences. He also understood that the way in which people read their own history influences their interpretations. His comments on the early church fathers, such as Origen, and their relationship to the Gnostic heresy, skewers particular modes of thought. 'Acknowledging that the literal sense is repugnant to every principle of faith as well as reason, they deem themselves secure and invulnerable behind the ample veil of allegory, which they carefully spread over every tender part of the Mosaic dispensation.'

He was, therefore, a historiographer as well as a historian, sceptical about the factual truth of beliefs while sensitive to the way in which what is believed to be true, and even written, determines its own reaction. David Hume wrote admiringly, 'You have the courage to despise the clamour of bigots.'

The History of the Decline and Fall of the Roman Empire is one of the high points of the Enlightenment. When he finished it, Gibbon mused on writing a 'dialogue of the dead', in which Lucian, Erasmus and Voltaire would compare their experiences in 'exposing an old superstition'; and fondly hoped he might write a series on 'the most eminent persons in Arms and Arts, in Church and State, who have flourished in Britain from the reign of Henry the Eighth to the present age'. Neither came about and it is, perhaps, sheer greediness to wish that there were more from his exquisite pen.

Johann Wolfgang von Goethe

(1749–1832)

Compared with such similar literary colossi as Homer or Shakespeare, we know a great deal about the life, opinions and amours of Goethe. This wealth of information and anecdote does not, however, make it any easier to neatly encapsulate the man who gave his name to a whole period – the *Goethezeit* – of German literature. His work resists any attempt to bracket it in a single adjective; the inelegance of an invention like 'Goethean' is surpassed only by its useless vacuity as a definition.

Describing Goethe is like drawing a silhouette: whatever line or angle you choose cannot compensate for the necessary loss of a dimension, nor can the inked shadow ever hope to illuminate the shades and wrinkles of skin. One cannot imply, while praising the *Sturm und Drang* individualism and cinematic scope of his early play *Götz von Berlichingen*, the beauties of the formal rigour of *Torquato Tasso* in his Weimar Classicism phase. An investigation into the Europe-wide sociopathic hysteria that accompanied his sentimentally melancholic, slightly overwrought novel *The Sorrows of Young Werther* does not simultaneously evoke the brilliantly recondite application of chemical experimentation to human emotions in *Elective Affinities*. The gentle charm of his epic of small romances, *Hermann and Dorothea*, seems radically at odds with the cynical panache of the *Venetian Epigrams*, or the classically erotic enthusiasms of the *Roman Elegies*. As Goethe himself said, he did not have a style: he had styles.

Goethe is, at one and the same time, the man attuned to the niceties of etiquette at the court and the bohemian poet who 'lived in sin'; an artist who thought his scientific studies meant more than his writings and a Promethean rebel combined with an Olympian judge. Yet he does not seem self-contradictory, and trying to contain him in a simple story about a daring youth who became a doctrinaire old man – or a feckless adolescent who was corrupted into a sycophantic reactionary – simply will not work. Too much of the plenitude of data seeps in, confuses, confutes the easy précis: the sixty-year-old very nearly entered into a *ménage à trois* with a woman half his age, and the twenty-year-old was drawn to Pietistic religion.

As a boy, Goethe was already ambitiously striving to create a work of magnitude, while doubting his own abilities to do so. An early poem, called 'A Song over the Unconfidence towards Myself' and written in English, is tortured between his admission that

> And other thought is misfortune
> Is death and night to me:
> I hum no supportable tune,
> I can no poet be

and an earnest invocation to the Muses, beseeching them: 'O Sisters, let me sing.' More evidence of his precocity, rather than ability, might have been found in the epistolary novel he conceived, written in six different languages. This particular demonstration of his desire to encompass everything is, alas, lost.

So too is his juvenile novel on Joseph and his brothers, which Thomas Mann was destined to write in the twentieth century. Goethe remembered his attempt ruefully, and suggested that the fact that Joseph 'has nothing to do but to pray' might have been the reason why it was discarded. But the idea that Goethe needed an archetypal hero to embody his talents would persist throughout his career.

Prometheus, Belshazzar, Socrates, Alexander, Julius Caesar, Ahasuerus (the so-called Wandering Jew) and Muhammad were all considered as apposite subjects for Goethe's own titanic aspirations. He even wrote an opening canto for an *Achilleis*, which would have continued Homer's epic through to the marriage and death of the Greek warrior, but abandoned it, along with the idea that it might be better as a novel. In the end it was a German magician who would supply him with his requisite protagonist; though the masterpiece would take him sixty years to write.

Goethe's first published foray into the legend of Faust's pact with the Devil appeared in 1790, and advertised itself as a glimpse of the *Gesamtskunstwerk* that the whole would be: it was *Faust: A Fragment*, not the 'total work of art' of which he was capable. The public would have to wait thirty-seven years for the next – again brief – instalment, entitled *Helen: Classical-Romantic Phantasmagoria. Interlude to Faust*, and it was only the niggling and cajoling of his friend and Boswellish confidant Eckermann that led to the final *Part II* being published at all, albeit posthumously. The very first draft, called the *Urfaust*, was rediscovered in 1887, at which point it became even more obvious just how far Goethe had gone in transforming an almost middle-class domestic tragedy about the arrogant scholar's seduction of Gretchen, who then commits infanticide and is executed, into a cosmological exploration of the nature of exertion, celestial intervention and the unification of Greece and Germany.

Faust combines pageantry, *Singspiel*, masques, *trionfi*, satirical swipes and epic swathes (act III of Part II, for example, covers 3,000 years of history and includes a symbolized version of Byron as the child of Faust and Helen). At a profound level, it is unstageable, except in the theatre of the mind. Goethe's facility in making new combinatory adjectives, his transubstantiation of low-brow poetic forms and his moments of almost supernatural grandeur make his masterpiece untranslatable as well. As the Goethe scholar and translator David Luke opined, in an introduction to a selection of Goethe's poetry, aiming to represent him at his best means representing him at his most intractable.

Part II of *Faust* was not the only sequel with which Goethe struggled. After having organized for a performance of Mozart's *The Magic Flute* at the Court Theatre in 1794, he spent two years trying to write the libretto for a sequel, *Die Zauberharfe, The Magic Harp*. In the extant fragments, we learn that the resurgent Queen of the Night has abducted the child of Tamino and Pamina and sealed him in a golden casket. The parents must undergo similar trials by flood and flame to free the infant; and their story is counterpoised to the misadventures of Papageno and Papagena and their children, born, with feathers, from huge eggs. Goethe seemed to want to outdo Mozart's spectacular stage effects: the Queen of the Night enters accompanied by ball-lightning and St Elmo's fire. Goethe claimed to lose interest in the project since no one could recapture the musical genius of Mozart (not even Beethoven); the fact that the original librettist, Schikaneder, produced his own follow-up in 1798 may also have contributed to the waning of his enthusiasm.

Faust was not, perhaps, the least ambitious work Goethe projected. 'The Romance of the Universe' would have been an equal to Lucretius' *On the Nature of Things*, a scientific exposition of immense extent. Goethe's standing as a scientist has been rather overshadowed by his eccentric fixation in disproving Newtonian optics: the fact that Goethe's theory of colours is for the most part completely wrong further diminishes his claims. In the field of morphology, however, he did make advances. Although his claim, in 1784, to have 'discovered' the intermaxillary bone in the human foetus is open to question (since Félix d'Azyr observed the same connection four years prior to Goethe, but did not publish his finding until 1784), and its meaning is open to interpretation (humans do not strictly speaking 'have' an intermaxillary bone any more than they have tails, gills or any of the other features which are embryonically discernible), it nonetheless earned him a place in the footnotes of Darwin's *The Origin of Species*.

Morphology is the study of shape and variation, and was the background to the long, incomplete series of poems Goethe intended for his 'Romance of the Universe' – the 'Metamorphosis of Plants' and the 'Metamorphosis of Animals' – and he also published a number of prose studies on the topic. He identified parallels between species (such as the similarity of air-sacs in fish and lungs in mammals, or between wings and arms) to posit the limitations under which forms can change. He had extravagantly wondered whether, on his trip to Sicily, he might even find the *Urpflanze*, the aboriginal form of which all other flowers, heathers and trees are merely elaborate extrapolations. Needless to say, he did not; nor did he complete his grand fusion of science and poetry.

When Goethe buttonholed a friend in 1830, keen to discuss the momentous events in Paris, one might be forgiven for thinking he was referring to the July Revolution. In fact, he was more concerned with the debate at the Académie des Sciences between Cuvier and Saint-Hilaire on comparative anatomy. The recent political history of France was a source of continuing concern for Goethe, and despite many false starts and fumbled attempts, he never adequately responded to the Revolution, the Terror and the rise and fall of Napoleon.

In 1792, Goethe accompanied Duke Karl August on the campaign by a coalition of German princes and French royalist émigrés to counter the Citizens' Army and, they thought, take back Paris. As the battle turned against them, Goethe famously commented, 'From here and now begins a new epoch in world history.' His similes for the Revolution tended to emphasize its inhuman, irreversible quality: it was an earthquake, an eruption, a cataclysm of Nature.

Goethe tried to analyse the preconditions that had led to the Revolution in the abandoned drama *The Mystified.* Elements from this work were incorporated into *The Great Copt* (1791), in which he obliquely commented on the so-called Necklace scandal (which Dumas was to make the central plot of *The Three Musketeers*), and castigated the negligence and naivety of the French aristocracy which had led to the Revolution. *The Great Copt* is a comedy on the notorious charlatan and supposed sorcerer, Count Cagliostro, whom Goethe had met in Sicily, and whose mendacity and trickery are reflected in the corruption and susceptibility of the court. Nonetheless, the Revolution failed to be contained within the conventions of comic drama, though Goethe tried again with *The Citizen General* and abandoned another attempt, *The Agitated.*

The Revolution provides a contemporary backdrop to *Hermann and Dorothea*, but little else. Similarly, the *Conversations among German Emigrants*, a work conceived along the lines of Boccaccio's convocation of stories, *The Decameron*, substituted the tactical withdrawal from General Custine's advance on the Rhine for the escape from plague-ridden Florence in the Italian version. Goethe did not even come close to finishing this prose collection, and the actual political setting barely impinges on the tales, or their tellers. A Rabelaisian satire, *The Journey of the Sons of Megaprazon*, contains some spirited nonsense and heavy-handed allegory about a 'fever' for factionalism that ruins a society, but remains fragmentary.

The Natural Daughter of 1799 was his most sustained attempt at a drama that dealt with the causes of the Revolution; and even its proposed sequel, or second and third volumes of a trilogy, remained unwritten. Derived from the memoirs of Princess Stéphanie-Louis de Bourbon Conti, the play re-creates her as Eugénie, who is abducted and forced into a marriage with a social inferior by her contemptible half-brother. The widespread abuses of the *ancien régime* are glimpsed through this minor, unpleasant incident, and in a prophetic speech delivered by a monk in the play, who describes an impending, unstoppable flood. But Goethe never completed the postulated continuation, and the actual guillotine itself is again avoided.

The Revolution was Titanism in Life, rather than Art; and in these fragmentary, oblique and unsatisfactory endeavours, it appears as if Goethe, for all his natural gravitation towards world-changing, doomed men of destiny, flinched from putting Robespierre, or Marat, or Danton – or even Napoleon – into his work. Not that he was averse to, or even concerned about using real figures. Goethe's early play *Clavigo* concerned the playwright Beaumarchais; and Beaumarchais himself saw it. He was not impressed, not even by the scene in which he murders a rival (when he had, in fact, just disgraced him), his wife dying on stage during the purely fictitious episode. Real people could be placed in literature, but the epic events between the fall of the Bastille and the battle of Waterloo remained a curious blind spot in Goethe's oeuvre. Famously, he once said, 'I prefer to sanction injustice than tolerate disorder': his reluctance to engage with the Revolution underlines the extent of these fears.

★

The sheer number of Goethe's lost, unfinished and never-started works is an indirect testament to his prodigious output and phenomenal achievement. Yet, increasingly, Goethe is the unread classic, consigned to a limbo of avowed genius and importance, yet shorn of any sympathetic understanding. In part, the political situation in Germany across the twentieth century misappropriated him maliciously and stranded readers in a similar indeterminacy. Soldiers carried copies of his poetry into the First World War. Hitler acknowledged his genius and approved of his travestied politics. The GDP of East Germany declared the triumph of scientific socialism to be the Third Part of Goethe's *Faust*.

Is Goethe relevant to the twenty-first century? Or rather, is the twenty-first century relevant to Goethe? Failed-successful, classical-romantic, libertine-curmudgeon, poet-biologist, novelist-physicist, artist-librettist, radical-conservative: Goethe might yet, in his refusal to be easy, signal the way in which we too might splice a dash and imagine a bridge between the past and the future.

Robert Fergusson

(1750–74)

Some physicists, including Leibniz, have speculated that there exist an infinite number of quantum universes, which reflect and encompass every possible eventuality. If so, there will be one in which Robert Fergusson did not die, aged twenty-four, in an Edinburgh Bedlam cell. The alternative Robert Fergusson would still have gone to St Andrews University, where his roister-doistering and sharp wit would lead another student to graffiti a copy of volume III of Fielding's *Miscellanies* with claims that Fergusson was a 'stinking fairy' and a 'snake in human form'. He would narrowly avoid being sent down through the protection of the tutor and poet William Wilkie.

He would still have been employed copying records in the Commissary Office when he returned to his native Edinburgh, and spend his evenings debating and carousing with the folk-song collector David Herd, the painter Henry Raeburn, the not-yet notorious William Brodie and other fellow members of the Cape Club. He would still have written the most innovative, exciting and daring Scottish poetry in nearly three centuries; but he would not have succumbed to mania and despondency, nor would he have burned all his manuscripts, nor would he have died in a frantic rage and filthy conditions.

Fergusson's poetic talents are seen most clearly in his poems in Scots; however, his vernacular verse is not a retreat into some couthy, cosy nostalgia. It brims with modernity and bristles with deft, half-mocking neoclassical grace notes, like the acciaccaturas of a Mozart sonata. In his poetry, Edinburgh was both the demotic, almost demonic Auld Reikie and the elegant, pseudo-Latin Edina; a place where Boreas blows over the Nor' Loch Brig and Phoebus jostles with Luckie Middlemist. Although his publications led some minor rhymers to invoke the late Allan Ramsay, who had done much to get old Scottish verse back in print, marvelling, 'Is Allan risen frae the deid?', Fergusson was no resurrected throwback, nor some kind of Caledonian Chatterton, but a fully contemporary writer engaged with the living reality of the city.

There is a joyously cocksure quality to his poetry. He cheekily rhymes Sir Isaac Newton with 'snout on' and 'dout on', forcing the English physicist into an arm-lock with Scottish pronunciation, and links 'dinna fash us' with 'Parnassus'. Samuel Johnson's visit to St Andrews inspires him to wish that the grandees of his alma mater had dared to give 'Samy' a haggis and a sheep's head rather than any imported delicacies. He flytes at Johnson in another 'English' poem, claiming to

> Loud encomiate thy puissant name
> Eulogiated from the green decline
> Of Thames's banks to Scoticanian shores,
> Where Loch-lomondian liquids undulize.

Fergusson's poetry evokes the smells and stinks of Edinburgh, its City Guard and foppish macaronis, the gormandizing in oyster-bars and the clanging of the Tron Kirk bell. In more sombre moments, perhaps indicative of his impending crisis, he paraphrases Job and pens a Villonesque last testament. His immersion in the city's glorious chaos came at a cost.

But what of the hypothetical alternative Fergusson? We can imagine him at least completing his most exuberant topographical Edinburgh work, 'Auld Reikie', of which only a single canto survives. Robert Burns, rather than writing an elegy for his 'elder brother in the Muse' and paying to put up a gravestone in the Canongate kirkyard, would meet the man himself in 1786. Burns, more rural, yet more adept at using irony to create characters in his poetry, might have learned much from Fergusson's dizzying cityscapes and linguistic high jinks; Fergusson likewise might have introduced more of a range of emotions, and more of a narrative impulse. In 1788, he would see his friend, the respectable Deacon Brodie, unmasked as a notorious, nocturnal thief, and hanged on the gallows: such a potent story might well have suited Fergusson's long-frustrated desire to write drama. His early attempt, the two acts of a tragedy entitled *William Wallace*, might not have been burned, but neither might they be taken up again, in the light of a more theatrical, urban tale to tell.

In 1796, the middle-aged Fergusson would write his own elegy to the younger Burns; and, as he approached sixty, would discuss the relative merits of Scott and Hogg, the rising stars of a new generation. He might even be tempted to write a novel himself. He might have done much more in an alternative, kinder universe. In this one, however, we must be content with the brief, all too parochial magnificence he did achieve.

James Hogg

(1770–1835)

Sir Walter Scott died a protracted, painful death. He was trepanned, doped with opium and still screamed for hours on end; his seemingly lucid moments relapsed into snatches of Shakespeare and incoherent whining. Crippled by successive strokes and exhausted through writing himself out of bankruptcy, he finally died at half-past one in the afternoon, on 21 September 1832.

Two weeks later, his son-in-law and future biographer, John Gibson Lockhart, received an unexpected epistle from James Hogg. Scott and Hogg had met when Scott was compiling his first notable work, *The Minstrelsy of the Scottish Border*, for which Hogg was able to supply the traditional ballads he had learned from his mother. Encouraged by Scott, Hogg had gone on to become a poet, magazine editor, novelist and anthologist of Jacobite lyrics. In addition to his writing, he had achieved an ambiguous celebrity by being written about. As 'The Ettrick Shepherd' in John Lockhart and John Wilson's long-running *Noctes Ambrosianae*, a persona was foisted on him – that of an uncouth, couthy rustic bard, an unpolished genius, Yarrow's own Falstaff.

Hogg's letter began:

> My dear Lockhart
> Having been disappointed in seeing you at Kaeside which I hardly expected to do considering the confusion and distress you were in yet I cannot help writing to you thus early as I find that now having lost the best and most steady friend that I ever had in the world I have none to depend on for advice or assistance but yourself.

If Lockhart was presuming that the rest of the letter would be a plea for pecuniary help or editorial guidance, he was about to be supremely surprised.

> I am thus going to begin by giving you a piece of advice. It is 'That you will write Sir Walter's life in my name and in my manner'.

Lockhart had spent his life preparing to write his father-in-law's biography. Suggesting the ghost-written 'Life of Sir Walter Scott by his friend, the Ettrick Shepherd, Mr James Hogg' to Lockhart was a grave miscalculation.

Hogg laid out his reasons for this ambitious impersonation. Lockhart had 'command of the documents', but 'for a son brother or husband to write an original and interesting biography is impossible'. If Lockhart adopts Hogg's 'forthright egotistical stile' (which, of course, countless issues of *Blackwood's* proved he readily could), then 'it will give you ten times more freedom of expression both as a critic and as a friend', and, by the by, Hogg had already promised some publishers that he would write a Life of Sir Walter.

The scheme was not as outwardly outrageous as might be thought. Authorship in the early nineteenth century was a game of smoke and mirrors. Scott's Waverley Novels had appeared anonymously, and speculation ran wild as to who the author was. 'Scott, or the Devil' was Maria Edgeworth's assessment. Hogg's own *Private Memoirs and Confessions of a Justified Sinner* presented itself as a genuine seventeenth-century document, edited by a nineteenth-century writer. Hogg himself appears in the last pages. He hid himself in his own text, and rumours abounded, abetted by Hogg, that Lockhart was the editor. One of Hogg's proposals was to 'collect a poem from every living author and publish them in a neat volume, by which I calculated I might make my fortune'. When Byron's submission never arrived, and Scott (who probably wondered why Hogg should profit from other people's industry) refused outright, the entrepreneurial James just sat down and wrote new works by these authors, with nary a second thought about permission, legality or decorum. The resulting volume of parodies, *The Poetic Mirror*, is a small gem.

Lockhart declined to have anything to do with Hogg's biographical masquerade. 'The man is no more qualified to delineate the intellectual character of the illustrious giant of modern literature than he is able to build a bridge of goats across the Hellespont,' he complained to friends.

When Hogg's *The Domestic Manners and Private Life of Sir Walter Scott* appeared in 1834, Lockhart may have wished that on this occasion he had taken a more conciliatory stance. The ghost-written volume would at least have constrained Hogg within Lockhart's judgements. *The Domestic Manners* was a very different volume. Thirty years of suppressed anger erupted in the work. Hogg had written under the stifling shadow of Scott, and the aristocratic Sir Walter had queered the pitch for the heav'n-taught Hogg. His novel about the Covenanters, *The Brownie of Bodsbeck*, had been dismissed as an imitation of Scott's *The Tale of Old Mortality*, even though, Hogg claims, Scott knew he was working on a story set in that period before he began his. Scott had criticized the plot of *The Three Perils of Man*, then plagiarized it for his own *Castle Dangerous*. Hogg may not have known that one English work of fiction, *Scotch Novel Reading* by Sarah Green (a witty Don Quixote in tartan), had suggested that 'James Hogg' might be another pseudonym of 'The Great Unknown', Sir Walter. If he did know, he kept remarkably quiet.

Hogg, the Ishmael to Scott's Isaac, the Sancho Panza to his Don Quixote, the ineffectual *doppelgänger* and genetically frayed clone, exploded. Scott's antiquarianism was amateur. He was a lickspittle Tory, fawning to the upper classes. His famous equanimity was a pose; indeed, when the critic Francis Jeffrey read his review of Scott's *Marmion* to him, during a boating trip, Scott had threatened to scupper them if the critique were not emended. Hogg dropped dark hints about the illegitimacy of Scott's French wife, and recorded that he seemed like a drunk man in his final illness. As for Lockhart, he had never told the truth in his life.

Lockhart, whose notoriously acidic reviews had led Hogg to christen him 'The Scorpion', retorted in kind. He stripped Hogg of any claims to genius and bestowed them instead on his editor. 'In Wilson's hands the Shepherd will always be delightful; but of the fellow himself I can scarcely express my contemptuous pity,' he wrote. Lockhart's official life appeared in 1838, three years after Hogg's death. Lockhart gave his father-in-law a peaceful death-bed benediction and the derring-do history of Charlotte Scott's parents in the French Revolution. But the book contained a final, furious sting at Hogg: 'it had been better for his fame had his end been of earlier date, for he did not follow his best benefactor until he had insulted his dust'.

Later writers would be less impressed by Lockhart's mixture of tact and venom: D. H. Lawrence wrote, 'Those damned middle class Lockharts grew lilies of the valley up their arses to hear them talk.' One doubts whether Lockhart impersonating Hogg would have been any less piously reverential, or whether Hogg's work on Scott could ever transcend his sense of inferiority.

Sir Walter Scott

(1771–1832)

Even before his bankruptcy demanded it, Sir Walter Scott was an immensely productive writer. Since *Waverley* appeared anonymously in 1814, he had released at least a novel a year, and managed a whole three in 1823, as well as innumerable articles, occasional poems and plays. He consistently refused to acknowledge his authorship of the series, and the press coined such soubriquets as 'The Great Unknown', 'The Author of *Waverley*' and 'The Wizard of the North' to identify the novelist.

Scott joined in the game: the novels usually opened with a tongue-in-cheek account of how the manuscript had been found, how the Author of *Waverley* had only edited it, or translated it, or tidied it up for publication. *Ivanhoe*, for example, was supposedly based on an Anglo-Saxon source in the possession of Sir Arthur Wardour, a character in *The Antiquary*; other phantom authors such as Jedediah Cleishbotham, Captain Clutterbuck and Dr Dryasdust peopled the prefaces.

Scott brought these personae together in the preface to *The Betrothed*. Jonathon Oldbuck – the antiquary in *The Antiquary* – called the meeting to order:

Gentlemen, I need scarcely remind you, that we have a joint interest in the valuable property which has accumulated under our common labours. While the public have been idly engaged in ascribing to one individual or another the immense mass of various matter, which the labours of many had accumulated, you, gentlemen, well know, that every person in this numerous assembly has had his share in the honours and profits of our common success. It is, indeed, to me a mystery, how the sharp-sighted could suppose so huge a mass of sense and nonsense, jest and earnest, humorous and pathetic, good, bad, and indifferent, amounting to scores of volumes, could be the work of one hand, when we know the doctrine so well laid down by the immortal Adam Smith, concerning the division of labour.

One strategy for writing off the £120,000 debts that Scott had accumulated was a definitive edition of his work, where he openly admitted authorship and provided autobiographical introductions to his voluminous oeuvre. The so-called 'Magnum Opus' edition, along with a *Life of Napoleon* and other new novels, would, with luck, restore his finances. Ill-health and nervous exhaustion, however, contributed to another economic principle that worked in tandem with his industrious endeavours: the law of diminishing returns.

In the 1830s, Scott's novels were declining in quality. *Count Robert of Paris* had been not only corrected, but substantially rewritten by Scott's son-in-law, John Gibson Lockhart. A series of strokes had further impeded Scott's abilities; a 'cloudiness of words and arrangement' necessitated the use of an amanuensis. When his health became ever more precarious, it was decided that a trip to the milder climes of Malta might assist in his recuperation.

Even though he was supposed to rest, and the final volumes of the Magnum were at the printers, Scott nonetheless embarked on a series of new works. As if addicted to the act of writing, and having to rely on his own unsteady penmanship, he began another novel. 'No persuasion could arrest him,' says Lockhart, as he commenced a work based on a 'history of the Neapolitan banditti, and covered many quires with chapter after chapter of a romance connected with the Knights of St. John.'

John Buchan, in his own life of Sir Walter Scott, discusses *The Siege of Malta* and *Il Bizarro*, as the works were called: 'Both are still extant in manuscript, but it may be hoped that no literary resurrectionist will ever be guilty of the crime of giving them to the world.' Lockhart, who received the new works in instalments, lamented that 'The MS . . . is hardly to be deciphered with any effort.' Neither is wholly telling the truth.

The manuscript is not completely extant, as various pages have been excised by souvenir hunters. Neither is it utterly illegible, although Scott's celerity means that many pronouns, conjunctions and prepositions are omitted; and his infirm handwriting renders the transcription of certain passages speculative at best. As usual with his drafts, there is hardly any punctuation, which Scott relied on the printers to supply.

The work itself is a ghost book: Scott was, if not technically, then artistically dead, and *The Siege of Malta* is a prose poltergeist, lingering in the world of the living. There are flashes of the old Scott wit – such as the suggestion that Miguel de Cervantes, with his honourable track record against the Moor, might join the defenders in Malta and entertain them in the evening. But as a whole, each line is written as if with no memory of the last, trapped in a perpetual present. The reader is introduced to Don Manuel de Vilhenya, an old-school chivalric knight, and his niece Angelica, who disappears from the narrative shortly after the opening. He has a flagged-up feud with Dragut, the Corsair and Viceroy of Algiers, yet their expected duel never materializes. It dwindles out, with even the main character slowly evaporating from the plot. James Skene compared Scott's pen to the staff of the seventeenth-century sorcerer Major Weir (about whom Scott had once planned a novel), which could move independently of its master. The necromantic comparison is uncannily correct.

Yet Scott thought it equal to *Ivanhoe*. He burned the opening and rewrote it, and intended to accompany it with a poem about St George and a dragon of Rhodes, the former residence of the Knights of St John, having seen his friend William Gell's sketch of a dinosaur skeleton embedded in the roof of a church. A travel book about Malta was promised, but never delivered. Hints that his mental health was none-too-sound can be seen in his behaviour before leaving England. His fears about the Reform Bill and the rumour that the Whig government might make the FitzClarences the legitimate heirs to the throne spurred him into conceiving a plan for the kidnap of Princess Victoria, securing her protection in Scotland and installing Wellington as dictator.

Scott had hoped to visit Goethe on their homeward journey; however, when he heard that Goethe had died, it strengthened his own desire to return, so that he too should die at home. On 11 July he reached Abbotsford, and died two months later, safe in the knowledge that the forthcoming *The Siege of Malta* was in the capable hands of his son-in-law and publisher.

Samuel Taylor Coleridge

(1772–1834)

No other author in the history of literature has been so detrimentally affected by that most poetic of embarrassing afflictions, *scriptus interruptus*. It is not the purpose of this book to offer a clinical diagnosis, outlining the high-risk life-style choices and genetic misfortunes that might lead to what is vulgarly termed 'premature ending'; however, the case-history of Samuel Taylor Coleridge may well prove invaluable to those who might wish to undertake such an investigation.

Coleridge's theory of poetic composition made him peculiarly vulnerable to untimely and terminal cessation, often even before the work in question had developed any form or coherent narrative that might allow it to be continued at a later date. Since a feeling of 'inspiration' was necessary, and that sensation was tacitly supposed to be untethered from the writer's conscious control, its sudden departure was equally unpremeditated, and must prove intransigent to any coaxings or pleadings from his rational mind. Furthermore, and this is typical, he somehow managed to simultaneously realize the ramifications of his condition and yet still believe that the exertion of his will, or a happier set of circumstances, might prevent any recurrence of the syndrome.

For our purposes, the most pertinent documentation of this ailment was written in 1816, some nineteen years after the incident in question took place. This delay in his revelation, in itself, is eloquent testimony to the deep-seated repressions and fear of social stigmatization that must have accompanied the original, dare we say, traumatic occasion. Perhaps it would be best, at this juncture, to hear from the man himself:

KUBLA KHAN:
OR, A VISION IN A DREAM. A FRAGMENT
The following fragment is here published at the request of a poet of great fame and deserved celebrity,

(Excuse me, he means Lord Byron.)

and, as far as the Author's own opinions are concerned, rather as a psychological curiosity, than on the ground of any supposed *poetic* merit.

(Again, might we just point out that the italicization of *poetic* might reveal a lurking anxiety? Is poetry somehow the opposite of psychology, something from beyond the brain? Or is Coleridge foisting on the term, even transferring on to it, his own deep-seated desire not to be held responsible or accountable for the result?)

In the summer of the year 1797, the Author, then in ill-health

(note: referring to himself as the Author instead of I: very dissociative),

had retired to a lonely farm-house between Porlock and Linton, on the Exmoor confines of Somerset and Devonshire. In consequence of a slight indisposition, an anodyne had been prescribed, from the effects of which he fell asleep in his chair

(Having, in fact, actively administered, ahem, some grains of opium.)

at the moment that he was reading the following sentence, or words of the same substance, in 'Purchas's Pilgrimage': 'Here Kubla Khan commanded a palace to be built, and a stately garden thereunto. And thus ten miles of fertile ground were inclosed within a wall.'

(It seems superfluous to mention that these lines do not appear in 'Purchas's Pilgrimage'.)

The Author continued for about three hours in a profound sleep, at least of the external senses, during which time he had the most vivid confidence, that he could not have composed less than two to three hundred lines; if that indeed can be called composition in which all the lines rose up before him as *things*, with a parallel production of correspondent expressions, without any sensation or consciousness of effort.

(What were the things? Pictures? Deliria? We should not be so naive as to think that a cinema projected behind his eyes: surely the vision was of lines of text! And as for effort, he had already succumbed to believing effort is not worth a fig.)

On awakening he appeared to himself to have a distinct recollection of the whole, and taking his pen, ink and paper, instantly and eagerly wrote down the lines that are here preserved. At this moment he was unfortunately called out by a person on business from Porlock, and detained by him for above an hour,

(Any attempt to fix the identity of the person is fruitless. Any number of cold-calling friends, debt collectors and anti-Muses has been supposed; but they ignore the obvious dichotomy: a business person whose habitation is as specific as his identity is anonymous.)

and on his return to his room, found, to his no small surprise and
mortification, that though he still retained some vague and dim
recollection of the general purport of the vision, yet, with the
exception of some eight or ten scattered lines and images, the rest
had passed away like the images on the surface of a stream into
which a stone has been cast, but, alas! without the after restoration
of the latter!

Mortification: obviously, humiliation, but with the queasy
sense of orgasmic release, imparted by the litotes of 'no small
surprise'. Did anyone arrive at all, or is this an unsubtle
admission that he interrupted himself before the inspiration
reached fruition? As to the meaning of the vision, the words of
William Hazlitt seem apposite. He thought Coleridge wrote
'better *nonsense* verses than any man in England'. Yet the
poem itself, despite its languorous and exotic tone, contains
hints that the vision had fled before he ever put quill to ink.
'Could I revive within me/Her symphony and song,' he
pleads; and the less said about the 'fast thick pants' leading to
'a mighty fountain momently . . . forced', the better.

Scriptus interruptus reached pandemic proportions among
the Romantic writers of the end of the eighteenth and beginning of the nineteenth centuries. Shelley's identification with
the 'uncontrollable' West Wind and 'unpremeditated' Skylark
captures some of the typical symptoms. Keats twice attempted
to write an epic on the Titans struggling against the Olympian
gods in *Hyperion* and *The Fall of Hyperion*, and failed twice.
They were published with the excuse that the reception given
to his previous work, *Endymion*, 'discouraged the author from
proceeding'. It had, admittedly, been described by John
Gibson Lockhart as 'calm, settled, imperturbable drivelling
idiocy'.

Coleridge, in moments of clarity, wrote affectingly on his
etiolated condition. 'By what I *have* effected, am I to be
judged by my fellowmen; what I *could* have done is a question

for my own conscience,' he wrote in his *Biographia Literaria*, shortly after detailing an epic poem on the progress of a brook from source to sea in the Quantocks. In a letter to his friend Allsop, after years of publishing little and writing less poetry, he nonetheless still harboured dreams of a restored condition:

Of my poetic works, I would fain finish the 'Christabel'. Alas! for the proud time when I planned, when I had present in my mind, the materials, as well as the scheme, of the Hymns entitled Spirit, Sun, Earth, Air, Water, Fire, and Man: and the Epic Poem on – what still seems to me the one only fit subject remaining for an Epic Poem – Jerusalem besieged and destroyed by Titus.

Too often, sufferers from this fearful incapacity are derided as delusional, lazy, vapid, unproductive, prima donna-ish, lackadaisical dreamers. They are not. They are ill. A freephone line or a support group should be set up.

Jane Austen

(1775–1817)

The divine Jane! Only forty-two, only six novels to her name, only four of them published, when a systematic erosion of her suprarenal cortex ushered her into the spinster-cold earth! A slight corpus from a diminishing body. Margaret Drabble was surely right, were we only discussing works in English, when she remarked that 'there would be more genuine rejoicing at the discovery of a complete new novel by Jane Austen than any other literary discovery, short of a new major play by Shakespeare'. 'Those six perfect novels', as the critic Sue Gaisford has called them, are a quiet rebuke to the voluminous acres produced to order by those Victorian sensationalists.

Sir Walter Scott, whose fame, for a moment, seemed to eclipse Austen's, realized that her work was destined for immortality. 'That young lady,' he wrote in his journal, nine years after her death, 'had a talent for describing the involvements and feelings and characters of ordinary life, which is to me the most wonderful I ever met with. The Big Bow-wow strain I can do myself like any now going; but the exquisite touch, which renders ordinary commonplace things and characters interesting, from the truth of the description and the sentiment, is denied to me.'

With such a slender oeuvre, it is understandable that every manuscript fragment, teenage letter and drafted project found its way into print. Austen's nephew, James Edward Austen-Leigh, first published some of the incomplete works in the second edition of his 1871 *Memoir*, against the judgement of his half-sister. The Oxford editor R. W. Chapman added a seventh volume, *Minor Works*, to the six novels of the 1925 Collected Works. The three scrapbooks of her teenage baga-telles have also been published; nearly every word of Austen's that has survived can now be bought in paperback. In these remnants and patches we glimpse a radically different author to the whalebone-corseted, elegantly quadrill'ing stereotype so beloved by television adaptors.

Austen's juvenilia was highly thought of by her family. Her father gave her the second volume, bound in white vellum, and inscribed in the third 'Effusions of Fancy by a very Young Lady Consisting of Tales in a Style entirely new'. Readers expecting the mature, sardonic politeness may be lulled into a false sense of security. In *Jack and Alice*, for example, nothing could seem more indicative of Austen's future writing career than a statement such as 'Every wish of Caroline was centred in a titled Husband . . .' Yet a few pages later, when another young girl relates her quest to catch a glimpse of her beau, things start to become peculiar.

On enquiring for his House I was directed thro' this Wood . . . With a heart elated by the expected happiness of beholding him I entered and had proceeded thus far in my progress thro' it, when I found myself suddenly seized by the leg and on examining the cause of it, found that I was caught in one of the steel traps so common in gentlemen's grounds.

Throughout these youthful *jeux d'esprit*, there is a streak of cackling sadism. Austen revels in violent altercations, drunkenness and bizarre switchbacks between professed goodness and despicable behaviour. In 'The Beautifull Cassandra', the heroine 'then proceeded to a Pastry-cooks where she devoured six ices, refused to pay for them, knocked down the Pastry-cook and walked away'. In *Henry and Eliza* the adopted child grew up 'Beloved by Lady Harcourt, adored by Sir George and admired by all the World' and lived 'in a continued course of uninterrupted Happiness, till she had attained her eighteenth year, when happening one day to be detected in stealing a banknote of 50£, she was turned out of doors by her inhuman Benefactors'.

Instead of wit, we have black comedy; instead of manners, mayhem. Austen's *History of England* of 1791 'by a partial, prejudiced and ignorant Historian' is a little comic masterpiece, which displays an assured feel for irony, a talent for understatement and a very writerly capacity to simultaneously postulate and subvert. Of the Earl of Essex she says,

he was beheaded, of which he might with reason have been proud, had he known that such was the death of Mary Queen of Scotland; but as it was impossible that He should be conscious of what had never happened, it does not appear that he felt particularly delighted with the manner of it.

More than in her romantic fables, *The History of England* shows a writer whose voice is beginning to flex.

Within four years her ambition was outgrowing such extravaganzas; her skill was smoothing as well as tightening. *Elinor and Marianne*, an epistolary novel, would be revised into *Sense and Sensibility. First Impressions* would metamorphose into *Pride and Prejudice.* Though scholars may lament the loss of these manuscripts, and the chance to dissect the development of her genius, the finished novels more than compensate for the loss.

Austen was realizing the limitations of the traditional, epistolary form. *Lady Susan* is such a novel, and although it has its moments, and Lady Susan herself is a more formidable, malign presence than later characters, the strictures clearly grate with the author. She ends it with a flourish of impatience: 'This correspondence, by a meeting between some of the parties and a separation between others, could not, to the great detriment of the Post Office revenue, be continued longer.'

Austen barely wrote anything between 1801 and 1811. Perhaps because of her disappointments at the hands of publishers who had accepted her work but refused to print it; perhaps because of the move from her idyllic Steventon to frosty, fashionable Bath; perhaps for countless reasons: she does not tell us. She did begin another novel, entitled *The Watsons*, which was set aside in 1805. Her nephew claimed that 'the author became aware of the evil of having placed her heroine too low, in such a position of poverty and obscurity . . . like a singer who has begun on too low a note, she discontinued the strain'. A more psychologically plausible reading might be that she intended her heroine, Fanny Watson, to face her father's death. Her own father, the Rev. George Austen, died in 1805; there are no depicted paternal deaths in any of Austen's complete or unfinished novels.

Towards the end of her life, after moving to Chawton and enjoying her first successes as a published author, Austen started a novel called *Sanditon*. She only lived to write twelve chapters: what we now know as Addison's Disease was rendering her weak, bilious, and, as she said in a letter, her skin had gone 'black & white & every wrong colour'. *Sanditon* is the most melancholy example of a work terminated by illness. Its tantalizing enigma lies not in its resemblance to her other works, but in its differences.

Austen had previously proscribed her matter and *métier* in a letter to her niece, Anna. She had written, 'Three or four families in a country village is the very thing to work on'; and yet *Sanditon* takes place in a newly emerging spa town, with families flocking to take the health-giving sea air throughout the chapters that are extant.

Whereas it is easy to see how the romantic conundrums of *The Watsons* might have panned out: the fragment of *Sanditon* had only got to the stage where the reader knows of four young women, all in want of a husband, and three distinctly ineligible men. One of them desperately wants to be a dashing cad. Whereas in previous works Austen had introduced young men whose nefarious agenda only became clear when their devious schemes came to fruition, *Sanditon* has an aspiring villain from the outset. Young Sir Edward Denham, whose title does not imply any cash in his pockets, is described thus: 'Sir Edward's great object in life was to be seductive.'

There are more than just moments when the Austenesque shines through. Some of these moments exemplify her mordant, precise style. Take, for example, this extract: 'the Miss Beauforts were soon satisfied with "the circle in which they moved in Sanditon" to use a proper phrase, for everybody must now "move in a circle", – to the prevalence of which rotary motion, is perhaps to be attributed the giddiness and false steps of many.' Perfect: not as a novel, but just, wholly, as a sentence.

Perhaps the oddest aspect of *Sanditon* is its satire. Austen knew she was ill, suspected she was dying, and wrote a novel in which hypochondriacs are skewered. Sanditon's founder has three siblings with variously comical and possibly self-induced nervous disorders: Arthur is a pudding-shaped stay-at-home who couldn't dream of being well enough to get a job; his sisters, Diana and Susan, rarely eat, get their teeth extracted for safety's sake and are clouds of static electricity desperate to earth themselves.

Although Austen described her writing as 'the little bit (two Inches wide) of Ivory on which I work with so fine a brush', we must remember that this is the interim judgement of a novelist who did not live to fully explore her genius. *Sanditon* amply demonstrates that she could tackle a wider canvas.

In 1816, Austen sketched out a 'Plan of a Novel, according to hints from various quarters'. She never intended to write it; the 'Plan' itself was sufficient to show up the folly of her critics. The heroine would be the daughter of a clergyman, who would be 'driven from his Curacy by the vile arts of some totally unprincipled and heartless young Man, desperately in love with the Heroine'. Father and daughter would 'never [be] above a fortnight together in one place', and would be pursued across Europe by the infamous and ardent inamorato. The heroine would have to work 'worn down to a Skeleton' to support them, eventually eking out an existence in Kamschatka, on the eastern borders of Russia. The father, 'quite worn down, finding his end approaching, throws himself on the Ground, and after 4 or 5 hours of tender advice . . . expires in a burst of Literary Enthusiasm' (supposedly the suggestion of a family friend, Henry Sandford).

Austen also includes some of the plots sent to her by James Stanier Clarke, the Prince Regent's librarian. Austen had corresponded with Clarke about permission to dedicate *Emma* to the Prince Regent – a request he was pleased to grant. By the by, Clarke modestly offered some possible stories:

Do let us have an English Clergyman after *your* fancy – much novelty may be introduced – see dear Madam what good would be done if Tythes were taken away entirely, and describe him buying his own mother – as I did – because the High Priest of the Parish in which she died – did not pay her remains the respect he ought to do. I have never recovered the Shock. Carry your Clergyman to Sea as the Friend of some distinguished Naval Character about a Court.

In the 'Plan of a Novel', this appears unchanged as the father's life-story.

Clarke was full of ideas, and his second attempt at a commission is unique, in that it posits a novel which one is heartily relieved that Austen never wrote.

The Prince Regent has just left us for London; and having been pleased to appoint me Chaplain and private English Secretary to the Prince of Cobourg, I remain here with His Serene Highness & a select Party until the Marriage. Perhaps when you again appear in print you may chuse to dedicate your volumes to Prince Leopold: any Historical Romance illustrative of the History of the august house of Cobourg, would just now be very interesting.

Austen's response is gloriously arch, and daringly candid:

You are very, very kind in your hints as to the sort of Composition which might recommend me at present, & I am fully sensible that an Historical Romance, founded on the House of Saxe Cobourg might be much more to the purpose of Profit or Popularity, than such pictures of domestic Life in Country Villages as I deal in – but I could no more write a Romance than an Epic Poem. – I could not sit seriously down to write a serious Romance under any other motive than to save my Life, & if it were indispensable for me to keep it up & never relax into laughing at myself or other people, I am sure I should be hung before I had finished the first Chapter. – No – I must keep to my own style & go on in my own Way.

If there was ever a book we can be glad is well and truly lost, it is surely Jane Austen's *The Magnificent Adventures and Intriguing Romances of the House of Saxe Cobourg*.

George Gordon, Lord Byron

(1788–1824)

The fact that Lord Byron's *Memoirs* were burned by his publisher, executor and biographer has not deprived them of an afterlife. According to the critic William Gifford, they were 'fit only for the brothel and would have damned Lord Byron to everlasting infamy'. Nonetheless, a moderately diligent browser could easily obtain Robert Nye's *Memoirs of Lord Byron* (1989), or Christopher Nicole's *Secret Memoirs of Lord Byron* (1979), or Tom Holland's *Lord of the Dead* (2000), which reveal that the 'bad, mad and dangerous to know' poet was a vampire to boot.

Harriet Beecher Stowe, through her friendship with Byron's widow and a hefty slug of inference, shocked the world in 1869 by announcing that the awful secret of the *Memoirs* was Byron's confession to having committed incest with his half-sister Augusta Leigh (a rumour first aired during Lord Byron's life). Most of her evidence was drawn from Byron's drama about an incestuous couple, *Manfred*. By her logic, the author of *Uncle Tom's Cabin* might be suspected of being an elderly black gentleman from the Southern States.

Only nine years after Byron's death, an odd poem appeared entitled *Don Leon*. Byron was named as the author, and it seemed to form 'Part of the Private Journal of his Lordship, supposed to have been entirely destroyed by Thos. Moore'. Since it refers to events after his death, the ascription is unlikely at best. All the first editions of this rhyming defence of homosexuality are lost; and it is doubtful whether the initial printing kept some clue to the author's identity.

The posthumous fame of Lord Byron was also blighted by a forger who called himself Major George Gordon de Luña Byron, who claimed to be an illegitimate son. After an erratic career in India and America, he eventually wound up in London, where he began blackmailing Mary Shelley with counterfeit correspondence. At this time, Mary was still vainly hoping some of her late husband's lost poetry might be found lining packing cases, and was more than susceptible to any chance to obtain his manuscripts. Having swindled Mary Shelley, the major then produced *The Inedited Works of Lord Byron*, a haphazard collocation of unpublished material, plagiarism and fakes. He even managed to gull Robert Browning, whose *Essay on Shelley* began with an inadvertent advertisement for some phoney epistles.

That John Murray, Thomas Moore and John Cam Hobhouse destroyed Byron's *Memoirs* is indeed objectionable; even more so, given that Moore's doubts were assuaged by £2,000. None of the men could actually bring themselves to perpetrate the deed, and two friends of Lord Byron's embittered widow did the actual kindling. But are critics wise to wring their hands and wish that 'Byron's autobiography might now have its place on the shelves alongside Rousseau's *Confessions*'?

The contents of the *Memoirs* are not as intangible as its postulated literary merits. Byron had written to Murray, his publisher, clearly outlining its contents:

The *Life* is *Memoranda* not Confessions. I have left out all my *loves* (except in a general way) and many other of the most important things (because I must not compromise other people) so that it is like the play of Hamlet – 'the part of Hamlet omitted by particular desire'. But you will find many opinions, and some fun, with a detailed account of my marriage and its consequences, as true as a party concerned can make such accounts, for I suppose we are all prejudiced.

Lady Byron had, before the *Memoirs* were ever in the hands of potential publishers and editors, scandalized London by hinting at some secret proclivities on the part of her former husband. That Byron wished to provide his version of events in no way justifies suspecting the *Memoirs* to have contained outrageous revelations.

Byron's supposedly explosive *Memoirs* are such a famous example of a book that cannot be read that it blinds us to his real, incomplete work. The mammoth *Don Juan*, at the time of his death, had already exceeded the twelve books that Byron had, half-seriously, claimed to be planning at the end of canto I. By the time that he was sending the fifth section to Murray in 1821, he knew that 'the 5th is so far from being the last of *D. J.* that it is hardly the beginning'. All thoughts of a Virgilian, measured epic, in the standard twelve books and with the prerequisite visits to the Underworld and catalogues of ships, had been shattered. *Don Juan* was a gossipy ragbag, a freewheeling satire that winked at conventional heroics while it lauded the protagonist's unshakeable sense of self, and self-preservation. It was 'a kind of poetical Tristram Shandy, or Montaigne with a plot for a hinge'.

The sixteen and a bit cantos we have go some way towards fulfilling Byron's claim in that letter that it would have 'a proper mixture of siege, battle and adventure'. Juan is sent away in disgrace after an affair with an older woman, is shipwrecked, avoids cannibalism and conducts an affair with Haidée, the daughter of a pirate. He is sold as a slave in Constantinople, escapes to join the Russian Army, and is sent by Catherine the Great on a diplomatic mission to England, where the poem breaks off, leaving him in the middle of country-house shenanigans with three insistent and ardent suitors.

Even this is but a fragment of what Byron felt he could achieve. Juan would tour Europe, becoming 'a *Cavalier Servente* in Italy, and a cause for a divorce in England, and a Sentimental "Werther-faced man" in Germany, so as to show the different ridicules of the society in each of those countries, and to have displayed him gradually *gâté* and *blasé*, as is natural'. One wonders if Goethe's high opinion of Byron would have altered, had the latter lived to apply his satirical lash to *The Sorrows of Young Werther*.

Byron never mentions Mozart's *Don Giovanni*, nor does he seem too preoccupied with the dramatic version Molière wrote. If we can say anything with a degree of certainty, it is that Byron's *Don Juan* would not have ended with the Commandatore, the Stone Guest. Don Juan may still have ended up in Hell, although Byron characteristically is unresolved on whether to send him there, or to an unhappy marriage: 'the Spanish tradition says Hell: but is probably only an Allegory of the other state'.

In the very same letter Byron suggests another closure. Don Juan might end his European tour in France during the Revolution, and be guillotined by Robespierre. Perhaps, he suggested, he would 'make him finish as *Anacharsis Cloots* [Clootz]', the Prussian nobleman who asked to be beheaded last that day, in order to complete some pertinent scientific observations.

Had Byron not died in the Greek swamps, who knows how many misadventures and animadversions the Don might have enjoyed? *Don Juan* could only ever be as long as the author's life itself. The *Memoirs* could only ever be a wry and rueful glance over his shoulder; the ongoing, reckless *Don Juan* could have easily ended up anywhere.

Byron's nonchalance about the *Memoirs* is radically at odds with the hysteria caused by their destruction. The very fact that he completed them, whereas *Don Juan* sallies on regardless, implies it was only one facet, a biopsy rather than a body. The *Memoirs* detailed a mere incident, a journalistic rejoinder; whereas *Don Juan* was the epic of his life, in all its comedy, ardour, outspokenness and opinion.

Thomas Carlyle

(1795–1881)

If being prolix, obscure, reactionary and immoderate were
the criteria for becoming lost, there would not be a single
page of Thomas Carlyle in existence. Fortunately, he was also
a genius: though that is no guarantee of survival either.

In *Sartor Resartus* (1833), Thomas Carlyle created a heady
mélange of spiritual autobiography and polemical vituperation,
under the guise of a philosophy of clothes written by an
eccentric German academic, Professor Herr Diogenes Teufelsdröckh. George Eliot thought it marked 'an epoch of their
minds' for the members of her generation; Ralph Waldo
Emerson wrote that the author possessed 'an equal mastery
over all the riches of the language', and a 'purity of moral
sentiment'.

The work evolved from diametric impulses: philosophical
investigation and religious angst, the treatise and the story.
Carlyle had been listlessly considering an Essay on Metaphors,
which was transformed into the meditations on language as
the warp, weft, fabric and wrapping of thought; he was likewise attempting to find a narrative form in which to express
his metaphysical crises and resolutions. An early foray into
novel-writing, *Illudo Chartis*, had been abandoned, as had an

unwieldy combination of didactic harangue and *roman à clef*, with the equally ungraceful title *Wotton Reinfred*.

Carlyle was never comfortable with the novel as a vehicle for his ideas, considering it slight and superficial; and his biographer Froude dismissed these youthful efforts, saying Carlyle 'could no more invent than he could lie'. Although most of *Wotton Reinfred* was burned in 1827, part of the manuscript was stolen by an amanuensis, Frederick Martin, and published after Carlyle's death, when he was, in the words of the *Saturday Review*, 'in the opinion of many capable judges, the greatest writer of his time'.

The autobiographical elements of *Sartor Resartus* are polarized between two extreme epiphanies. In a 'Baphometic Fire-baptism', Teufelsdröckh experiences 'the EVERLASTING NO', where 'the Universe was all void of Life, of Purpose, of Volition, even of Hostility: it was one huge, dead, immeasurable Steam-engine, rolling on, in its dead indifference'. This is superseded by 'the EVERLASTING YEA', where Teufelsdröckh realizes 'there is in man a HIGHER than Love of Happiness'. He is reconciled to the world through his own sense of creative purpose.

I too could now say to myself: Be no longer a Chaos, but a World, or even a Worldkin. Produce! Produce! Were it but the pitifullest infinitesimal fraction of a Product, produce it in God's name! . . . Up! Up! Whatsoever thy hand findeth to do, do it with thy whole might. Work while it is called To-day, for the Night cometh wherein no man can work.

In, and between, these poles, the glimmerings can be seen not only of Carlyle's mature ideas, but of his inimitable style: the PERPETUAL ACH. In infuriated, frustrated prose, he railed against the mechanistic reduction of 'the sole nexus between man and man' to 'Cash-payment', while simultaneously preaching the inherent virtue of work, even to the slaves of the West Indies. His elliptical, apocalyptic sentences raised and exorcized the terror of anarchy, and, as he grew older, the perceptive analysis of the problems of the era was replaced with the conviction that the only solution lay with the 'Strong Man' and 'the few Wise' who must 'by one method or another . . . take command of the innumerable Foolish'.

Carlyle's Gospel of Work faced its own test on 6 March 1835. He and his wife had moved to 5, Cheyne Row in Chelsea, London. Carlyle's literary ambitions and financial security were pinned on his forthcoming work, *The History of the French Revolution*. He had lent the first volume, for comment, to his friend, the philosopher John Stuart Mill, who, in turn, and perhaps indiscreetly, had left it with his lady-friend, Harriet Taylor. Writing, as always, had been a strenuous task; on 7 February he had written, 'soul and body both very sick'. Mill appeared at their door in the evening, ashen-faced and barely comprehensible. Taylor's maid had mistaken the manuscript for scrap paper, and kindled the fire with it. Apart from a few sheets, the first volume was 'irrevocably annihilated'.

'The thing was lost,' wrote Carlyle,

and perhaps worse; for I had not only forgotten all the structure of it, but the spirit it was written with was past; only the general impression seemed to remain . . . Mill, whom I had to comfort and speak peace to, remained injudiciously enough till almost midnight, and my poor Dame and I had to sit talking of indifferent matters; and could not till then get our lament freely uttered.

Carlyle's working methods exacerbated the problem. He did not take notes, and selectively incinerated drafts as he progressed. His manuscripts – and we should, perhaps, not judge the maid too harshly in the light of this – were a torrent of crossings-through, excision, revisions and inkings-out, with scraps of paper glued to the edges to accommodate the emendations. Though he would later praise Dr Johnson, for refusing to 'whine over his existence', at the time Carlyle was utterly distraught. He had 'never at any period of my life felt more thoroughly disconsolate, beaten-down . . . simply *impossible* it seems that I should *ever* do that weariest, miserablest of tasks'. 'My will is not conquered;' he rallied, 'but my *vacuum* of element to swim in seems complete.'

The French Revolution was published in 1837: Mill had offered £200 compensation, of which Carlyle accepted half. Mill also reviewed it fulsomely in the *London and Westminster Review*. They remained friends until the 'Eyre Affair', in 1866, when Carlyle typically defended the 'excessive force' with which the Governor of Jamaica had quelled a rebellion, an action deplored by the liberal Mill.

Their parting of the ways mirrors the critical reaction to Carlyle in the twentieth century. The insistence that might is right, that there must be 'Order, were it under the Soldier's Sword', cannot be read without our knowledge of the horrendous culmination of these ideas. Carlyle's political stance cannot be extricated from his literary reputation, any more than that of his idol Goethe. That Hitler was reading Carlyle's *Frederick the Great* in the bunker as the Allies advanced does little to endear him to contemporary readers.

But even before the rise of totalitarian regimes, Carlyle's posthumous high standing was jeopardized by a book he wanted burned. In 1866, Jane Welsh Carlyle died. It 'shattered my whole existence', and, as he struggled to cope with his grief, Carlyle believed he could find some therapeutic relief in editing her letters. As well as deep respect and actual love, he found resentment, sarcasm, impatience and unhappiness. He incorporated her letters and his memories into a reminiscence, as an act of penitence and masochistic self-revelation, even including the evidence that he had physically harmed her: his doctrine of brute force applied to the drawing room as well as the imperial palace. 'I will write of this no further . . . is not all this appointed by me rigorously to the fire?' This was a different form of suffering to merely rewriting *The French Revolution.*

'I still mainly mean to *burn* this Book before my own departure, but feel that I shall always have a kind of grudge to do it,' he insisted. He always hesitated, as if he could not extinguish the last link to the living Jane. He 'solemnly forbid [anyone] to *publish* this Bit of Writing': it was personal contrition, not public confession. When Carlyle died in 1881, the manuscript remained intact.

The typical Victorian 'Life of' was a hagiographic affair: it drew a veil rather than exposed its subject. When Froude prefaced his monumental work with the words: 'Mr Carlyle expressed a desire in his will that of him no biography should be written', he signalled that this was a distinctly different proposition. The correspondence contained in the biography, along with the posthumously published memoirs, had a frankness that perturbed the nineteenth-century readership's penchant for uplifting, adulatory commemoration.

Edward Fitzgerald, the translator of the *Rubáiyát of Omar Khayyám*, moped that it would have been 'better . . . kept unpublished, for some while at least', and suggested that Carlyle 'must have "lost his head"' if not when he recorded them, yet when he left them in any one's hands to decide on their publication'. Charles Norton, a later editor, fulminated that 'The letters of lovers are sacred confidences, whose sanctity none ought to violate. Mr. Froude's use of these letters seems to me, on general grounds, unjustifiable, and the motives he alleges for it inadequate.' Froude's sin was to show that the Sage of Ecclefechan was also the Bully of Cheyne Row, prompting another biographer, David Wilson, to lament that 'the impartial critic is reluctantly driven to use very strong language indeed'.

Personal failings and political naivety, even political culpa-

bility, aside, what keeps Carlyle in the canon? 'Strong language', or what the Spasmodic poet William Aytoun referred
to as 'dislocated' language, is Carlyle's legacy. He writes
ecstatically, and though the solutions he proffered were
unspeakably wrong, the iniquities he sought to redress have
rarely been more profoundly unpicked. His psychology, and
his society, were complex, and his language reflected that:
one does not go to Carlyle for simple answers, or soundbite
slogans. Walt Whitman, no lover of Carlyle's authoritarian
leanings, captured his importance exactly: 'no man else will
bequeath to the future more significant hints of our sorry era,
its fierce paradoxes, its din, and its struggling parturition
periods, than Carlyle'.

Heinrich Heine

(1797–1856)

Life resists synopsis. In the case of Heinrich Heine, any attempt at summary is especially likely to be a distortion: he is everywhere evasive and contradictory, and every outright opinion is elsewhere balanced by qualification or mockery. The 'last king of Romanticism', the 'first man of the century', he was the high priest of the cult of self, and that self was incorrigibly multiple.

Heine's broad spectrum of acquaintances reads like a Who's Who of nineteenth-century European culture. He was taught by August Schlegel and Georg Wilhelm Friedrich Hegel. His lyric poems were set to music by Schubert, Schumann, Mendelssohn and Brahms, and he provided the plot for Wagner's *Flying Dutchman*. At salons he mixed with Balzac, Nerval, Hugo, Dumas, George Sand, Hans Christian Andersen and Karl Marx. Yet he seems not to have had a single, true friend, with the possible exception of his long-suffering publisher, the radical Julius Combe, whom he berated and praised in equal measure.

In addition to being a lyric poet, Heine was a journalist, travel writer, political agitator and cultural mediator between

France and Germany, often infuriating both. His most exquisite poems of romantic longing and frustrated desire are shot
through with ironic self-deprecation and satirical swerves. He
was committed to the ideals of Liberty, and yet impugned
the socialists, saying, 'I agree we are all brothers, but I am the
big brother and you are the little brothers.' He underwent a
religious conversion at the same time as he was incapacitated
by eight years of excruciating paralysis, but quipped on his
deathbed that he did not fear judgement since forgiveness was
God's stock-in-trade. He was born into a Jewish family, and
was prone to virulent outbursts of anti-Semitism.

It is easier, in some ways, to describe what Heine was not.
Although he was a voluminous writer, there were nonetheless
projects which eluded him and manuscripts which he
destroyed. After his conversion, he burned poems which had
the merest whiff of blasphemy about them: 'better to burn
the verses than the versifex', he maintained.

He was not a novelist, even though he attempted three
times to write a novel. The first foray, *The Rabbi of Bacherach*,
was started in 1824, and published in part in 1840. The second,
From the Memoirs of Herr von Schnabelewopski, was an imitation
of *Tristram Shandy*, but, according to Heine, it 'miscarried' in
1833. *Florentine Nights* was rejected by his regular publisher
in 1837 as being too short to escape the automatic censorship
required by the Metternich government. The mob, apparently, did not read long books, hence the exemption.

Heine was not a philosopher, though he claimed to have
burned his study on the works of Hegel. He claimed Hegel
was 'the greatest philosopher Germany has produced since
Leibniz', but lampooned him in correspondence, saying that,
when reading him, 'one's brain freezes in abstract ice'. Heine's
study of Hegel may have been destroyed, but one cannot
help but suspect that Hegel's deathbed words – 'only one
person has understood me and he doesn't understand me
either' – would have been singularly apposite.

Throughout his life, he begged from and vilified his fantastically wealthy Uncle Salomon, and protracted negotiations about his will widened an already gaping chasm with the rest of the family. Heine's trump card was a piece of rather distasteful blackmail. He threatened to write about the family. Although his published *Memoirs* have a glowing encomium to Uncle Salomon, they are typically cavalier with other facts. Heine's brother, Maximilian, incinerated five or six hundred pages of autobiography after his death: we might presume that this manuscript gave a more explicit account, and one which the family feared might be libellous. That said, it was the sycophantic version Heine chose to publish. He was not un-self-interested.

In his earliest play, the rather dire *Almansor*, Heine again seems shockingly prescient: 'when books / are burned, sooner or later people will be burned as well'. He destroyed his works in a futile attempt to burn away his own inconsistencies.

Joseph Smith Jnr

(1805–44)

If the 'quotation' below looks like gobbledygook, that is because it is. Nonetheless, this fictitious orthography, denominated by its inventor as 'Reformed Egyptian Hieroglyphics', is responsible for the founding of Salt Lake City. It is the only evidence of the language from which Joseph Smith Jnr claimed to have miraculously translated *The Book of Mormon*. It comes from a slip of paper headed 'Caractors',

which was given to Martin Harris, who later paid for the publication of the book. Harris had shown it to a Columbia professor in order to establish the authenticity and provenance of the antique texts. Whatever scholarly mayhaps, possiblys and perchances the academic hedged around his opinion evaporated in the mind of the gullible Harris, and the poor classicist had to issue strongly worded denials when it transpired he was being quoted as authoritatively declaring the squiggles to be genuine, ancient writing.

The 'Reformed Egyptian Hieroglyphics' are not the most far-fetched aspect of the Joseph Smith story: he himself said, 'I don't blame anyone for not believing my history. If I had not experienced what I have, I could not believe it myself'. He was the poorly educated son of an impecunious farmer and one-time ginseng exporter, who became a prophet, a self-appointed lieutenant-general and a presidential candidate, and is venerated today by millions. He was murdered, or martyred, by a lynch-mob in the jail of Carthage, Illinois, where he had been imprisoned for wrecking the printing press of an opponent.

In 1827, though, he was an outwardly unexceptional figure, except for a brush with the law over his claims to be able to locate Indian gold using a 'peep-stone'. All that was about to change: for four years he had supposedly been visited by an angel, Moroni, who had promised to deliver into his hands a set of golden plates, when the time was right. In 1827, it was. These plates, written in the 'Reformed Egyptian Hiero-glyphics', detailed the religious history of the aboriginal inhabitants of America, the virtuous Nephi and the wicked descendants of his brother Laman, and Smith was to make their content known to the world.

Once he had possession of the inscribed plates, he guarded them jealously, and would transcribe their contents whilst hidden behind a raised sheet. Knowing Joseph's lack of any formal acquaintance with ancient languages, Moroni con-veniently provided a pair of magic spectacles, called the Urim and Thummim, which allowed him to understand the chron-icles. After an infraction, Moroni confiscated the glasses, and Joseph was forced to read the symbols by putting his head inside a large hat containing his peep-stone, with the actual text beside him. Secretaries took dictation, but were for-bidden to look at the golden plates on pain of divine punish-ment. In 1829, the results of his endeavours were published as *The Book of Mormon*.

Setting aside the celestial messenger, and whether or not the golden plates really existed, we might start with the glasses, or rather their name. The Urim and Thummim are mentioned in the Pentateuch and the early historical books of the Old Testament, though what they actually are is open to contention. Exodus 28:30 and Leviticus 8:8 tell us they adorned the breastplate of Aaron, the brother of Moses and first High Priest. They evidently had some prophetic function, since at 1 Samuel 28:6, Saul cannot communicate with God, either through dreams, prophets or the Urim. Numbers 28:21 confirms that they were used for some form of divination. It has been suggested that they were used in rhabdomancy or bone-casting. Nowhere is it said that they can be balanced on the nose and ears, or that they are in any way translucent.

A little piece of outré biblical knowledge was embellished into a whole legend. What is striking about *The Book of Mormon* is not how extravagant its notions are, but how closely they reflect its own time. Smith's choice of Egyptian was perfectly canny, given that the Rosetta Stone would not unlock the meaning of hieroglyphics for an English audience until 1837. Likewise, the final battle where Mormon and the Nephite remnant succumb to their Lamanite oppressors makes sense of Indian burial mounds, which amateur anthropologists of the period believed could not have been erected by the indigenous tribes. No less a person than President Harrison subscribed to the belief that the barrows were the result of a cataclysmic battle where the 'Moundbuilders' were extirpated by the Iroquois. Cotton Mather believed the Indians to be a lost tribe of Israel. *The Book of Mormon* chastises, allegorically, Freemasons and Roman Catholics; it freely adapts less well-known biblical passages and parts of an anthropological study entitled *A View of the Hebrews* and even incorporates dreams recorded by Joseph Smith's mother.

Mark Twain's witticism, 'chloroform in print', ably

describes the book. It is repetitive (140 of the first 200 sentences begin 'And', and Twain himself counted over 2,000 occurrences of 'And it came to pass'), ludicrously anachronistic (wheels and cities being two of the most unlikely pre-Columbian features) and frequently prone to theological error (Jesus, for example, is born in Jerusalem). Yet it somehow founded a religion. Whether we attribute its success to the provision of a peculiarly American testament, or its justification of European settlement (the white Nephites being the true owners of the New World, not the redskinned Lamanites), or the particular foment of dissenting sects in the years following the Revolution makes little difference to its impact.

From the outset, the new 'Mormonites' were keen to stress the veracity of the Prophet's vision. Three men, including Martin Harris, swore an affidavit affirming the reality of the books, the presence of Moroni and the divine nature of the transmission (although all three were eventually excommunicated). Smith obtained a papyrus with genuine hieroglyphics, which he translated as 'The Book of Abraham'; and though experts are now able to compare an informed translation with the account of the star Kobol and a racist explanation of Africans that Smith came up with, the Mormon church has become no less expert at countering such claims. 'Egyptian hieroglyphics had at least two (but more probably three) meanings, the one understood by the masses – the other comprehended by the initiated, the priesthood,' wrote George Reynolds in 1879. Smith did not 'get the translation wrong'; he was translating a different, allegorical level of the text. It is much the same reasoning that Origen applied to the New Testament.

There was, however, one document which would prove to be a thornier problem for the Mormon church. Smith began his translation in 1828, with Harris committing it to paper. His wife was less than convinced by the story of golden plates, magic spectacles and angelic intervention, and Harris pleaded with Smith to allow him to take the 116 completed pages to her, in order to prove their reliability. She stole the manuscript. 'I have lost my soul!' Harris wept. 'All is lost!' groaned Joseph. 'If this be a divine communication, the same being who revealed it to you can easily replace it,' Lucy Harris argued.

Moroni must have been less than impressed that the Chosen One had managed to go and lose the new Bible. After all, Jibra'el had never had this kind of problem with Muhammad. He petulantly retracted the use of the Urim and Thummim, and, instead of simply starting from scratch again, insisted that the lost pages would be replaced by a different work, the Plates of Nephi, which concentrated on the ecclesiastical history. It would, of course, differ slightly, but not, hopefully, materially.

The pages purloined by Lucy Harris have never been dis-covered, and, given the extent of anti-Mormon propaganda in the 1830s, it seems likely that if she had been able to produce the first version of the revelation, she would have done so. Even with the caveat that it was derived from a different source, any inconsistencies would have been difficult to explain away, and it might have proven to be a mortal blow to the nascent cult's credibility. It is presumed that she destroyed the manuscript: however, there is a slim chance that it still exists somewhere, a sheaf of handwritten pages that could topple a religion. Unless it is already safely under lock and key in Salt Lake City's copious archives.

Nikolai Gogol

(1809–52)

In 1845, Gogol burned the manuscript of part II of *Dead Souls* for the first time. 'It was hard to burn the work of five years, achieved at the price of such morbid tension, every line of which cost me a nervous disorder,' he wrote; 'the moment the flames had consumed the last sheet of my book, its contents were reborn, luminous and purified, as the phoenix from the ashes, and suddenly I saw how chaotic was all I had supposed to be orderly and harmonious.'

Even before this drastic action, Gogol had been cagey, to say the least, about the continuation of the book. He had reluctantly read some of it to a friend, Alexandra Smirnov, but had desisted abruptly when the first rumbles of thunder began to crack. 'God himself,' he said, 'does not want me to read something unfinished.' Many of his friends knew that he had staked much on part II of *Dead Souls*. To both Vassily Zhukovsky and Pyotr Pletnyev he had compared part I to an overture for a work of unsurpassed importance. It was 'no more than the portico of a palace rising within me'.

Part I of *Dead Souls* introduces Chichikov, a jovial, dandyish, vaguely abominable businessman, who arrives in the town of N. He rapidly makes the acquaintance of all the officials and landowners, and inveigles himself into their social calendar and provincial hierarchy. After a while he makes a tour of the landowners with a curious proposition. In order to tax them, the state reckons the size of their estates according to the number of serfs, or souls, they possess, and a census is carried out to determine this figure. Chichikov's proposal is to buy the serfs that have died, but whose names still feature on the census. It alleviates their tax, and he gains – well, he tells different people different stories as to why he needs dead souls. Is it illegal? No one knows. If it is a crime, it is born out of Byzantine bureaucracy and feudal oppression. After all, selling living, breathing humans is perfectly acceptable.

Eventually, suspicions are aroused; but they are inflamed more by an anxiety that Chichikov has not paid each landowner the same amount for their dead souls than by any inkling of a demonic pact. But Chichikov escapes scot-free, his carriage speeding through N. and Gogol delivering a paean on the troika. The last direct speech is attributed to the typical Russian, who loves the speed and 'mad carouse' of a hurtling troika: 'To hell with it all!' The editor Mikhail Pogodin captured some of its sinister power when he described it as being like 'a long corridor along which he dragged the reader and his hero Chichikov, opening doors left and right and showing a monster seated in every room'.

When *Dead Souls* appeared in 1842 (with the title altered by the censor to *Chichikov's Adventures, or, Dead Souls*, since the soul was immortal: Gogol had mordant fun with this in Part II), it was to thunderous applause. Pletnyev wrote an enthusiastic review under a pseudonym in *The Contemporary*, where he echoed Gogol's conception of Part I. It was 'a curtain raiser intended to elucidate the hero's strange progression'. Vossarion Belinsky, the radical, rising critic, called it 'the pride and honour of Russian letters'. Gogol left Russia for Europe, claiming the continuation involved some kind of pilgrimage.

Although Gogol's friends sympathized with his aesthetic ambitions, they were becoming increasingly aware that there was a manic element to Part II. Gogol believed that literary Russia had been 'awaiting me as though I were some sort of Messiah'. The triptych he envisioned of *Dead Souls* covered Crime, Punishment and Redemption: it was nothing less than a Divine Comedy of the Steppes, to use Henri Troyat's phrase. Gogol referred to it as 'the history of my soul', and dropped odd hints that he had now 'acquired the strength to undertake my sacred journey . . . only then will the enigma of my life be resolved'.

Part I did contain passages implying something greater to follow. At the beginning of chapter VII he contrasts two kinds of writer. There is one who 'feels drawn to characters which reveal the high dignity of man', by whom 'young, ardent hearts are thrilled' and for whom 'responsive tears gleam in every eye . . . He had no equal in power – he is a god'. The other is forced to show 'all the terrible, shocking morass of trivial things', and the public will 'rob him of his heart and soul'. Which kind of writer would Gogol be?

Gogol had never been particularly reliable, or honest, with his friends, and had often relied on them to extricate him from financial crises. His behaviour, now, exasperated them. The long-suffering and sponged-from Pletnyev referred to him as a 'devious, selfish, arrogant and suspicious creature'. Gogol dropped ever more arcane insinuations about the true meaning of Part I. 'For the time being it is still a secret, which will suddenly be revealed to the stupefaction of one and all (for not a single reader has guessed!).' 'I shall starve to death if I must,' he wrote to Stepan Shevyrev, 'but I shall not produce a superficial and incomplete work.'

A few chapters of part II have survived. There are satirical cadenzas on eccentric reformers, utter gluttons and world-weary loafers, these are joined by unbelievable paragons: the landowner Kostanjoglo, the official Murazov and the Prince who is both the 'callous instrument of justice' and the 'inter-cessor for you all'. From these brief glimpses, little can be gleaned of Chichikov's moral conversion. Part III, it was hinted, would have taken him to Siberia, as a penitent. The complete *Dead Souls* would do no less than precipitate a total religious transformation of Russia.

Having burned his first attempt at Part II, Gogol's fanati-cism intensified. He had intended to go to Jerusalem to give thanks for Part II: now he would go there to pray for inspiration. He also published the ill-advised *Selected Passages from Correspondence with Friends* in 1847 before leaving. This justification of absolutism, which contained such sentiments as 'A State without an absolute monarch is an orchestra with-out a conductor' and 'The peasant must not even *know* there exist other books besides the Bible' earned him the unremit-ting enmity of Belinsky and caused profound embarrassment to his friends. Sergei Askakov lamented that 'the best that can be done is to call him a madman'. Belinsky, more irate and more eloquent, berated the 'apostle of ignorance' and main-tained that 'everything must be done to protect the people from a man who has lost his mind, were that man Homer himself'.

Jerusalem did not provide any divine editorial advice, and Gogol, plus manuscript, returned to Russia, where he became deeply embroiled with the equally unstable Father Matthew Konstantinovsky, who believed everything except the Rus-sian Orthodox church was inspired by Satan. He encouraged Gogol to enter a monastery and forgo the paganism of litera-ture. God's wish was clear, and the penance exacted for the publication of Part I was the destruction of part II.

At about 3 a.m. on 24 February 1852, Gogol summoned a servant and ordered him to kindle a fire. He started to feed manuscript pages into it. When the boy begged him not to, Gogol growled, 'This is none of your business – better pray.' He clogged the fire with paper, and had to remove the charred bundle, containing Parts II and III, and feed them in one by one. When it was done, he crossed himself, kissed the boy, and collapsed in tears.

He then stopped eating. When he was asked by the attending priest, 'What prayer do you want me to read?' he answered, 'They're all good,' and after nine days of self-enforced starvation, died.

Charles Dickens

(1812–70)

On 9 March 1870, Charles Dickens gave a private reading to Queen Victoria from his new work, *The Mystery of Edwin Drood*. Set in the sleepy cathedral town of Cloisterham, the novel involves the opium-addicted choir-master John Jasper, who is secretly obsessed with the fiancée of his ward and nephew, the eponymous Edwin Drood. Rosa has also come to the attention of another orphan, the hot-tempered Neville Landless, and when Drood disappears, his watch and shirt-pin found in the river, Jasper immediately accuses Neville of murder.

Dickens offered the Queen the opportunity to know, in advance of her subjects, how the story would conclude. Whether through indifference, or the understandable desire not to have the ending spoiled, Victoria declined. Dickens died less than three months later, with *The Mystery of Edwin Drood* less than half-finished. Its title had become eerily apposite: Dickens left no notes, no plans and no clues as to the outcome.

He might have been more careful. Only six years beforehand, Dickens had been on a train that derailed at Staplehurst, leaving only his carriage on the tracks. After helping two ladies off the train, Dickens went back to secure the manuscript of *Our Mutual Friend* that he had left on board, and a hip-flask of brandy. This brush with mortality did not change his working methods.

A disappointed public speculated about what would happen to the work: would, perhaps, Wilkie Collins supply an ending? Eager to scotch rumours of a continuation, Dickens' publishers Chapman and Hall sent a letter to *The Times*, insisting that 'no other writer could be permitted by us to complete the work which Mr Dickens left'. That said, Collins revealed in 1878 that he had been asked to finish the novel, but had 'positively refused'. No such firm declarations of principle fettered Collins' own publishers, who contracted Sir Walter Besant to complete *Blind Love* ten years later.

Others had significantly fewer qualms. One Orpheus C. Kerr in New York adapted and burlesqued the plot of *Edwin Drood* under the title *The Cloven Hoof*, which appeared in Britain in 1871 as *The Mystery of Mr E. Drood*. The American market, unrestrained by too strict an interpretation of British copyright law, also produced *John Jasper's Secret* in 1872. In 1878, a female writer from the north of England under the pseudonym Gillan Vase wrote another continuation, *The Great Mystery Solved*. Most curious of all, Charles Dickens also completed the novel through the help of a spirit medium from Brattleborough, Vermont, and even puffed his next, posthumous novel, *The Life and Adventures of Bockley Winkleheep*.

Although, in time, the number of full-length impostures and reconstructions dried up, speculation about *The Mystery of Edwin Drood* did not. Inspired by Edgar Allan Poe, who had famously, and to Dickens' chagrin, deduced the ending of *Barnaby Rudge*, countless bookish sleuths attempted to solve the riddle. Andrew Lang, the polymathic poet, translator, fairy-tale-writer, biographer, mythologist and editor (a man whose talents were so various, it was even claimed he was a committee), and M. R. James, the quintessential English ghost-story-writer, both contributed solutions to the Drood enigma.

★

To put the conundrum simply: we know the criminal but not the crime. Dickens' manuscript list of projected titles offers *The Loss of . . ., The Disappearance of . . .* and *The Flight of . . .* as well as *The Mystery of Edwin Drood. Edwin Drood in Hiding* and *Dead? Or Alive?* are also considered. Against this, Dickens' biographer John Forster maintained that the novelist had told him that 'the story was to be that of the murder of a nephew by his uncle'. In the first chapter, as John Jasper enters the cathedral fresh from the opium-den, he does so to the 'intoned words, "WHEN THE WICKED MAN".' Jasper is the villain, and Drood may or may not be dead.

Dickens took a great deal of care in the commissioning of covers for his works. The illustration for *The Mystery of Edwin Drood*, by Luke Fildes, is no exception. On the right-hand side, Jaspers appears to be leading a search for the murderer, and points, inadvertently, to another picture of himself at the cloisters.

In the novel itself, Rosa seems to attribute to Jasper almost psychic powers of manipulation: she confides in Neville's sister Helena that she feels as if 'he could pass in through the wall when he is spoken of'. The reader knows, moreover, that Jasper has an unhealthy interest in the graveyard, and has even drugged the stonemason Durdles in order to obtain a set of keys. Durdles also reveals to him the presence of a lime-pit 'quick enough to eat your bones'. If all this were not sufficient to cast Jasper in a sinister light, it should be added that Jasper mentions to the jeweller that the only decorative accessories Edwin ever wears are his watch and shirt-pin, the very articles found in the river. In his opium-daze, the reader knows that Jaspers fantasizes about strangling.

So it seems clear that Jasper is the guilty party. But what is the crime? Did he succeed in murdering Drood? Or is Edwin still alive, working to unmask his perfidious uncle?

M. R. James and Andrew Lang were both of the opinion that Drood was still alive. Chapter XIV, which narrates the events leading up to the reconciliation dinner between Drood and Landless at Jasper, after which Edwin disappears, is entitled 'When shall these three meet again?', presuming some future reunion (though it could well be the two adversaries and a corpse). In addition, Hiram Grewgious, Rosa's benevolent uncle, takes against Jasper very suddenly: because (so goes the theory) Drood has secretly informed him of Jasper's attempt on his life.

Another twist occurs in chapter XVIII. It opens with a new character, a 'white-haired personage, with black eyebrows'. His name is Dick Datchery, and he has a strange interest in the habits of John Jasper. He announces himself by having the waiter look into his hat, and throughout the descriptions of him, particular importance is attached to this hat, and his shock of white hair. As he walks with the pompous Mr Sapsea, he 'had the odd momentary appearance upon him of having forgotten his hat . . . and he clapped his hand up to his head as if with some vague expectation of finding another hat upon it'. Dick Datchery, it seems, is in disguise.

Datchery, if you like stories where the murder victim is not actually killed, is Drood in disguise. A variation of this argument supposes that Jasper knocked Drood unconscious and placed the body in the lime-pit: Drood revived, but not before his hair was bleached and his skin burned (forensic pathology not being Dickens' strong point). However, there are minor problems with this solution. For example, Datchery has to ask for directions to Jasper's house, even though, if he is Drood, he knows full well where his own house is. Or is this a complicated double-bluff, a misdirection to convince people he really is a stranger?

On the other hand, let us suppose that Drood is dead. Unbeknown to Jasper, Drood was carrying the diamond engagement ring which he was to return to Grewgious. If his corpse is in the lime-pit or the Sapsea monument, the ring becomes an incriminating token of identification. He was taking the ring back to Rosa's guardian as they had agreed to amicably separate. When Jasper hears this he is distraught, because his murder, motivated by jealousy, was actually unnecessary.

But if Drood is dead, who is Datchery? Many of the other characters in the story might be in disguise.

We know that, during their abysmal childhood in Ceylon, Neville Landless and his twin sister Helena ran away from their guardian, and 'each time, she dressed as a boy and showed the daring of a man'. Is Helena putting her cross-dressing to good use, to clear her brother's name?

Grewgious has a clerk, a failed tragedian named Bazzard. His acquaintance with the theatre might suggest him as the perfect person to don a costume, and act as Grewgious' eyes and ears around the town. Is he Datchery?

Then again, there's Lieutenant Tartar. Both he and Datchery have sunburned complexions and a military air. In addition, there is an odd echo between them: Tartar is, he says, 'an idle fellow'; and Datchery describes himself as 'an idle buffer living on his means'. Is Tartar Datchery?

Is Grewgious Datchery? Is everyone Datchery? This is becoming chaotic!

Perhaps Datchery is simply Datchery; a wholly new character in the plot. It has been mooted that he could be a professional detective, hired by Grewgious to keep tabs on Jasper. Datcherys everywhere and not a clue as to who he really is.

The novel as we have it ends with Datchery making a connection between Jasper and the 'Princess Puffer', the crone who supplies him with opium and who has observed his psychotic episodes when under the influence. Dickens had already set up the idea of a split personality: 'As in some cases of drunkenness,' he wrote, '. . . there are two states of consciousness which never clash, but each of which pursues its separate course as though it were continuous instead of broken (thus, if I hide my watch when I am drunk, I must be drunk again before I can remember where).' The drug would, one supposes, reveal the murderous truth that the rational side of Jasper can suppress. The net is undoubtedly tightening, though the conclusion still eludes the reader. In this way, *The Mystery of Edwin Drood* is a gloriously perfect murder novel.

What is regrettable is not that we lack the neat summing up, but that we do not know how the tantalizing undercurrents of the story would have played themselves out. Despite its quaint Englishness, *The Mystery of Edwin Drood* is shot through with oriental images: Edwin plans to become an engineer in Egypt, the Landlesses are criticized for the 'drop of what is tigerish in their blood', Lascars and Chinese immigrants flit through the opium smog of the East End. The 'large black scarf of strong close-woven silk' which Jasper wears has even been seen as evidence that he is an initiate of the Thuggee cult.

And it would have ended, says John Forster, with Jasper. 'The originality . . . was to consist in the review of the murderer's career by himself at the close . . . The last chapters were to be written in the condemned cell, to which his wickedness, all elaborately elicited from him as if told of another, had brought him.'

Like Jane Austen's *Sanditon*, *The Mystery of Edwin Drood* shows a novelist eager to expand the range of their work. In the opening chapter of *The Mystery of Edwin Drood*, Dickens imagines himself in the hazed mind of an addict with cinematic precision: on waking, the unnamed character seems to see the cathedral spire, which gradually resolves itself into the bed-post. Twins, ghosts, exotic incomers and repressed residents of small towns; drugs, murder, psychosexual manipulation and moments of unutterable kindness: Dickens, in his last work, sets up a series of resonances and ambiguities that seem comparable to the films of David Lynch.

Herman Melville

(1819–91)

There are a great many novels that remain unwritten: the spark of inspiration might fail to kindle, the work might warp in being moulded, the nib might be split by mortality. *Agatha*, however, is unique, in that two men of genius failed to write it. The original idea that the life story of Mrs Agatha Robertson, née Hatch, was worthy of some novelistic transfiguration belongs to an elderly lawyer from New Bedford whom Herman Melville met in Nantucket, in July 1852.

The story of Agatha Hatch ('but you must give her some other name,' Melville wrote to Nathaniel Hawthorne) has a moment of high drama, many years of patient, though ferociously painful, suffering and a denouement of sorts. Setting aside chronology momentarily, the catalyst that unveils the whole story is a Mr Janney of Missouri, who had become the executor of his mother-in-law's second husband's $20,000 estate. He tried to locate the descendants of Mr James Robertson, and discovered in the process that his real name was Mr Shinn. However, these assiduous researches bore less fruit than the unexpected arrival of a letter addressed to the deceased. It was from a woman called Rebecca Gifford of Falmouth, Massachusetts, and it called him 'Father'.

Cut back twenty years. Shipwrecked by a sudden tempest,

James Robertson is washed up on the shore at Pembroke, Mass., and is nursed back to health by a local girl, Agatha Hatch. The confluence of care, relief and a brush with death slowly evolves into something like love, and Agatha and James are duly married. He undertakes two further sea-voyages, and together they have a daughter, Rebecca. Robertson leaves again in search of employment, and does not return.

Over the next seventeen years, Agatha is left in limbo. That she does not remarry might indicate she believes her husband is still alive; she has certainly never had any confirmation that he has died. The sea, supposedly, can wait a long time to recapture those that managed to elude a watery destiny. How long does it take for hope to shade into resignation, for acquiescence to crumble into despondency? The fact that would allow grief is endlessly deferred. She makes a living through nursing and struggles to send Rebecca to the foremost Quaker school. Then he comes back.

He sends a message through her father that he will understand if she does not want to see him, but would like to be allowed to see his daughter. He is cagey about where he has been, and somehow manages to convince them that trying to follow or find him is unwise, possibly even dangerous. He promises to return for good within a year, and settles on them a handsome sum of money.

Robertson does return, the day before Rebecca's wedding. But he disappears again, and sends letters asking the whole family to move to Missouri. He sends shawls that seem to have been worn by someone beforehand. Eventually, he confesses to Rebecca's husband what had prevented him from being with Agatha and his wife. Mrs Irvin, a widow, became the second Mrs Robertson, and their daughter married Mr Janney. Janney mentioned later that his stepfather-in-law had been an oddly suspicious man, who would always wait to find out who visitors were before agreeing to see them. Agatha maintained that she had 'no wish to make either of them unhappy', and that to expose his bigamy would only have driven him far further away. Neither Agatha nor Rebecca pressed to have his settlement on the Janneys annulled.

Melville wrote to Hawthorne, saying that he had considered using the story himself, 'but, thinking again, it has occurred to me that this thing lies very much in a vein, with which you are peculiarly familiar. To be plump, I think that in this matter you would make a better hand at it than I would.' Given the rapturous applause that had greeted Hawthorne's 1850 study of Puritan hypocrisy, *The Scarlet Letter*, and his subtle characterization of the self-sacrificing, infinitely patient Hester Prynne, one can see why Melville gravitated towards thinking *Agatha* should be written by Hawthorne.

In addition, Melville was most likely still smarting from many of the less positive reviews of his 1851 novel *Moby-Dick*. 'So much trash belonging to the worst school of Bedlam literature,' thundered the *Athenaeum*. 'Sheer moonstruck lunacy' – the *London Morning Chronicle*. 'Mr Melville is evidently trying to ascertain how far the public will consent to be imposed upon . . . the very ultimatum of weakness . . . bad rhetoric, involved syntax, stilted sentiment and incoherent English' – the *New York United States Magazine and Democratic Review*. Having, it seemed, failed so spectacularly with his metaphysical romance of whaling, monomania and masculine camaraderie, a Stoic, feminine domestic tragedy would certainly be a departure.

Melville's letter to Hawthorne reveals the extent to which he was seriously shaping his own *Agatha*. Her father is made a former mariner, and lighthouse keeper, who has made her swear never to marry a sailor. The mailbox Agatha walks to each day is described in a stop-frame sequence of deterioration and mouldy decrepitude; an opening long-shot dwells across the land and seascape, the cliffs from which she will not fling herself in despair. Her faithless husband is treated empathetically: 'the whole sin stole upon him insensibly – so that it would perhaps have been hard for him to settle upon the exact day when he could say to himself, "Now I have deserted my wife".' Nonetheless, it was Hawthorne who should 'build about with fulness & veins & beauty' this 'skeleton of actual reality': 'And if I thought I could do it as well as you, why, I should not let you have it.'

Hawthorne started to write an *Agatha*, but soon tired of it. In October 1852, Melville wrote again, suggesting plot lines, specifically that Robertson's bigamy might 'be ascribed to the peculiarly latitudinarian notions, which most sailors have of all tender obligations of that sort', an idea Melville is sure that Hawthorne has already pondered.

By November, Hawthorne had decided against *Agatha*, and encouraged Melville to write the novel himself. Melville agrees, asks permission to use the 'Isle of Shoals' name Hawthorne had woven into his fragment, and declares he 'shall begin it immediately upon reaching home; and so far as in me lies, I shall endeavor to do justice to so interesting a story of reality'. With that, *Agatha* vanishes from literary history.

Hawthorne and Melville's friendship cooled around 1856. 'I have just about made up my mind to be annihilated,' Melville wrote. Although he lived for another thirty years, he ceased to publish fiction completely: after the brilliant, darkly ironic study in illusion and bad faith, *The Confidence Man* of 1857, Melville the novelist disappeared as completely as James Shinn Robertson Robinson. When he died, the unfinished manuscript of *Billy Budd, Sailor* was found among his papers. The manuscript of *Agatha* was not.

Gustave Flaubert

(1821–80)

Had he had his once-upon-a-time wish for obliteration, there would be very little to say about Gustave Flaubert. In 1851 he was thirty years old, living at home with his quarrelsome mother and a cupboard crammed with jottings, scribbles and juvenilia. His only major previous attempt at a serious and sustained literary composition was a High Romantic phantasmagoria, *La Tentation de Saint-Antoine,* a work inspired by Bruegel's painting which he had seen in Genoa some years before. The anguished prose-poem had baroqued like a shot plant from his initial note on the picture: 'Naked woman lying down, Love in one corner'.

Flaubert read it to his friend Louis Bouilhet, whose critical response was succinct – 'I think you ought to throw it in the fire and never mention it again.' He did not.

Dispirited, he left, and listlessly trudged around North Africa, gazed at the face of the Sphinx and the navel of a stripper whose arms were adorned with Koranic tattoos. He meandered back to France, unsure, but in the knowledge he would have to do something. He should begin what Louis had suggested: 'a down-to-earth subject, some little incident from bourgeois life'. Furthermore, Louis had prompted a plot – 'the story of Delphine Delamare', a local adulteress, driven to suicide. The idea had obviously pushed tentative roots into Gustave's mind: at the summit of Djebel Abousir, above the seething Nile, he had exclaimed, 'Eureka! I'm going to call her Emma Bovary!'

But back at home with his mother, it was going less well. Beginnings never did for Flaubert; the conception may be sudden and exhilarating but when pen reached paper, it bled an agonizing parturition. The corpulent author sprawled, prostrate, on his settle, taunted by blank pages. He indulged himself in torrents of tears and tantrums of masturbation. Writing disgusted him, it was like 'having to drink up an ocean and then piss it all out again'; publishing was a horrific *faux-pas*, 'like letting someone see your bum'. At the pitch of this, he fantasized that the ideal would be 'to be buried in an enormous tomb, with all my never-published manuscripts, like a savage buried alongside his horse'. Had he had his way, all of Flaubert's works would be lost within some off-road sepulchre.

Eventually, finally, after five years of writing and revising, *Madame Bovary: The Story of a Provincial Education* (1857) appeared in *La Revue de Paris*, initially advertised as the work of one Monsieur G. Faubert. The editor, his erstwhile friend Maxime Du Camp, had required further cuts. Even so, the printed version was sprinkled with demure dashes to protect easily offended eyes from gutter words. These absences were material evidence in its eventual trial, where the wily defending lawyer, Sénard, insisted that the considerate blanks had merely inflamed the suspicions of the dirty-minded prosecution, who obviously knew far worse words than the blanks suppressed.

The *scandale* ensured healthy sales. The reclusive, overweight de Sade aficionado had commenced a career that would take him even as far as being welcomed into the bosom of the Imperial Family. *Madame Bovary* was followed by a Carthaginian orgy, *Salammbô* (1862), the 'moral history of . . . my generation', *L'Education sentimentale* (1867), which the ever-helpful Du Camp thought should rightly be called *Mediocrities*, the thrice-revised *Saint-Antoine* (1874) and the late, luminous *Trois contes* (1877). A relatively slight corpus from a self-confessed Behemoth. But there were other writings, planned novels, aborted projects, unfinished epics . . .

Flaubert had written since infancy. He had coloured in an illustrated copy of *Don Quixote*. He had demanded his nursemaid take dictations. While still at school, family friends gathered some of his youthful works, including a comedy entitled *The Miser*, an elegy on a local dog and a treatise replete with puerile mischief, *The Splendid Explanation of the Famous Constipation*, and bound them in a volume. As a student, he had written to a schoolteacher, claiming he was working on three stories, a lifetime before the appearance of the *Trois contes*. At the same time as he was struck by the nightmare vision of Bruegel's painting, he was sketching a version of *Don Juan*.

Flaubert was notorious for hoarding his manuscripts, unable to discard the slightest inked scrap. We know that in 1871, with the Prussian Army sweeping across France, a wary Flaubert buried a box full of letters – and, perhaps, other papers? – in his garden. Did it also contain more on his proposed satire on socialism, or the working drafts of *Harel-Bey*, his novel on the contemporary Orient, where the Europeans degenerated as the Arabs improved? The year after his death, the house at Croisset was demolished. The box, as far as anyone knows, remained beneath the soil. As one biographer speculates, a treasure-trove of Flaubertiana might lie beneath the concrete dockland development of Rouen.

More tantalizingly, he took copious notes for a novel on French society under the Second Empire, whose highest echelons had embraced him so wholeheartedly. The work was schemed out after the political upheavals of 1870–71, and the extant remarks reveal a skewed hindsight: Babylon is mapped on a decaying Paris. The planned work would be a counterpart to his equally dyspeptic *L'Education sentimentale*, a tale that would expose 'the great lie that we lived by', a novel teeming with 'a fake army, fake politics, fake literature, fake credit and even fake whores'. If the impersonal psychology of *Madame Bovary* heralded Modernism, would the unwritten Second Empire novel, replete with illusion and delusion, have intimated what came after? Another work would certainly be claimed to do just that.

Bouvard et Pécuchet occupied most of the remainder of Flaubert's life; a bitter-sweet, encyclopedic, ultimately unfinished and potentially impossible-to-finish book. Two clerks, with a comfortable income, run through the gamut of human knowledge. Flaubert's *Dictionnaire des idées reçues* catalogued the inanity of bourgeois opinion in all its various forms. In *Bouvard et Pécuchet*, Flaubert gave his triumphant celebration of the manic compulsion to observe the world.

The two fictional obsessives and guileless eccentrics attempt to taxonomize the universe, much as the eighteenth-century *philosophes* had done. Like a frock-coated double act, they are unravelled at every turn, unable to discern the distinction between an old wives' tale masquerading as wisdom and the proverbial pearl.

Flaubert himself abandoned and restarted the work constantly, read over 1,500 books researching it. The work, he claimed, was like 'trying to put the ocean into a bottle'. Was it a quixotic venture from the outset? Perhaps, although he was prone to begin each venture with a fathomless fear of its conclusion: as he hobbled through the opening chapters of *L'Education sentimentale*, he had griped it was as difficult as 'fitting the sea into a carafe'. In note form, Flaubert imagined one possible ending: having exhausted every field of human knowledge, the two former copyists joyfully purchase 'register and instruments, erasers, sandarach, etc.', and order the construction of a double-sided desk. They return to being clerks, having rid themselves of the terrible 'desire for concluding'. Tentatively, they even attempt to make amends to Mélie, the young woman embroiled in their fantastical schemes.

Flaubert may have declared, 'Madame Bovary, c'est moi', but he never started the novel which might have touched on the dark secret of his own life. He described *La Spirale* as 'a large fantastical metaphysical loudmouth novel' which advanced the proposition that 'happiness is in the imagination' – a strange elision: did he mean that true happiness is achieved, in Romantic poet style, through an act of imagination? Or that all happiness is a mere figment of the fancy? Although the initial impetus towards the novel was his reading of Dante's *Inferno* in 1852 and the vagaries of his relationship with the flighty and none too faithful Louise Colet, its wellspring was buried deeper and earlier in himself.

During his early twenties, whilst travelling home with his more respectable brother Achille, Flaubert suffered a debilitating and inexplicable attack. It seemed to be sparked by the complex relationship between a fixed light in a distant inn, and the swinging lantern on an oncoming carriage. These points created an indeterminate triangulation with something in his mind. The event caused a psychic dislocation, as if trying to focus on the shapes wrenched the brain's equivalent of a muscle. As a child he had faded and phased out of conversations: this was more serious. It was a 'golden fire', an 'irruption of *memory*', a 'yellow cloud', 'a thousand fireworks', 'Bengal lights'. He collapsed, frothed at the mouth, babbled. In retrospect, it seems likely that Flaubert suffered from some form of epilepsy.

La Spirale was 'a novel about madness, or rather about *the way* in which you go mad'. Achille-Cléophas Flaubert, the novelist's father, had founded the Rouen Hospital, and the young Gustave had witnessed autopsies and operations, wandered amongst the imbeciles and the insane. He, more than many, had the material from which to construct a scientifically accurate fiction on illness. But, as he said, 'it is a subject that frightens me'.

La Spirale remained locked in Flaubert's body, never to be manifested on the page. Corruption, insanity, a foreboding that these knots and flaws were not only in the grain of the self, but striated through society, traumas walking abroad: Flaubert did not dare embark on such an investigation. How could he? When his cult of authorial impersonality demanded that the author must love, fight and drink without being a lover, soldier or drunk: under such strictures, how could the tortured elucidate torment? In the hateful hiatus between each completed work and the dreaded embarkation on another, the idea glimmered, taunted and was deferred. 'I shall have to wait until I am far enough away from those experiences,' he wrote. He never did acquire such distance.

Fyodor Dostoyevsky

(1821–81)

'Like a rat, slithering along in hate' was D. H. Lawrence's verdict on the novelist Fyodor Dostoyevsky. Hatred did indeed motivate the author: hatred of socialists, anarchists, the corrupt aristocracy, the feckless peasants, Germans, Jews, the French ('they make me sick'), himself, the gaming tables of Baden-Baden, the 'Baal' of London, Turgenev, publishers, critics, the complacent and the radicals. 'Let the nihilists and Westerners scream that I am a *reactionary*!' he boasted in the 1870s.

Yet this was the man who, in 1849, had stood before a firing squad, fully expecting to be shot for sedition. The sentence was commuted to four years' imprisonment in Siberia, followed by four years as a private soldier: the whole ritual of blindfolding and waiting was part of an elaborate state ritual designed to bring the condemned to the brink of execution, before the Tsar's benevolence exiled them to the wastes of Omsk.

At the time of the capital punishment charade, Dostoyevsky was a minor, but not unimportant, writer. His debut work *Poor Folk* (1846) had caused quite a stir. The poet Nikolai Nekrasov had read the manuscript, and dashed to see the eminent critic Vossarion Belinsky, whose imprimatur guaranteed a book's success. Nekrasov lauded the appearance of 'a new Gogol', to which Belinsky retorted, 'Gogols sprout like mushrooms in your imagination.' The arch cultural arbiter, however, was won over, and praised the young novelist who had shown the garret-dwelling underclass to the pampered bourgeoisie, saying, 'These men too are your brothers.'

Belinsky was to be tangentially responsible for Dostoyevsky's Siberian incarceration. In 1847, the increasingly unstable Nikolai Gogol had shocked his friends and admirers by publishing an almost lunatic justification of Tsarist autarchy, *Selected Passages from Correspondence with Friends*. Belinsky had responded with the so-called 'Gogol letter', condemning it as an 'inflated and sluttish hullabaloo of words and phrases'. The censors acted quickly, and it became a crime to distribute the 'felonious missive'.

Dostoyevsky was, at this juncture in his life, an ardent acolyte of Belinsky's socialism and an uncommitted observer of his atheism; he was also involved with the Fourierist 'Petrashevsky Circle'. He was arrested, charged with 'orally disseminating' and 'failing to report the dissemination of' Belinsky's letter. In the harsh conditions of his penal sentence in Siberia, Dostoyevsky's views took a swerve similar to Gogol's. He recanted his former allegiances, and excoriated his former friends. Belinsky was a 'dung beetle . . . the shit', 'the most stinking, stupid and shameful phenomenon in Russian life'. It was this new, ultra-conservative Dostoyevsky that would go on to write *Crime and Punishment* (1866), *The Idiot* (1868), *The Devils* (1872) and *The Brothers Karamazov* (1880).

After his release, Dostoyevsky's attempts to re-enter literary life trapped him in a spiralling morass of debts and creditors. With his brother, Mikhail, he started a magazine, *Vremya* (*Time*), which serialized the novelization of his Siberian experience, *Memoirs from the House of the Dead*. Arguments with the censors forced the closure of *Vremya*, and the brothers started another journal, *Epokha* (*Epoch*). The death of Mikhail in 1864 not only left the periodical without a safe pair of financial hands, it left his brother with the responsibility for supporting Mikhail's wife and children as well. Despite a grant from the Society for Assisting Needy Authors and Scholars, Dostoyevsky became entrapped by the unprincipled publisher Stellovsky, who had bought up his outstanding IOUs and strong-armed him into a decidedly inequitable contract.

Stellovsky had demanded a new work of at least 160 pages, by November 1866, which if not delivered would result in the forfeiture of copyrights on all writings past, present and future. Dostoyevsky did not wish to hand over his work in progress, *Crime and Punishment*, and engaged a secretary to take dictation of what would become *The Gambler* for Stellovsky. At the same time, he was attempting to raise sufficient funds to quit Russia, and was consequently hawking a new novel, *The Drunkards*, around the editors of *Homeland Notes* and *The Russian Herald*, with a price-tag of 3,000 roubles. Neither was interested. Perhaps the meagre conditions of the Siberian camp had taught Dostoyevsky how to cannibalize and recycle even ideas. *The Drunkards*, and its anti-hero Marmeladov, became incorporated into *Crime and Punishment*. As he fell in love with his stenographer Anna, and completed both *The Gambler* and *Crime and Punishment*, he prepared to escape with her from St Petersburg.

Their married life in Continental Europe bounced from city to city like a roulette ball jumping the numbers. Apart from working on an essay on Belinsky, which never saw the light of day, Dostoyevsky plotted continuously for a grand novel that would settle scores with his enemies and his former selves. In 1868 it was called *Atheism*, about a 45-year-old civil servant who loses his faith in God. 'He gets mixed up with the younger generation, the atheists, Slavophils, and Europeans, Russian religious fanatics, monks and priests; gets deeply involved, among others, with a Jesuit propagandist, a Pole; sinks as low as the sect of flagellants and in the end – regains his faith in Christ as well as in Russia,' he wrote to the poet A. N. Maykov. 'For God's sake don't tell anyone about it: so far as I am concerned, I am going to write this last novel if it kills me.' Elements of *Atheism* were eventually grafted into the character of Stavrogin in *The Devils*. But, he told his niece, he could not write *Atheism* in Europe.

By 1870 the masterpiece was to be called *The Life of a Great Sinner*, and would be 'as long as *War and Peace*'. Dostoyevsky conceived of the work in three, then five inter-related but discrete novellas. The Sinner was to be an illegitimate child, brought up by grandparents, whose noble family was 'degenerate to the point of swinishness'. He detests the moral aberration of his kin, and is drawn to two individuals: a beatific crippled girl called Katya, whom he forces to worship him, and a family retainer Kulikov, a member of the self-whipping Khristy sect. The first volume ended with the 'wolf-child, nihilist' murdering a notorious brigand.

The second volume, after his confession, was set in a monastery school. There, the Sinner befriends Albert, with whom he desecrates icons but whom he beats for blaspheming, and the debauched Lambert, whom Dostoyevsky scavenged into *A Raw Youth* (1875); as well as being influenced by a character based on the Russian mystic Tikhon Zadonsky, later transformed into Father Zossima in *The Brothers Karamazov*. The Sinner would, by the last volumes, become an ascetic, tempted by suicide, and the founder of an orphanage.

The Life of a Great Sinner was variously renamed *The Forties*, *A Russian Candide*, *A Book of Christ* and *Disorder*.

The whole idea of the novel is to show that universal disorder now reigns everywhere in society, in its affairs, in its leading ideas (which for that reason do not exist), in its convictions (which do not exist, either), in the disintegration of family life. If passionate convictions do exist, they are only destructive ones (socialism). There are no moral ideas left.

All these hypothetical novels would be synthesized into *The Brothers Karamazov*, a work as equally indebted to the falsely convicted parricide Dostoyevsky had met during his time in Siberia. Even that is an incomplete manifestation of the book he was trying to write.

The introduction to *The Brothers Karamazov* makes clear that we are learning the vast background, the inherited and acquired traits of a new kind of novelistic hero. 'The trouble is,' he wrote,

that while I am dealing with one biography, I have two novels on my hands. The main novel is the second one – it deals with the activity of my hero in our own day ... The action of the first novel, on the other hand, takes place thirteen years ago and is not really a novel but just a chapter out of my hero's adolescence. It is quite impossible for me to dispense with the first novel because without it a great deal in the second novel would be unintelligible.

The Grand Duke Alexander Mikhailovich recorded what a journalist, Alexei Suvorin, maintained the second volume would have involved. The central character was the saintly Alyosha Karamazov, younger brother to the atheist writer Ivan, the dissolute but endearing Dmitry and the murderous half-brother Smerdyakov. 'It seems to you that in my last novel, *The Brothers Karamazov*, there was much that was prophetic. But wait for the continuation. In it, Alyosha will leave the monastery and become an anarchist. And my pure Alyosha will kill the Tsar!'

Dostoyevsky died on 28 January 1881. At the end of February 1881, Tsar Alexander II was assassinated.

Sir Richard Burton

(1821–90)

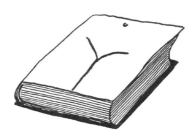

Witnessing cannibalism was one of the few ambitions Sir Richard Burton failed to satisfy. As an explorer, author, intelligence agent and diplomat, he had chalked up an astonishing number of firsts, and an equally honourable number of bizarre near-misses. He was the first European to perform the *haj*, the ritual pilgrimage from Medina to Mecca, disguised as a practising Muslim. He discovered the Great Lakes in the interior of Africa, though, through illness, did not succeed in locating the source of the Nile. He studied Mormons in Salt Lake City, and met the religion's own Saint Paul, Brigham Young. He toured the battlefields of Paraguay after the disastrous war waged by Francisco López and his mistress Eliza Lynch.

He was the first Christian to enter the Ethiopian Islamic stronghold of Harar, which was forbidden to outsiders, and, with his redoubtable wife, Isabel, he reached the city of Palmyra without the help of the Bedouins who controlled the routes. During an ambush in Somaliland, a spear was thrust through his cheeks. Burton's search for gold in the Midian failed, though if he had been looking for oil he would have become a rich man. Similarly, during his consulship in

West Africa, he failed to appreciate the pecuniary potential in an 'exceptionally sweet' drink combining water and kola nuts, though he did patent a beverage called 'Captain Burton's Tonic Bitters'.

His peregrinations were distilled into a remarkable literary oeuvre, comprising geography, ethnology, anthropology, poetry, swordsmanship, translation, satire and a complete, unexpurgated and annotated edition of *The Arabian Nights* in sixteen volumes. He mastered over twenty languages as well as countless local dialects, wrote definitively on the Portuguese poet Camoens, and published forty-seven works in his lifetime, followed by several posthumous volumes.

Physically courageous and intellectually daunting, he should have been a Boy's Own hero, but a sticky film of innuendo and rumour clung to his reputation, and not without cause. Burton never suffered fools gladly, and his indiscreet criticisms of Imperial policy in the Indian subcontinent and Africa earned him the disapprobation of his superiors. He was arrogant, ambitious and fond of bitingly sarcastic reproaches. Perhaps most damagingly for his hopes of advancement, his insatiable curiosity extended into the realms of the erotic.

As a young soldier in Karachi, with a proven flair for languages and an unparalleled ability to pass himself off as a native, he was asked by Sir Charles Napier to prepare a confidential report on alleged homosexual brothels. The resulting document was authoritative to a shocking degree, sparing the reader no detail about the relative practices of eunuchs, pederasts and catamites. Although the report was supposed to be destroyed, it was skimmed by the eyes of Napier's successor as Governor of Sindh, the civilian R. K. Pringle, who was so shocked he forwarded the document to the authorities, recommending that Burton be immediately dismissed.

The actual report has never resurfaced in the annals of

bureaucracy, but the beginnings of Burton's notoriety as a Byronic libertine were established. Furthermore, his successful impersonation of a Muslim pilgrim led to persistent rumours that he had actually converted, and that he harboured a deep animosity, not only to missionaries, but to the Christian religion in general.

Burton, half-jokingly, later claimed that he had broken every one of the Ten Commandments. That any respectable Victorian woman would marry the infamous Burton was unlikely: that an ardent Roman Catholic girl from an aristocratic family would elope to do so is even more surprising. Isabel Arundell had been in love with Burton since she had met him at the age of nineteen, and bolstered by a gypsy prophecy that she would marry a Burton, she turned down countless suitors, flew in the face of her mother's protestations, and ran off with him.

Isabel, in many ways, was the ideal companion. She combined self-will and submissiveness to an extraordinary degree. Having single-mindedly won her man, she then advised future brides to tolerate everything. In a phrase rich with metaphorical possibilities, she counselled them to let their husbands smoke at home, since they would assuredly find someplace else to, should it be frowned upon. She shocked guests by wearing trousers, and accompanied him on some of his most dangerous escapades. Unstintingly loyal, she acted as his literary agent and harangued lukewarm reviewers. It was only after his death that erstwhile, life-long friends launched a cacophony of animosity against her. After her own death, numerous biographers colluded in depicting her as an unfit, inferior partner.

Richard Burton made Isabel his literary executrix in the year of his death. He had already published his translation of the *Kama Sutra* and the explicit commentary on sexual behaviour that accompanied *The Tales of 1001 Nights*. Both of them were aware of the levels of censorious prudery in late

Victorian society: the *Edinburgh Review*, in its notice of Burton's *1001 Nights*, compared rival translations and declared, 'Galland is for the nursery, Lane for the study and Burton for the sewers.'

Burton's attitude was one of frustrated defiance. If he were prosecuted for obscenity, he intended to arrive at court with the Bible, Shakespeare and Rabelais and ask how much of those works was to be suppressed. A vein of utter devilry runs through some of his correspondence. When working on a study of the geographical limits in which sodomy was permissible, he hoped that 'Mrs Grundy' – the personification of nineteenth-century puritanism – would 'howl on her big bum to her heart's content'.

Isabel had always been more cautious. She had prepared a bowdlerized version of the *1001 Nights*, dedicated 'To the Women of England', and her frequent defences of Burton's views became the targets for gleefully malicious reviewers. Nonetheless, before he died, Burton trusted her with his extant manuscripts and prepared an inventory of what was to be burned.

In later years, the myth of Lady Burton's embittered and ignorant act of arson would be elevated to the status of fact. The poet Swinburne, who had admired Isabel as a wife, would refer to her as a harpy when she was a widow, his vitriol exacerbated by the fact she had organized for her unconscious, agnostic husband to be given Extreme Unction. Isabel Burton did burn some papers, most notably the entire 1,200 pages of his translation of the Arabic erotic classic *The Scented Garden*. Burton had previously written a version based on French translations, entitled *The Perfumed Garden*, and had been engaged in an edition from the original language at the time of his death.

Isabel did, however, prepare various posthumous works for publication. When news of the destruction of *The Scented Garden* broke, rumours started that Isabel had actually secreted the manuscript in her husband's crypt. Unscrupulous publishers kept hinting that they had access to another copy, which would shortly appear, alongside other works 'by' Burton. In light of the difficulties managing the estate and fending off unauthorized or counterfeit editions, her own will stipulated that everything should be burned: her papers, her manuscripts, his unpublished works, his remnants. It was not wholly successful: a work which Burton had wanted destroyed – an essay on a mysterious Arabian sect of Jews who supposedly performed human sacrifices – appeared after Isabel's death.

It was following Isabel's, not Richard's, death that the real literary cremation took place. Burton's journals from 1872 to 1890, alongside her own teenage diaries, their letters, his unfinished manuscripts on the Lowlands of Brazil, North, Central and South America, Syrian proverbs, notes on the eunuch trade, translations of Ovid, Ausonius and Ariosto, studies of polygamy: all were erased. Isabel had already destroyed her own book on *The Sixth Sense*. It was not out of spite, but out of love, that she had ever burned anything at all. Had their correspondence alone been spared, the speculation about the relationship between these two remarkable and devoted people would have been instantly stilled.

But her detractors had done their job well, and Isabel would be blamed for the pyre in subsequent biographies. Few would mention that Burton had already lost a lot of unpublished material during a warehouse fire in 1860. Amongst those papers was one study which might have proved more interesting than yet more erotological investigations. As a soldier in Karachi, Burton had kept forty monkeys in a house, and was attempting to use his formidable literary abilities to understand their language. The results of this experiment – a vocabulary of sixty words – were lost thirty-six years before the more conspicuous conflagration.

Algernon Charles Swinburne

(1837–1909)

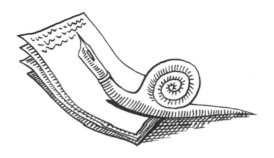

'I am told that Mr Swinburne is the best poet in my dominions,' said Queen Victoria. Such high estimation of his voluminous work did not even last as long as her reign.

The unfortunate poet, with his preternaturally large head and shock of red hair, became a byword for the aesthetic excesses and sexual peccadilloes of the so-called 'Decadent' period. His enthusiastic interest in spanking and his ostentatious display of classical mythology seemed dated and, frankly, immature, even before the Great War. He yearned to be *un poète maudit*, an iconoclastic libertine in the manner of Baudelaire or Villon, and yet the closest he came to being tortured was convoluted grammar and the occasional birching.

It is, indeed, difficult to take lines like these, from 'Dolores', seriously:

> O lips full of lust and of laughter,
>> Curled snakes that are fed from my breast,
> Bite hard, lest remembrance come after
>> And press with new lips where you pressed.
> For my heart too springs up at the pressure,
>> Mine eyelids too moisten and burn;

> Ah, feed me and fill me with pleasure,
>   Ere pain come in turn.

Swinburne himself admitted being wary of his 'tendency to
the dulcet and luscious form of verbosity', and could even
compose passable self-parodies of his alliterative and meander-
ing verse, such as:

> Life is the lust of a lamp for the light that is dark till the dawn
>   of the day, when we die.

It is regrettable that his wit was rarely in evidence in his
poetry. As an undergraduate, he regaled his acolytes with satirical squibs, where contemporary events were retold as if they
were historical dramas in the style of Victor Hugo. A friend,
W. H. Mallock, recollected one in which Queen Victoria was
embroiled in a love-tryst between the politicians Lord John
Russell and Sir Robert Peel. Perhaps it was during this comedy
that Swinburne also composed Victoria's anguished confession
that she had been seduced by an elderly William Wordsworth.

After which, Mallock remarks, Swinburne tossed off
another glass of port and collapsed into an inebriated slumber.

Later, in this vaudeville of Victorian high politics, the focus
moves to the illegitimate daughter of the monarch and Lord
Russell, who becomes a courtesan under the pseudonym
'Miss Kitty' and enthrals various princes and statesmen. 'She
may have done everything which might have made a Mes-
salina blush, but whenever she looked at the sky, she murmured "God", and whenever she looked at a flower she
murmured "mother",' lauds one of her suitors.

After which, Mallock remarks, Swinburne tossed off
another glass of port and collapsed into an inebriated slumber.

Puerile, yes, and to an extent just silliness. But if Swinburne
had forgone the all-too-frequent jiggers and snifters, and
dashed down these skits in manuscripts for his friends, we
might now remember him as a precursor to alternative comedy and the satirical irreverence of the 1960s, rather than as a
fey and eminently forgettable minor poet of the 1860s.

Emile Zola

(1840–1902)

On Friday 22 September 1893, Emile Zola, the most controversial French novelist of his day, addressed the English Institute of Journalists at Lincoln's Inn Hall in London. It was an
influential gathering, and a rare accolade for the author, fresh
from the completion of his monumental twenty-volume cycle
of novels, *L'Histoire naturelle et sociale d'une famille sous le Second
Empire*; better known as *Les Rougon-Macquart*.

The subject on which he was asked to speak was curiously
apposite: anonymity. Although Zola was indisputably infamous (reviewers had called him everything from a 'hysterical
pornographer' to a 'literary sewer-man') he was also uncom-
promisingly private, even unknowable. From this self-
imposed distance, Zola seemed more – or less – than a man.
He was a factory through which the raw materials of the
world were transformed into novels.

Unrelentingly prodigious, Zola categorized the upper
echelons and abysmal depths of French society, rigorously
abiding by his motto *Nulla Dies Sine Linea*: no day without
a line. George Moore, the philosopher whose professorial
writings would have such an impact on the Bloomsbury
Group, described the Institute of Journalists congress in the

Illustrated Magazine and captured something of this over-whelming productivity, when he lamented that, although the *Rougon-Macquart* sequence was now concluded, readers were 'now threatened with a novel on Lourdes, which is to be written in seven months; by a novel on Rome, and by another on the Russian Alliance'. The first two titles duly appeared, followed by *Paris* (1897) to comprise the *Trois Villes* trilogy. In a rare deviation from his intentions, the Russian Alliance fiction evaporated.

Zola had not always been so unswervingly modern. As an earnest young Romantic, he considered himself a poet. 'In this materialist age,' he hymned, 'when commerce absorbs every-one, when the sciences, which have grown so big and robust, render man vainglorious and make him forget the supreme intelligence, a holy mission awaits the poet: at every moment and everywhere to show the soul to those who think only about the body, and God to those in whom science has killed faith.'

God, however, proved no match for the literary critic Hippolyte Taine and the scientist Prosper Lucas. By reading Taine's *Histoire de la littérature anglaise*, with its creed of 'race, milieu and moment', and discovering genetic determinism in Lucas' *Traité de l'hérédité naturelle*, Zola threw off his dreamy chasuble and reinvented himself as the scientist of literature. Studied through the lens of inherited characteristics and environmental adaptations, the seeming flurry of humanity crystallized into perfect regularity. The unpredictable was factored out. Tragedies were inevitable but their causes com-prehensible. Mankind, thought Zola, would slowly learn to adjust its negative propensities: he did not envisage that later generations would derive, from the same half-understood science, eugenics.

Thérèse Raquin (1867) explored how this mechanized aes-thetic might be programmed into a novel. The critics loathed it, and against their aghast denunciations, Zola depicted him-self as an impersonal clinician who had 'simply applied to . . .

living bodies the analytical method that surgeons apply to corpses'. A one-off *succès d'horreur* was, however, hardly sufficient for his ambitions. From the outset, he was drawn to grandiose schemes. A trilogy on heroism had already been abandoned, as it was considered too light a theme. Looking at a blank wall, a few years earlier, he had come up with *La Chaîne des êtres*, a poem in three cantos, entitled 'Past', 'Present' and 'Future', that would trace humanity from the Stone Age to its 'magnificent *divagation*', while providing a comprehensive survey of 'what physiology tells us about the physical man and philosophy about the moral man'. He only had time to jot down eight lines.

The obsession with multi-volume structures may be linked with a certain eccentricity of Zola's: a psychological condition called arithmomania. He had to count continually. Daundering down the boulevard, he checked off lamp-posts, trees, doorways. Taxi registration numbers had to be subjected to some abstruse personal calculus, to divulge if they were lucky or unlucky. When it became transparent that the *Histoire d'une famille* would overrun the ten novels he had allotted, it was revised, not to eleven or twelve, but twenty. The family tree developed a few quirks and offshoots along the way – a brother materialized out of thin air in *La Bête humaine*, his brothers blissfully unaware of their sibling during *L'Assommoir*, *Germinal* and *L'Œuvre*, and the childless pander Sidonie Rougon, from *La Curée*, nonetheless transpired to have a mystery child, Angélique, the heroine of *Le Rêve* (though even reading the whole of the *Rougon-Macquart* would not enlighten the poor girl about her parentage). Nonetheless, a quarter-century before its completion, Zola already had the architecture of the series fixed.

From *La Fortune des Rougon* (1871) to *Le Docteur Pascal* (1893), Zola created 'a simple exposé of the facts of a family, showing the inner mechanism that makes it run'; a panoramic vision of department stores and gin-traps, railway engines and secret gardens, peasants and politicians, tortured artists and high-class doxies; in short, 'the tableau of a dead reign, a strange era fraught with madness and shame'. It brought him vilification and celebration. It had turned him into a perpetual-prosification device, an inexhaustible reamm-machine. And although tit-bits and titles of his future projects were leaked in London, no one could have predicted the drama that would occupy his final decade: the Dreyfus Affair.

In 1894, Alfred Dreyfus, an artillery captain, was arrested and found guilty at a court martial of treason. According to the prosecutor, he had sold secrets about military placements and the specifics of weaponry to the Germans. He was transported the following year to Devil's Island. He was later discovered to be innocent. Dreyfus was Jewish: a fact almost incidental to himself but of material significance to his accusers. In 1896, the intelligence chief, Colonel Picquart, suspected that the evidence for the conviction was unsound and on investigation discovered that one Major Esterhazy was actually the spy. He made his concerns known to his superiors and was swiftly reassigned to North Africa.

In the ensuing struggle for justice, a seam of anti-Semitism opened that convulsed the press and the nation with poisonous intensity. The Jews, it was whispered in print, had a syndicate to fund Dreyfus' appeal. They were profiting from both sides of the conflict. Most of Zola's friends were unabashed about their distrust of 'the parasite among nations . . . the cursed race which no longer has a country of its own' (those words, incidentally, are Zola's: Saccard in *L'Argent* reflects his era). Dreyfus' brother and the vice-president of the Senate sought Zola's support, and expertise with the papers, a support which he readily gave. When his third article on the affair was published in *Le Figaro*, he was promptly sacked. Cartoons depicting an obese Zola, tattooed with pigs and Stars of David, began to appear in the so-called 'loyalist' papers.

It is difficult, accustomed as we are to monotonous shock-

horror revelations, to recapture the sheer power of the front
page of *L'Aurore* of 13 January 1898. Under the stark title
'J'Accuse . . . !', Zola named the conspirators who, in his
opinion, had framed Dreyfus, and those whose incompetence,
apathy or stupidity had consolidated the plot. He ended this
blistering denunciation with a challenge: 'Let those who dare
do so try me at assize court and let the inquest take place
openly, in broad daylight. I shall wait.' They did, and found
him guilty. Six months later, when his appeal against conviction failed, Zola assessed the situation, weighed his options,
and fled to London, as Paris echoed to the sound of lynch-
mobs baying for their own particular brand of justice. He had
already written, 'So there exists such a thing as anti-Semitic
youth . . . fresh young brains and souls that this idiotic poison
has already deranged? How very sad, and how ominous for
the coming twentieth century!'

Under the alibi 'M. Jacques Beauchamp', he settled into a
fugitive's exile in Sussex. He tried to read the *Daily Telegraph*
with the help of an English dictionary, watched a bit of cricket
and worked as furiously as ever. Ernest Vizetelly, a long-term
supporter, nearly blew their cover by describing Zola's English sojourn in *The Athenaeum*.

He certainly intends a book on it [the Dreyfus Affair] in due season
and has made many notes with that object – meantimes, between
chapters of *Fécondité* – his new novel, and the start of a new quartet,
The Four Evangelists – M. Zola has been preparing an account of
his adventures, experiences and observations in exile. This will be
completely illustrated from photographs and sketches.

With the exception of a rather dull ghost story, based on a
haunted house at Penn, but relocated to the Médan in *Contes et
nouvelles*, the album of English anecdotes failed to materialize
(a shame, since Zola was an accomplished photographer).

Zola's first inclination on learning the full details of the

Dreyfus miscarriage of justice was that it was prime, prospective material. He considered it as a sub-plot in a novel, and indeed elements of the case were used in *Vérité*, the third of *The Four Evangelists* alongside the tedious Grand Guignol of a murderous, sexually deviant Catholic priest. He made a 'mental reservation' that the Affair might do as a drama. But no work truly captures the intensity, the power and the significance of the episode, except its own history. Henry James claimed – not without a note of rancour – that Zola's zeal stemmed from being a man 'with arrears of personal history to make up'. After a life devoted to the aloof vivisection of the world, he had become embroiled in a situation that required action, not redaction. To James, Zola was 'treating himself at last to a luxury of experience'.

In 1899, Dreyfus was cleared, and Zola was free to return to France; albeit a France where the unleashed anti-Semitic antipathies still seethed, barely in secret. He worked on: he could do little else. With three of the *Four Evangelists* completed, he toyed with a set of dramas that would 'do for the Third Republic what I did for the Second Empire'. But the prose robot was succumbing to its inevitable entropy. The critics were bored rather than scandalized. Zola spoke wistfully of retiring to the Balearics.

Justice – the final part of the final quartet – remained to be written. In *The Four Evangelists*, Zola had written about the lives of the children of Pierre Froment from the previous *Trois Villes* trilogy. The auspiciously named Mathieu, Marc, Luc and Jean represented the new virtues: wholesome families, honest and well-rewarded labour, adherence to the truth and determination for justice. One reviewer archly noted that the new Septuagint of novels showed the Froments as the Rougons who conquered the world. Zola described the final volumes as 'a great prose poem, full of life and sweetness', ruefully adding 'and then perhaps they won't accuse me of insulting mankind'. Did he recall his own unwritten poem 'Future' as he laboriously attempted to manufacture his own vision of an earthly paradise? 'I have been dissecting for forty years . . . You really must let me dream a little in my old age.' The book would envisage a United States of Europe, an alliance of all the nations, the 'kiss of Peace' in a New Jerusalem.

More controversially, Zola's friend Maurice le Blond claimed that *Justice* 'was to have as its theme Zionism'. How many others knew this? How many others suspected that the Dreyfus material, the taxonomy of anti-Semitism, might well work its way into a novel? Given that his talents were fraying, his phenomenal voltage faltering, perhaps it is better that the triumphal unveiling remains forever hypothetical, rather than half-glimpsed underneath a prolix and turgid last gasp. And yet the reason it must remain so reveals the extent to which the world was not ready for his vision of tolerance.

Zola died before he could finish *Justice*, and *Vérité* appeared with a black border on the cover. The coroner recorded that Zola died from carbon monoxide poisoning. At three in the morning on 29 September 1902, he had complained of nausea, headaches and dizziness. He opened a window, collapsed and choked to death. Reconstructions of the state of the fireplace in his bedroom and demolition of the flue failed to explain the lethal build up of gas; indeed, several guinea pigs later spent an untroubled night in the same room under similar conditions. Worried by how news of any suspicion surrounding Zola's death might be taken by the volatile public, the coroner recorded accidental death.

In 1953, one M. Haquin, an elderly reader of the paper *Libération*, responded to an article on Zola's death. A chimney-sweep friend of his, one of the many anti-Dreyfusards who considered the author nothing more than a traitor, had confessed: 'I and my men blocked the chimney while doing repairs next door. There was a lot of coming and going and we took advantage of the hubbub to locate Zola's chimney and stop it. We unstopped it the next day, very early. No one noticed us.'

Arthur Rimbaud

(1854–91)

In May and June 1886, the French literary magazine *Vogue* published a work called *Les Illuminations*, a haunting sequence of prose-poems. The effect was galvanic. Critical acclaim was immediate: the author, in the words of one enthusiast, was 'a sort of legendary figure', whom younger poets already 'claim as their Master'. His hallucinatory, synaesthetic texts were replete with alchemy, socialism, drunkenness and adolescence. He was literature's fallen angel. Nearly all his poetry had been written before he was twenty years old. According to the magazine, this titanic talent was 'the late Arthur Rimbaud'.

Rimbaud, in fact, was not dead. He had left France for Africa in 1880 and was currently living in Tadjourah, awaiting a consignment of guns he intended to sell to King Menelik. A taut, tanned adventurer, it was as if a Baudelairean poet had been transformed into a cohort of Richard Burton. His new attitude towards writing can be seen, askance, when his business partner, Pierre Labatut, dies suddenly the next year. Despite his widow's pleas and in front of her eyes, Rimbaud burns all thirty-four volumes of Labatut's memoirs, 'a great misfortune, I later learned,' he says, 'as certain property deeds were shuffled in amongst these confessions.'

He had never been particularly reverential with manu-scripts. *Les Illuminations* had been constructed from a sheaf of papers handed by Rimbaud to his ex-lover, the poet Paul Verlaine, in 1875. Almost the entire print-run of *Une Saison en enfer* (*A Season in Hell*) was mouldering in a warehouse in Brussels, eventually to be rediscovered ten years after Rim-baud's actual death. The editors of the Pléiade edition described his 'slim and flashing work which, at the end of the nineteenth century, Arthur Rimbaud left to us with a kind of disdain, and without having bothered to publish almost any of it'.

Rimbaud's corpus is slight; but as thin and sharp as a stiletto. Had Verlaine, in one of his jealous rages, discarded the papers, Rimbaud's reputation would be as the ghostly memory of a petulant and deliberately impudent youth on Verlaine's arm, and a few scattered works in literary magazines. His entire oeuvre could well have stretched from the school-book, where phrases like 'Arthur / The infinitely little' sit beside his denunciations of Latin ('maybe it's some sort of made-up language') and his arithmetical notes ('If 2 cubic metres of wood cost 32F how much would 7 decimetres cost?'), up to the African accounts ('35 Abyssinians @ 15 Thalers for the journey and two months back pay @ 3 Thalers, payment promised on arrival, 34 × 21 . . . 714 Thalers'), with nothing in between.

Assiduous scholars and opportunistic friends have attempted to enlarge this smattering of genius. Verlaine, for example, quoted as an epigraph to his poem 'Ariettes oubliées' a line by Rimbaud – 'It rained softly on the city' – which does not appear in any of his works. Rimbaud's school-friend Ernest Delahaye had remembered by heart two rather copro-philic little sonnets, which were published in 1923. He could also recollect a snatch of a satire against pro-monarchist grocers, though the text no doubt ended up in the bin at the newspaper to which it was supposedly sent.

Another school-friend, Paul Labarrière, waited until 1933 to confess that he had managed to lose a notebook containing fifty or sixty of Rimbaud's poems, whilst moving house in 1885. Apart from remembering a poem about 'geese and ducks splashing around in a pond', almost all he could recollect was a line full of the typical Rimbaud bravado: 'And the drunken poet rebukes the Universe'.

Desperate for any extra scrap, how many scholars must have lamented the aside left by another of Rimbaud's colleagues in Africa, Ugo Ferrandi? 'He provided me with some precise and lucid observations about Tadjourah which I once intended to publish, along with some notes of my own, but fate did not decree this to be. I still have several pages of these notes by Rimbaud.' The trail goes cold just there.

There is a blank at the heart of Rimbaud. How did the homosexual, blasphemous, drunken, demonically gifted poet transform himself into a reputedly temperate merchant who discussed the Qur'an with local Muslims? Are the poems some kind of ciphered message that can explain, or enact, the metamorphosis? Is it all supposed to *mean* something? Is the answer lost in a misplaced notebook?

'If I don't write to you any more it's because I'm very tired and also because with me, as with you, there is nothing new to write about,' he wrote to his family in 1882. And two years later: 'In the end, as the Muslims say: It is written! That's life and it's no laughing matter.'

Frank Norris

(1870–1902)

Twelve years after his death, a novel by Frank Norris which was thought destroyed in the San Francisco earthquake of 1906 was found. *Vandover and the Brute*, his study of moral degeneration and lycanthropy, was Norris' second post-humous novel. Literature is so rarely found, once lost, that *Vandover and the Brute* should be a cause for celebration. But the pleasure was subdued, given that another, possibly more significant, work was irretrievably gone.

Norris had found fame in 1899 with *McTeague*, an unremit-tingly ferocious novel about human greed and inhuman desires. With its deviant psychologies and frank depictions of brutish sexuality, critics immediately associated it with the work of Emile Zola. It was a comparison relished by Norris, who signed letters and autographed books with his self-given nickname 'The Boy Zola'. Just as Zola had announced himself with the shocking *La Bête humaine* and then progressed to a more ambitious project, so too would Norris.

Even before *McTeague*, he had fixed his eye on his major literary goal. In 1897, in a letter to the Literary Editor of the *San Francisco Examiner*, he had written, 'There are two ways

of considering the question of the "great American novel".
One as to the best novel produced by an American author,
and the other as to the novel which is the most thoroughly
American in its tone and most aptly interprets the phasos of
American life'. Norris' intention was to produce the latter.

In 1899, he had the Idea, an idea so immediate and vast he
woke his friend Bruce Porter at 5 a.m. to tell him. He wrote
to the novelist and critic William Dean Howells, explaining
it in detail. It was 'thoroughly American', and took California
as its background:

My Idea is to write three novels around the one subject of *Wheat*.
First, a story of California (the Producer), second, a story of Chicago
(the distributor), third, a story of Europe (the Consumer) and in
each to keep to the idea of this huge Niagara of wheat rolling from
the West to the East.

The business of America was business: before Calvin Cool-
idge's dictum, Norris was using an economic process as the
structural underpinning of his epic trilogy. Although it was
'straight naturalism with all the guts I can get into it', Norris
was presenting a radically different vision from Zola. Whereas
Zola's characters were driven by inherited conditions, Norris
was to explore economic conditions. As Cedarquist in the
first part of *The Octopus* presciently puts it: 'The Great Word
of the nineteenth century has been Production. The Great
Word of the twentieth century will be – listen to me, you
youngsters – Markets'.

The Octopus appeared in 1901. It deals with the conflict
between Californian farmers and the Pacific and South-
western Railway Trust. The farmers have leased the land,
irrigated it, planted it, and expect to buy it for around $5 an
acre. The Company, however, alters its prices, pushing them
up to $40 an acre. Political machinations and corrupt bureau-
cracy spawn armed resistance and internecine violence. It is

an archetypal American conflict: the individual frontiersman versus the capitalist monopoly. Norris researched thoroughly, and even in its journalistic factionality and fidelity (though some called it muckraking) *The Octopus* was a new benchmark in the American-ness of American novels.

When the second volume, *The Pit* – about the brokerage of the wheat on the Chicago exchange – appeared, Norris was already dead from peritonitis. He was only thirty-two. Nonetheless, the preface was published as he had planned. It announced a book he would never write.

The Trilogy of The Epic of the Wheat includes the following novels:
THE OCTOPUS, a Story of California.
THE PIT, a Story of Chicago.
THE WOLF, a Story of Europe.

The Wolf, we are told, 'will probably have for its pivotal episode the relieving of a famine in an Old World community'. Norris was planning his trip to Europe, and another trilogy on the Battle of Gettysburg, only days before his death. Welcome though *Vandover and the Brute* is, if we had *The Wolf*, Norris' reputation might now be far higher. William Dean Howells captured the elegiac quality of the incomplete epic precisely:

The two novels he has left behind him are sufficient for his fame, but though they have their completeness and their adequacy, one cannot help thinking of the series of their like that is now lost to us. It is Aladdin's palace, and yet,

'The unfinished window in Aladdin's palace
Unfinished must remain,'

and we never can look upon it without an ache of longing and regret.

Franz Kafka

(1883–1924)

Franz Kafka was exceptionally clear about what should happen to his literary remains. In 1921 he said to his friend Max Brod, 'My will is going to be quite simple – a request to you to burn everything.' Brod refused, and Kafka never made a will, but amongst his papers, two notes were found.

DEAREST MAX, my last request: everything I leave behind me (that is, in the bookcases, chest of drawers, writing-table, both at home and in the office, or wherever anything may have got to, whatever you happen to find), in the way of notebooks, manuscripts, letters, my own and other people's, sketches and so on, is to be burned unread to the last page, as well as all writings of mine or notes which either you may have or other people, from whom you are to beg them in my name. Letters which are not handed over to you should at least be faithfully burned by those who have them.

In pencil, rather than in ink, was what appeared to be a draft of this note:

DEAR MAX, perhaps this time I shan't recover, pneumonia is likely enough after the month of pulmonary fever I have had, and not even setting it down in writing will keep it off, although there's some power even in that.

Just in case, then, this is my last will concerning all I have written:

Of all my writings the only books that count are these: *The Judgement, The Stoker, Metamorphosis, Penal Colony, Country Doctor,* and the short story: *Hunger-Artists.* (The few copies that exist of the *Meditation* can be left; but I don't want to give anyone the trouble of pulping them, but there's to be no reprinting.) When I say that these five books and the short story count, I don't mean that I want them to be printed again and handed down to posterity; on the contrary, should they disappear altogether that would be what I want. Only, since they do exist, I don't mind anyone's keeping them if he wants to.

But everything else of mine that I have written (printed in magazines or newspapers, written in manuscripts or letters) without exception, so far as it can be got hold of, or begged from the addressees . . . – all this without exception and preferably unread (though I don't mind you looking into it, but I would much prefer that you didn't, and in any case no one else is to look at it) – all this, without exception, is to be burned, and that you should do it as soon as possible is what I beg of you.

To Gustav Janouch, an aspiring poet and the son of one of his colleagues, Kafka was equally adamant. Janouch had bound some stories in leather, and Kafka insisted that his 'own materialization of horror . . . should be burned'.

It was not that Kafka lacked the mettle to destroy his work himself. In 1923, he and Dora Diamant, his last love, committed a large amount of material to the flames. This conflagration included letters, the final pages of the short story 'The Burrow', a play and a story about ritual murder in Odessa. He had burned manuscripts to keep warm, wrote all night and then immediately destroyed the results, and constantly edited his slender oeuvre in the most drastic manner.

Brod refused to honour his friend's wishes. He rationalized

his decision by maintaining that Kafka had always known he would refuse to comply, and that by addressing the instructions to him, Kafka had entrusted his works to the one person he knew would preserve them. Thus, the letters' ostensible meaning was, at best, adolescent posturing and, at worst, evidence that he was not in sound mind at the time of their writing. So in 1925, *The Trial* appeared, followed by *The Castle* (1926), *Amerika* (1927), *The Great Wall of China and Other Stories* (1931) and *Diaries 1910–1923* (1951). Seven hundred pages of letters he sent to Félice Bauer, who was twice his fiancée, became available to the public in 1967, fifteen years after his equally distraught and self-lacerating correspondence with his lover and Czech translator Milena Jesenká had been published.

Did Max Brod do the right thing? The fact that Kafka's reputation rose exponentially after his death, to the extent that he has become one of the central figures of twentieth-century Modernism, would seem to suggest that Brod's transgression was eminently forgivable. There are, however, certain ironies that complicate the picture of an unrecognized genius.

Kafka did not complete any of the novels, and both *Amerika* and *The Castle* are unfinished. If he had prepared *Amerika* for publication, certain anomalies might have been resolved. Karl Rossman, the protagonist, is confronted at the end with the 'Nature Theatre of Oklahama' (the misspelling being preserved from Arthur Holitscher's *Amerika heute und morgen*): whether this strange, fake, commercialized heaven was to be a fool's paradise or a genuine redemption is unknown. Likewise, the ultimate fate of K, the central character in *The Castle*, is beyond our reach. Brod claimed it would end with K dying of exhaustion, and in the extant version we have K seemingly at the nadir of his fortunes, deserted by Frieda, confounded in his scheme to enter the Castle and aware that he will never meet the mysterious and powerful Klamm. But with a writer as profoundly sensitive to the vertiginous depths to which humanity can sink, we cannot be sure that even this apparent pit might not belie some even deeper despondency. We cannot underestimate Kafka's sense of *worst*.

The Trial, at least, has its ending. Joseph K, about whom someone must have been telling lies, buffeted and rebuffed in his attempt to clarify the exact nature of the accusation against him, and the nature of the trial itself, throws himself into the arms of his executioners. The form in which we read *The Trial* is not, however, unimpeachably Kafkaesque. Although the manuscript was divided into chapters and the chapters had titles, Brod had to 'depend on [his] own judgement' as to their arrangement, based on having heard Kafka read sections of his work in progress. His editorial decisions were 'supported by actual recollection': not the firmest of critical foundations. Brod admitted that 'various further stages of the mysterious trial should have been described', but argued that since we know from the last chapter that Joseph K never reached the highest court, the intervening, torturous section 'could be prolonged into infinity'. With an almost arrogant assurance, Brod believed that if readers did not know about the book's lacunae, they 'would scarcely notice its deficiencies', such as the jump from late autumn to late spring between the penultimate and final chapters.

The absence of a trial in *The Trial* is a central tenet of Modernist aesthetics, and yet to attribute this to authorial design rather than textual fragmentation is a mistake. As Kafka again said to Brod, 'I am not going to include the novels. Why rake up these old attempts? Only because they happen not to have been burned yet?' In a typically self-obliterating sentence, Kafka suggested that if someone 'hoped to create a whole out of the fragments, some complete work' it would be 'impossible here, there is no help for me in these. So what am I to do with these things? Since they can't help me am I to let them harm me, as must be the case, given my knowledge about them?'

It is too easy to cast Kafka as a twentieth-century Virgil,

demanding that since *The Aeneid* is not perfected, it should be burned. But Kafka's insistence on the destruction of his papers is not retroactive vanity in the face of bad reviews. In some way, the latent incendiary quality, the transitory nature of his texts, is paramount.

Of all writers, Kafka is the most shatteringly aware of the abuse of power. This self-awareness led him to earnest protestations of his worthlessness, as he recognized those impulses in himself; he was 'infinitely dirty', he told Milena. He knew the inefficacy of writing as a defence against the horrors: in a chilling passage he relates a 'swoon' that comes over him as he criticized a piece of theatre: 'What are you talking about? What's the matter? Literature, what is that? Where does it come from? What use is it?'

He knew, at some visceral level, about peremptory and non-reversible judgements, implacable, unjust rules and meek submission to the eventual knife. Although he was the least willing to impose his will or exert his force, he knew that writing was an act of violence, and that when we talk about the 'power' of a text, this is not unrelated to the power wielded by tyrants. He wrote:

Altogether I think we ought to read only books that bite and sting us. If a book we are reading does not shake us awake like a blow on the skull, why bother reading it in the first place? So that it can 'make us happy', as you put it? Good God, we'd be just as happy if we had no books at all . . . what we need are books that hit us like the most painful misfortune . . . that make us feel as though we had been banished to the woods . . . a book must be an axe for the frozen sea within us.

Kafka wanted his manuscripts burned because they were meant to hurt.

Ezra Loomis Pound

(1885–1972)

The Bookman for July 1909 announced that Ezra Pound, whose collection *Personae* had just been published, had already destroyed considerably more than he had written, his 'faculty for self-criticism' having incinerated 'two novels and three hundred sonnets'. As always with Pound, his customary bluster concealed a grainy irritant of truth. Apart from a slender pamphlet *A Quinzaine for this Yule*, the only work available to the English-reading public was *A Lume Spento*, a volume privately printed in Venice and currently malingering in A. R. Orage's bookshop. The earliest work of the man who would transform twentieth-century poetry cannot be described more accurately than by Walter de la Mare's later phrase 'patchoulied fallalaries'.

He told friends that he wrote a Petrarchan sonnet every morning, and immediately ripped it up. By such regular, technical exercise, he built up the formidable metrical skills that are evident in his later work. Fiction, however, was more troublesome. Two short stories, 'La Dogesa's necklace' and 'Genoa', were certainly sent to the American magazine *Smart Set*, but they declined to publish them and the sole copies disappeared. Pound claimed to lack the 'feminine power of endurance' that was necessary for full-length novels, but he was sufficiently astute to realize that the five chapters he wrote of one were just an 'interminable beginning', and 'damn bad'.

At the time he was dallying with prose narrative he had little to write about anyway. He knew he was a great poet, but he had not written any great poetry yet. He was a talented, if bumptious, American in Europe who had been bullied at university, listlessly engaged a few times and thrown out of a teaching job in Wabash College, Indiana, on account of bohemian philanthropy towards a wintering circus performer. A publicist without a product, but a very effective self-promoter nonetheless, he was assiduously courting the great and the good of London, making more impact with his shock of hair than with the shock of the new. Ezra was distinctly ersatz, a charge that would be flung at him repeatedly.

His patient mother helpfully suggested he might make his fortune by writing an epic poem about the Wild West – a *Billythekidiad* – but Pound was already cultivating a disdainful, dismissive tone towards most things American. He was, however, planning an epic. As early as 1904, he had been struck by his tutor, Joseph Ibbotson, talking about Bentley's edition of Milton and the germ of an idea of a 'forty-year epic'. At the time, he was more enthused about writing a trilogy of plays about the thrice-married, ostentatiously obscure tenth-century Lady Marozia. It is not known if he even started the work; but recondite pieces of Italian history would also find their place in his eventual epic. She herself is mentioned, very much in passing, in Canto XX.

The first instalment, *A Draft of XXX Cantos*, finally appeared in 1930, once Pound had left England. He spent the rest of his life writing it, and to this day, its ending, if it has one, is uncertain. *The Cantos* resembled his working method for short stories, as he outlined it to his father – 'I write them in the first person of any character that comes into my head & say anything I can think of that might make them sell' –

and, although personal financial benefit was hardly the *raison d'être* of the work, the nature of money would become a major theme.

At the outset, Pound seemed at ease with the open, unresolved structure of *The Cantos*. He told James Joyce it was 'an endless poem, of no known category, Phanopoeia or something or other, all about everything'. The range of subject matter is vast: Sigismundo Malatesta, 'a failure worth all the successes of his age', Confucius, the rise of usury in a hellish rendition of modern London, Captain Acoetes (whom, for a while, Pound considered for the narrator of *The Cantos*, 'only I dont see how I cd. get *him* to Bayswater') telling of the voyage of the god Dionysos, Pound's grandfather Thaddeus and his railway schemes, scraps of all of Ezra's obsessions from the Troubadours to Eleusinian Mysteries to Anglo-Saxon to Social Credit. The languages veer between erudite quotation, semi-mystical transfiguration and cracker-barrel antics. As with the radio, the reader could only 'tell who is talking by the noise they make': like an untuned radio, a crackle of interference allowed only snatches of the voice through.

If there is a theme, it is perhaps indicated by the title. The 'canto' division was used by Dante for his *Divine Comedy*, and Pound's *Cantos* seem like a godless, unlaughing, unforgiving version of absolute judgement. As T. S. Eliot realized, Pound's Hell 'consists of other people'. He himself was exempt from the condemnations and punishments. He was not a fellow sufferer, but the implacable judge. *The Cantos*, like *The Divine Comedy*, opens descending into Hell, although this inferno is typified by liberalism, capitalism, warmongering and cultural desiccation. As Pound wrote more of *The Cantos*, the inferno to paradise undercurrent strengthened: a later volume was called *Thrones* in imitation of Dante's blessed spirits, and was a movement towards the heavenly. 'I've been around a bit, and know Paradise when I see it,' he claimed.

Unfortunately, he saw it in Fascism. Pound moved to Italy in 1925, and found in Mussolini the rise of a cultural superhero who could remedy many of the ills against which he was painstakingly raging. His ever more incoherent theories about money supply, economic stagnation and cultural rejuvenation made him deeply susceptible to the balmy palliatives of Fascist rhetoric. As he waged a private war against 'usury', he segued seamlessly into pitiably predictable anti-Semitism. He started to broadcast for the Italian government, lauding Mussolini and fulminating against the pernicious Americans.

The Cantos themselves reflected this: paper money was only a symbol for wealth, and just as Pound's brief-lived, self-christened phase of 'Imagism' had forgone lazy metaphors and easy similes in poetry, he now fulminated against the phoniness of banknotes. Monetary philosophy and fiscal metaphysics became the circulating medium of the poetry. They became so obscure and personal that even the Fascist government, on receipt of a letter outlining his pet theories and copies of his poetry, was inclined to view his Utopia as 'the botched plan of a nebulous mind devoid of any sense of reality'. Nevertheless, they allowed him to broadcast his opinions. At the time, one of them involved the idea that the USA should cede Guam to the Japanese in exchange for 300 film reels of Noh drama.

As the Allies advanced, Pound gave himself over to them. He was kept in a cage, exposed to the sun and surrounded by barbed wire at a compound near Pisa and gradually assembled his Cantos for that period. 'Pull down thy vanity,' he says in Canto LXXXI, though the reader is unsure whether this refers to his captors, or the sudden impinging of regret. He was transferred to America to stand trial for treason, and, after a plea of insanity, spent twelve years in an asylum, St Elizabeths, where acclaimed poets and deluded racists would sit at his feet.

It was there that he won, in 1949, the Bollingen Poetry

Prize for the Pisan Cantos, those 'insane and verified ravings of a confessed madman', as Radio Moscow put it. Though *The Cantos* contain multitudes, at least Pound's belief that he was going to learn Georgian to speak to Stalin was omitted. He did not write much, but mused on what this ever-swelling epic actually meant. The Dante parallel warped, but did not change. Cantos I to L were 'a detective story. Looking around to see what's wrong.' The rest would be his glimpses of an ideal city, a perfect order: but, on the page, it rarely appeared except as shuffled snippets of outré information.

When he was released in 1958, Pound was already the centre of reverential academic interest in the phenomenon of *The Cantos*, as well as scalding asides about the politics contained therein. On one hand, the playwright Arthur Miller denounced his work as 'sheer obscenity', while on the other Hugh Kenner cautioned his team of pre-publication readers not to emend Pound's frequent misspellings, since they might be ruining some yet-to-be-got joke.

Scholars read the fragmentation of the poem as a reflection of its time, as a reflection of his mind. Pound himself had counterpoised the 'principle of order / vs split atom', and various interpretations posited chaotic descent, Dantean voyage and autobiographical confession as the way to read *The Cantos*, even when the project was unfinished. The poem was not, however, heading for a glorious conclusion. Armageddon and Utopia vacillated as closure. Exhausted, broken and ill, Pound welcomed the critic Donald Hall, saying, 'You – find me – in fragments.'

Excerpts from some mental vision of the finished Cantos were scribbled down: 'Let the Gods forgive what I / have made', 'to be men not destroyers'. With the lines 'Her name was Courage / & is written Olga', he transfigured his mistress, 'These lines are for the / ultimate CANTO / whatever I may write // in the interim'. The poem has different endings depending on the editor's assessment of these final utterances.

The final sputtering-out of the Cantos, was, in a way, pre-figured by Malatesta's maxim 'tempus loquendi, tempus tacendi' – a time to speak, a time to be silent.

The Cantos remains a challenge to contemporary poetry, a labyrinth of meanings and methods, a gauntlet thrown down to those who think poetry should be easy. Its difficulties are not just problems caused by Pound's idiosyncratic hoard of knowledge, but lie in facing the density and ambiguity of that period. Whatever Pound's mendacious and idiotic beliefs, his poem resists final solutions.

Allen Ginsberg had managed to hear a recantation of Pound's anti-Semitic and anti-democratic prejudices, a change corroborated in some of his final letters, where, in a searing realization, he saw avarice, not usury, as the aboriginal sin, and saw his hate-filled broadcasts as an example of the small-mindedness he had always claimed to abhor. But as for the poem, this irruption of truthfulness came too late for his stricken powers to express it. His own epitaph on the interminable, unfinishable *Cantos* is a stark monosyllable: 'botched'.

Thomas Stearns Eliot

(1888–1965)

Nineteen twenty-four did not look as if it would be any better a year for T. S. Eliot than 1923, or '22, or '21 had been. Although his poem *The Waste Land* had been published in 1922 and won the Dial Prize for the best work published that year, reviewers still tended to stress its difficulty, claiming it to be 'ensorcelled mazes' and 'labyrinths utterly'. With the help of Ezra Pound, the poem had been unearthed from the much longer draft entitled *He Do the Police in Different Voices*, Eliot having managed to edit it during his recuperation from a mental breakdown in 1921. A similar crisis was narrowly averted in 1922. The following year, his wife Vivien came close to death: her own psychological and physical illness had, in part, precipitated his own.

In 1924 Eliot had spent seven years working for Lloyds Bank, using his linguistic skills to read not Jules Laforgue's symbolist poetry, but Continental financial reports. Solvency came at a price, and Pound had been soliciting patrons and friends to raise enough money for Eliot to leave the bank. In addition to the quotidian business of business, he had taken on the onerous responsibility of editing *Criterion* magazine. In only a year, a position would become his at the publishers

Faber & Gwyer: such a prospect seemed inconceivably remote at the time. Eliot was writing little, though the title of his 1925 poem 'The Hollow Men' would supply any biographically inclined critic with sufficient material to deduce how he viewed his time with Lloyds.

Readers of the *Harvard College Class of 1910 Quindecennial Report*, published in 1925, would have been forgiven for thinking that Eliot had reached some accommodation between the spheres of avant-garde poetics and monetary exchange rates, for, amongst his publications, they would have seen *Literature and Export Trade*. Writing to his bibliographer in 1936, Eliot claimed that the title was either a 'small leg-pull of my own' or the result of some misunderstanding on the part of the alumni report editors. At the time, he was writing articles for the monthly in-house magazine *Lloyds Bank Economic Review* on foreign currency movements. The articles in the journal were anonymous, and Eliot teased that only 'internal evidence' might distinguish his own contributions from those of the previous post-holder, and the successive one. In economic theory, as in poetry, the extinguishing of the self seemed paramount. Suffice it to say that, to date, no one has uncovered any Lloyds reports on the inflation of the deutschmark that contain anything like 'Present expenditure and past investment are both perhaps dependent on future predicted rates, in order for their risks to be sufficiently evaluated', or 'Between the outlay and the return falls the Shadow of an unstable international market, still recovering from the recent war'.

Since *Literature and Export Trade* was never, it seems, even a possibility, should we mourn its absence? Pound embroiled himself in the worst excesses of the period through his hastily conceived notions of economics, and it might be salient to show that Eliot's more measured understanding inoculated him against enthusing over Social Credit or legal tender with built-in obsolescence. Similarly, if *Literature and Export Trade* had examined how the differing literary markets in America and Britain operated, or how the importation of experimental foreign literature influenced writers in a way that then impacted back on to the original culture, it would have been intriguing.

But as it is, *Literature and Export Trade* is most likely two fingers flicked by a bored and depressed writer at the relentlessly mundane profession he reluctantly espoused. The existence of just a title permits a modicum of insight and a plethora of possibility.

Thomas Edward Lawrence

(1888–1935)

The myth of T. E. Lawrence ('of Arabia') frequently threatens to supplant the man. The gaunt good looks of Peter O'Toole playing Lawrence on film surreptitiously overwrite his actual jut of jaw. Lawrence could, in fact, imagine himself on celluloid, but only as a creation of Walt Disney. Versions and variations multiply: a mental patient was discovered impersonating him. He changes his name by deed-poll after his own breakdown. One friend sees in him a mirror for all men; another thinks that the only hope for Britain is a pact between Lawrence and Hitler. One biographer describes him as evolving into 'the Truly Strong Man'; another denounces him as an 'impudent mythomaniac' and a closet homosexual prone to panic attacks. The image fabricated for him jostles with the image projected by him. He was an illegitimate child who nonetheless became, in his own words, 'a sublimated Aladdin, the thousand and second knight'. He colluded in and distanced himself from his own persona. In *The Seven Pillars of Wisdom* he claims to have personally destroyed seventy-nine bridges during the Arabian revolt: in fact, he had blown up twenty-three.

Given the manifold contradictions, evasions, self-aggrandizements and mystifications of his character, it is in keeping that the manuscript history of his most famous work, *The Seven Pillars of Wisdom*, is also tainted by these traits. Lawrence may have helped liberate the Middle East from Turkish rule, but he aspired to being a small publisher of modernist prose. The form as we have it was first published in 1922 – the Oxford Edition – with a print-run of six copies. A subscriber's edition, lavishly illustrated with avant-garde colour plates, was issued in 1926, at the exorbitant price of thirty guineas. Lawrence was cagey about how many copies actually existed: 128 were sold to subscribers, and several other copies were given to friends. George Doran published twenty-two copies in the USA, with ten going on sale at $20,000 per volume. Although an abridged edition was available, there was no full edition for the general public until after Lawrence's death. Enigmatic as ever, Lawrence wrote a book he thought the equivalent of *War and Peace* or *Moby Dick*, but attempted to control its reading; unless, of course, it was a superbly managed promotional campaign.

Lawrence's account of the part he played in the Arab Revolt between 1916 and 1918 began its existence as a travel book. According to Robert Graves, Lawrence started a book in 1910 about the crusaders and Cairo, Smyrna, Constantinople, Beirut, Aleppo, Damascus and Medina, but destroyed the manuscript. All that remained was the title, reused for his wartime memoirs. Lawrence also burned the second manuscript version of this work, a version he referred to as the 'original-and-to-be-kept secret', while rewriting the text that was eventually published. This problematic approach to authorship continued after *The Seven Pillars of Wisdom* finally appeared; in his study of RAF life, *The Mint*, written under the pseudonym 352087 A/c Ross. Lawrence's dedication to Edward Garnett reads: 'You dreamed I came one night with this book crying, "It's a masterpiece. Burn it." Well – *as you please.*'

The first draft disappeared in Reading station. Lawrence was travelling from London to Oxford in the autumn of 1919, and stopped in the refreshment room, with the manuscript in a black banker's bag, which he put under the table. Although he claimed the bag was stolen, he also confided to another biographer, Liddell Hart, that perhaps he *involuntarily* allowed it to be lost. The subsequent versions were 'shorter, snappier and more truthful'; but, given his propensity for tweaking and finessing the truth, even that statement cannot be taken as definitive.

Take, for example, the infamous Der'a incident. In the Oxford edition, Lawrence clearly, though subtly, refers to some kind of sexual molestation when he was captured by a Turkish bey. Despite graphically described torture, he none-theless escapes and is back in active service remarkably quickly. One letter has been widely interpreted as hinting at a certain willing submission, despite the assertion in the same epistle that Lawrence even found that writing about what happened made him sick. Legions of biographers must have dreamed that the manuscript lost at Reading made clear not only what had happened, but what Lawrence felt about it. That such a traumatic event could be immediately and unambiguously poured into words seems psychologically implausible.

What is certain is that if the first draft was stolen, then the light-fingered culprit had a bag of papers more valuable than bank notes or bullion, had he or she the patience to allow the contents to maximize their value. With copies of the printed version changing hands at auction for between £20,000 and £30,000, and individual autograph letters reaching as much as £2,000, a nearly complete first draft would be an excep-tionally precious commodity – indeed, most auction houses would only venture a whistle and repeat the word 'thousands' a few times. The price of Lawrence's private pain increases exponentially, as collectors and biographers alike conspire in the idea that behind the array of self-made and imposed icons, there must be a confession with the aura of incontrovertible truth.

Bruno Schulz

(1892–1942)

I am simply calling it The Book without any epithets or qualifications, and in this vast sobriety there is a shade of helplessness, a silent capitulation before the vastness of the transcendental, for no word, no allusion, can adequately suggest the shiver of fear, the presentiment of a thing without name that exceeds all our capacity for wonder.

So begins 'The Book', the first piece in Bruno Schulz's second collection, *Sanatorium Under the Sign of the Hourglass*. Like its predecessor, *Cinnamon Shops* (in English, retitled *The Street of Crocodiles*), it is a series of linked short stories, where the Galician town of Drohobycz is transmogrified and metamorphosed through the eyes of the narrator, Joseph N. The Book in 'The Book' was an epiphanic volume glimpsed in childhood: his father would later attempt to pass off the Bible as the Book; another character maintains they have been using its pages to wrap up sandwiches and butcher's meat. Recapturing the vision of this lost book is a subterranean motif in Schulz. It also, tragically, mirrors the fate of his own work.

★

Bruno Schulz was a quiet, frightened man, who taught drawing at the King Władysław Jagiełło State Gymnasium in his beloved Drohobycz. His graphics, depicting grotesque, squat men – weird hybrids of Chagall and the Golem – and impossibly elegant women, were gradually earning acclaim, though barely replacing his income. He was also, along with his friend Władysław Riff, experimenting with prose. When Riff died in 1927, Schulz lost a creative spur as well as a trusted friend: it would take him six years to present his stories to a publisher. Riff died of tuberculosis, and the sanitary officers who disinfected his lodgings, through fear of an epidemic, or in sheer carelessness, burned all of Riff's manuscripts, and his letters from Schulz. He was, at one time, engaged to be married to Józefina Szelińska, whom he helped to translate Kafka's *The Trial* into Polish: his name was erroneously substituted for hers on the title-page.

Drohobycz was the universe for Schulz. It was itself and a cabbalistic symbol for everywhere; not a microcosm so much as a metaphor. Although he spent one vacation in Paris, he scurried, like an inverted smolt, back to the village, in that piece of Poland that had become Austrian Galicia and would soon careen between Germany and the Soviet Union. It is today part of the Ukraine.

Schulz knew he had to leave. He hoped, no doubt, that he would return. And he made sure his manuscripts were safe. Zbigniew Moroń, a friend of Schulz, remembered his saying he had left his work with 'someone else whom I did not know, he told me the name, but unfortunately I completely forgot it'. To Izydor Friedman, with whom he was sorting Landau's hoard of books, Schulz confided that a 'Catholic from outside of the ghetto' had his papers for safekeeping.

As early as 1934, Schulz had mentioned a novel in progress, entitled *Messiah*. The work was painstaking, and frequently deferred, or laid aside: sometimes he was silent about it, other times he merely said he was stalled. Those who heard him read sections claim it began with Joseph N being woken by his mother, who tells him, excitedly, that the Messiah has been seen in a village only 30 kilometres from Drohobycz. No one knew much more than that. In a letter Schulz described the book as a 'regression' to a time of 'fullness and limitlessness . . . My ideal is "to mature" into childhood'. As he worked on *Messiah*, the past must have seemed increasingly Edenic.

He was planning to leave the day he was shot. Fake travel documents and Aryan identity papers had been obtained through sympathetic friends. He had survived the German occupation since he was the protégé of the local Gestapo officer, Felix Landau, for whom he painted his children's nursery, catalogued his looted books and even produced a portrait. Landau was not, however, some SS Schindler. He had murdered the Jewish barber designated as a 'necessary Jewish worker' to the neighbouring Gestapo chief, Karl Günther. Günther, in return, killed Schulz, and later boasted to Landau, 'You killed my Jew – I killed yours.'

In 1987, the Polish poet and renowned Schulz scholar Jerzy Ficowski was telephoned by a man who announced himself as the illegitimate son of Bruno Schulz's elder brother, Izydor. Alex Schulz had been contacted in California by a New Yorker who claimed to be from Lwów, near Drohobycz. This unnamed individual had seen a package, weighing approximately 2 kilograms, containing eight drawings, the rest being made up of manuscript pages written in Polish. Two kilograms is approximately 1,500 printed paperback pages. It was, he said, by Bruno Schulz, and worth, he presumed, $10,000.

Time passed. Alex Schulz contacted Ficowski to say their mysterious seller had been in touch again, then went silent. Ficowski later learned that Alex had suffered a cerebral haemorrhage. He never passed on the name of his contact. Had that been the end of the story, one would be forgiven for thinking that a tragic accident had curtailed an unseemly plot to con a professor and a relative.

But in 1990, the Swedish Ambassador to Poland, Jean Christophe Öberg, contacted Ficowski. At a diplomatic meeting, a Soviet civil servant had let him know that a packet of papers had been found, mis-shelved, in the KGB archives relating to the Gestapo. The top sheet announced the novel *Messiah*.

The USSR was in the last throes of collapse. Visas were denied, for duplicitous and then paranoid reasons. Öberg died of cancer. His discreet lips had never passed on the name of the source in the archive. The Soviet Union fragmented. This particular *Messiah*'s first coming is hopefully still in the pending tray of a minor bureaucrat in a former superpower.

Ernest Hemingway

(1899–1961)

If there were a prize for the most accident-prone author, Ernest Hemingway would have won it before he received either the Pulitzer or the Nobel. He broke bones in several car crashes, escaped from one plane crash, contracted anthrax, was grazed by several bullets, and on occasion actually shot, cut his eyeball, suffered congestion of the kidneys and liver problems, pulled a skylight down on himself and endured countless bashes, scrapes, knocks, collapses and tumbles.

One accident, however, rendered even this most macho of authors speechless. In 1922, Hadley Hemingway (the first of his four wives) was travelling to Switzerland with her husband's effects. At the time, Ernest had written much, but very little had been published. He had managed 'six perfect sentences', and was already well advanced in a novel about his experiences in the First World War. Amongst the valises and trunks Hadley was transporting was a case with everything Ernest had written to date. Somehow, it was stolen.

He had been developing a theory that even if something was edited out of a work of art, its trace would linger. Now he had to face the full ramifications, the *reductio ad absurdum*, of this idea. The fact that both Ezra Pound and Gertrude

Stein had told him to ditch everything he had written and start again must have been little comfort. Every author produces juvenilia. Most destroy it. The theft of Hemingway's manuscripts short-circuited the whole process. Had he spent the next ten years trying to perfect his immature jottings, we might never have seen the novels of which he was capable.

The image of Hemingway – 'Papa', the boxer, fisher, hunter, brawler – almost eradicates the fresh-faced, unpublished and nervous boy of 1922. Of course, he harboured the germs of his combative persona: apropos of the death of Joseph Conrad, two years later, Hemingway wrote in *Transatlantic Review* that if 'by grinding Mr [T. S.] Eliot into a fine dry powder and sprinkling that powder over Conrad's grave' he might resurrect the novelist, then 'early tomorrow morning with a sausage-grinder' he would leave for London. But the bullish façade was still under construction, not yet concrete. The day after Hadley, distraught, arrived without a significant piece of luggage, Hemingway travelled to confirm that everything – every sheaf, notebook and carbon copy – was truly gone. They were.

'I remember what I did in the night after I let myself into the flat and found it was true,' he wrote, but never revealed whether rage, or booze, or even tears were his response. Despite his fame as a crack shot and tenacious angler, what grizzled Old Hem really felt about the books that got away is unknown – though he later claimed he would have opted for surgery if it might remove the memory of the loss. His motto – *il faut (d'abord) durer* – one must (above all) endure – was tested as much by pen and ink as on the savannah and the open seas.

Dylan Marlais Thomas

(1914–53)

If nothing else, Dylan Thomas is most people's idea of a modern poet. He is the hybrid of celebrity and poverty, swanning around in New York and schlepping about in Swansea, a pot-bellied genius and an evangelical boozer, with a permanent fag at a chipper angle in the corner of his mouth. Honey-tongued and beery-breathed, he is heading for the grave and immortality. What's more, his poetry is supposedly incomprehensible. The critic Kenneth Hopkins referred to the battle between 'the scoffers and the understanders', and academics challenged their students to discern meanings in the one-night stands between words. What did 'a grief ago' or 'flowered anchor' actually signify?

Thomas was allergic to the notion that his poetry was meaningless. He hated Surrealism, and joked that in Hell, particular sinners (like the editor of *Verse*) will 'for all eternity . . . read the cantos of Ezra Pound to a company of red-hot devils'. The poems are oblique, even cryptic, but they are not inchoate blathering. Riddles have solutions, ciphers can be decoded: as he said to his publishers, 'every line *is* meant to be understood.' The poems had their *veritas*, even though it sprung from, and might only be glimpsed again, *in vino*.

How many good ideas did Thomas piss up against a wall? The BBC commissioned a translation of Ibsen's *Peer Gynt*, and Thomas' unreliability, strident demands for more money and chaotic personal life ensured that we can never know what he would have made of that irrepressible, feckless, flamboyant failure. In July 1940, he assured Laurence Pollinger, who was standing in for his regular agent, David Higham, that his publishers would see a short novel, *Adventures in the Skin Trade*, 'quite soon'; in September 1953 he was telling E. F. Bozman of J. M. Dent publishers that he was 'so glad' that they would reconsider the same book, and that 'when I come back from America, I intend to settle down & finish it'. Thomas died in New York on 9 November of that year.

Given the intricacy and complexity of his poetic output, it is surprising that Thomas took so readily to radio broadcasting. He adapted to the necessary immediacy of the form, and one work which he consequently produced, *Under Milk Wood*, remains his most popular, even though it was only performed on the stage before his death. The genesis of *Under Milk Wood* is a peculiarly haphazard mishmash of abortive projects. It was not even, initially, imagined as 'a play for voices'.

In March 1948, Thomas was pitching to the *Picture Post* that he would love to write an article about Laugharne, where he had settled briefly, and which he would return to as a permanent address the next year. During the course of his proposal, he mentioned, *en passant*, that he was writing a radio play set there. The project would variously be called *The Town That Was Mad* and *LLareggub* (which, in typically Thomasy form, needs to be read backwards to get the joke). *Picture Post* declined to offer a commission, and another attempt to capture the cadences and accidents of rural Welsh life was postponed.

Ten years beforehand, Thomas had tried another tack. Writing to the aspiring poet Meurig Walters, he outlined a concept which he said he had sent to Keidrych Rhys, the editor of *Wales* magazine: a 'mass-poem'. Based on the principles of mass observation, the notional poem 'Wales' would involve all the contributors to the magazine writing a 'verse-report of his own particular town, village or district'; and the resulting entries, by random arrangement rather than editorial decision, should comprise a whole poem. Thomas was eager to solicit Walters as the Rhondda writer. However, no letter to Keidrych Rhys has ever surfaced, and it may be that Thomas, in true drink-sodden fashion, mistook a promise to himself to do something with the sense that he actually had.

Even once he was writing, and reading from *Under Milk Wood*, Thomas' propensities and fondnesses jeopardized the work ever seeing the light of day. In 1953 he wrote to Charles Elliott, of University College, Cardiff, asking a favour:

Do you remember that I had with me a suitcase & a briefcase, & that I transferred, some time in the evening, some of the contents of the briefcase into the suitcase? Well, anyway, I left the briefcase somewhere. I *think* it must be in the Park Hotel. I've written to the manager; but could you possibly; when & if passing by, drop in & see if it is there? It's very urgent to me: the only copy in the world of that kind-of-a-play of mine, from which I read bits, is in that battered, strapless briefcase whose handle is tied together with string.

If the thing isn't there, do you think you *could* find out where the hell I left it?

It was indeed so urgent, that, as Paul Ferris, the editor of Thomas' *Collected Letters* notes, he managed to lose it again in America, and then again in London, where it was found in a pub. Luck, for once, was on Thomas' side. For all his attempts to misplace *Under Milk Wood*, it refused to be lost. What was lost, however, was the poet himself. The self-styled 'Rimbaud of Cwmdonkin Drive' expired only three years older than his hero.

William S. Burroughs

(1914–97)

Reading *The Naked Lunch* is a disorientating experience. This is not solely because of its subjects: the drug-addled hallucination, the riddling sphincters, the paranoid intimations of impending disaster, the sexual degradation that unleashes psychic illumination; nor is it merely a product of the shifting tenses, coalescing characters and outrageous imagery. The text itself trembles with a sense of instability, a monstrous capacity for paranormal mutation, as if, on finishing it, the reader might start again and find a wholly different book in their hands. *The Naked Lunch* is an intoxicating, volatile volume.

Three different readers, one with a first edition from the Olympia Press in France, one with a US edition and the last with John Calder's UK edition, would find themselves embroiled in cross-purposes. Was it called *The Naked Lunch* or *Naked Lunch* or *Dead Fingers Talk*? Did everyone experience the fearful *déjà vu* of finding parts of the first paragraph also on page 170? When Allen Ginsberg, before the book had even been delivered to the publisher, referred to it as 'an endless novel that will drive everyone mad', he inadvertently described the experience of more than just a clutch of bibliographers trying to make sense of its publication history.

Myths cling to it like stains. Take the title. Burroughs once explained that *The Naked Lunch* referred to a 'frozen moment when everyone sees what's on the end of every fork', a sickly epiphany when consumption and greed become evident. The first publisher, the genius, pornographer and maverick Maurice Girodias, was told that it referred to the post-work, pre-dinner period for adulterous relationships, what the French refer to as the *cinq à sept*. Yet another explanation refers to Burroughs' first attempt at novel-writing, a detective story he and Jack Kerouac took turns penning, the still-unpublished *And the Hippos Were Boiled in Their Tanks*, where, supposedly, Burroughs mistyped 'naked lunch' for 'naked lust'. Which story is true? In the chaotic, quantum-fractured Burroughsverse, all of them contain a grain, or gram, of truth.

The book evolved out of what Burroughs had cut from his previous works, *Junkie* and *Queer*, as well as the so-called *Yage Letters* he sent back from Mexico. Given his nomadic existence and manner of working, the fact that anything resembling a manuscript was finally assembled is nothing short of miraculous. Girodias recalled Burroughs in Paris, as a 'grey phantom of a man in his phantom gabardine and ancient discoloured phantom hat, all looking like his mouldy manuscript', and insisted, against the testimony of Burroughs' friends, that the typescript had in part been eaten by rats.

Brion Gysin, Burroughs' collaborator, helped him move from London, organizing his twenty box-files, seventeen of which were marked 'Miscellaneous'. Paul Bowles offers a manic glimpse of Burroughs at work in Tangiers: he would type, or, when the typewriter was sold to pay for drugs, write longhand, tossing each page on to the floor where a pile of papers, covered with footprints and burying sandwiches, festered like an archaeological midden, occasionally blowing out of the window.

When it was assembled, nowhere near his entire output

was distilled into the various forms of *The Naked Lunch*. The *ur-text* was possibly a thousand pages long. Some pages, according to Brion Gysin, were later being sold at a dollar a sheet by Algerian street boys, salvaged from a suitcase of papers that Burroughs had hastily abandoned. The primordial swamp of words which had evolved into *The Naked Lunch* was not, however, spent effluvia. Burroughs developed, with Gysin, his 'cut-up' technique, where the reams were torn, folded and patched together to create new works. He believed that such ritualistic incisions could make the words reveal their true meaning: like a forensic shaman, he slaughtered and sacrificed quires and sheafs. The remnants were obliterated, reimagined, transformed and edited into *The Soft Machine* and *The Ticket That Exploded*.

'The fragmentary quality of my work is inherent,' Burroughs told Allen Ginsberg. The world was a wreck, shattered and splintered, yet full of hidden meanings and dark significances: squinting into the maelstrom might allow a man to realize that he was a sleeper, pre-programmed by occult espionage operatives, who could then escape from the tentacles of their influence. Everything was infected, except filth; everyone was hypocritical apart from the double-agents. If you could focus on the undulating pattern of the blur, rather than attempt to clarify the mirage, you might glimpse a quality beyond disillusion.

If Burroughs were merely a writer of copious first drafts, his manuscripts would be a curiosity, and ample fodder for an eager graduate student. But his methodology creates a kaleidoscope of possible books, an infinite number of sequences, each of which could, hypothetically, have revealed a different story altogether. His published work exists purely by virtue of its attendant swarm of virtual books, winking into and vanishing back out of our particular dimension.

Robert Traill Spence Lowell IV

(1917–77)

When Robert Lowell was fifteen years old, and had already earned the nickname 'Cal' (for Caligula), the poet Hart Crane jumped overboard and drowned. There was no causal link, though it raises a host of disturbing similes.

Crane, born in 1899, was only just too young to be in the vanguard of Modernist experimental poetry. He cruised the whole gamut of stylistic innovation: he imitated Pound's robust imagism and Eliot's vitreous ennui before realizing that neither model suited his ambitions or could adequately convey his experiences and enthusiasm. Eliot's disgust at the burgeoning metropolis and Pound's hankering after the medieval, the archaic and the obscure must have seemed equally pessimistic and equally elitist. Crane, as opposed to these self-imposed exiles who berated the philistinism of the States, wanted a 'mystic synthesis of America', a modern epic that lauded Chaplin and the Brooklyn Bridge as much as it shunned the neat, buttoned-up little quatrains of traditional poetry. Crane knew that the Modernists had opened radical new fields of expression, but wanted a voice that could 'go *through*' them towards a different engagement with the present.

As one of the many self-appointed laureates of America, Crane had a formidable, and internal, opposition to the role. Despite his louche good looks, he was hardly in the running for beau to the Homecoming Queen of the States Muse: high-school drop-out, gay, alcoholic and working in his father's candy store when he wasn't writing advertising copy. Eventually he was allowed to go to New York, where he indulged in dangerous affairs and problematic friendships, and gradually assembled the materials that would become *The Bridge*. He could have stayed at home and been but one more little suburban tragedy, rather than the operatic disaster he made of himself.

The Bridge (1930) was the Modernist epic, and, as such, critics denied it was an epic at all. Fragmentary and allusive, it was a book of loneliness and crowds: but where was heroism? Where was narrative? After winning a Guggenheim fellowship, Crane travelled to Mexico, in order to write another epic on the original encounter between America and Europe: the humiliation of Montezuma II before Cortés. In short, it was a poem that could address the perceived gap between the epic tradition and modern verse. He failed to write it, and became mired in drink, brawls and opportunistic sex, alienating his friends and frittering away his money. Returning home by boat, he declared to Peggy Cowley, 'I'm not going to make it dear, I'm utterly disgraced,' and bowed out over the railings of the S S *Orizaba*.

Robert Lowell also tried to write an epic, when he was at Harvard, a few years after Crane's death. The subject was the Crusades, and he was rebuffed by the poet Robert Frost, who pronounced that the poem '*did* seem to go on a bit'. But the whisper of Crane, as poet, man and symbol, kept needling in Lowell's mind: Crane's friend, and Lowell's tutor, Allen Tate wrote an 'Ode to the Confederate Dead', which Lowell, of old best-Bostonian stock, countered with 'For the Union

Dead'. Lowell wrote a remarkably sour elegy to Crane, where he ambiguously praised him as the 'Shelley of my age' who 'scattered Uncle Sam's / phoney gold-plated laurels'. By 1960, Lowell would, with patrician hauteur, admit that Crane was 'less limited' than his contemporaries. Most tellingly, when Lowell was suffering one of his frequent mental breakdowns, he would, as a friend wrote, 'talk about himself in connection with Achilles, Alexander, Hart Crane, Hitler and Christ'.

At school, Lowell had penned an essay entitled 'War: A Justification', foreshadowing his recurrent interest in belligerence, violence and resistance. The Crusades also provided him with an arena in which to vent his confusions about religion in general, and militant Catholicism in particular. Lowell, like Crane, was also concerned with how best to respond to the advances in aesthetic technique pioneered by the previous generation; and how to introduce American history and landscape into modern poetry. At first, he wrote elaborate, tightly mannered meditations on New England themes, suffused with Catholic symbolism at odds with his Puritan heritage, reminiscent of the Metaphysical poets. But the lure of the epic did not pass away entirely, and when he started on his 'long poem', it had nothing to do with the *Mayflower*, the Aztecs or the Fall of Jerusalem.

Lowell imagined that his collection *Life Studies* was 'a small scale *Prelude*'; an autobiography in metre 'written in many different styles and with digression'. The 'continuing story' evolved further into the free-verse sonnet sequences of *Notebook*, which itself was revised into *History*, *For Lizzie and Harriet* and *The Dolphin*. Magpie-like, Lowell stretched the form to accommodate newspaper copy, critical reviews of his work and even his ex-wife's anguished letters and telephone calls. As he says in 'The Misanthrope and the Painter', 'I pick lines from the trash'; and in the eyes of the poet Adrienne Rich, this stench of the garbage stuck to Lowell. Her review of *The Dolphin* berated him for the inclusion of 'private' materials, and denounced his 'bullshit eloquence'. 'A kind of aggrandized and merciless masculinity' typified the poetry; and though Rich intended this as a cutting insult, its sense of an almost Homeric palette and intensity applied to the life of a depressive, late-twentieth-century man is also oddly apposite. 'History has to live with what was here . . . it is so dull and gruesome how we die, / unlike writing, life never finishes' may not be as thrilling as Achilles' rage, but it captures a seriousness and resonance that might fittingly be termed epic.

Unlike Crane, Lowell never reached a quintessence of shame from which he could not return, despite behaviour that went far beyond disgracing himself. In his manic periods he had allegedly held Allen Tate out of a second-storey window while reciting 'Ode to the Confederate Dead'. In the asylum he had become inordinately attached to a piece of metal, which he claimed was 'the Totentanz' Hitler used to implement the Final Solution. Despite lithium treatment and electro-convulsive therapy, he was readmitted, hurt and crying, time and again.

One episode stands out, encapsulating Lowell's productivity, ambitious range and pitiable megalomania. He discharged himself from Greenways clinic in 1975, and was found in the fashionable L'Escargot restaurant, where he buttonholed fellow diners to help him write an *Anthology of World Poetry*. He was, he informed them, the King of Scotland.

Sylvia Plath

(1932–63)

In a poem unpublished in her lifetime, 'Dialogue over a Ouija Board', Plath described a glass which spelt out the phrase 'INPLUMAGEOFRAWWORMS'. Any writer attempting to grasp her life, death, art and reputation must face a similarly vermicular, seething corpus.

Sylvia Plath committed suicide on 11 February 1963. She died intestate, and, although she was separated from her husband, the poet Ted Hughes, divorce proceedings had not commenced. Hughes therefore became her literary executor, and controlled the copyright of her work, published and unpublished. The management of the estate was given over to Hughes' sister Olwyn, a move which, despite being pragmatic, was nonetheless highly contentious. Sylvia had not liked Olwyn, a fact confirmed by more than just the lacunae in her eventually published correspondence with her mother; nor did Olwyn like Sylvia, whom she described to one biographer as having 'something of the terrorist' about her. Plath's mother chose not to read her final, unsent letter, which Hughes offered to give her: its final instruction, accusation or bequest is shrouded. Nor did Plath leave a suicide note.

At the time of her death, Plath had only published one

collection of poems, *The Colossus*, and a pseudonymous semi-autobiographical novel, *The Bell Jar*. She had, however, been working on a number of projects, as well as continuing to keep her extensive diaries. In 1965, Hughes edited a new selection of her work, based on the collection she had been completing prior to her suicide. Hughes' *Ariel*, however, differed significantly from Plath's *Ariel*. The forty poems of the published version contained only twenty-seven of the forty-one poems Plath had grouped together as *The Rival*, then *A Birthday Present*, then *Daddy* and finally *Ariel*. Some of the excerpted works were eventually released in another posthumous collection, *Winter Trees*. Hughes wrote in the introduction to Plath's *Collected Poems* (1981) that *Ariel* 'was a somewhat different volume from the one she had planned' and that he had 'omitted some of the more personally aggressive poems'. In the preface to a selection of her prose, *Johnny Panic and the Bible of Dreams* (1977), he stated that he had taken the decision to burn her journals for the final months, since he did not want 'her' children to read it.

Robert Lowell, himself no stranger to psychosis, described her poetry as like 'playing Russian roulette with six cartridges in the cylinder'. But the effect of reading her work was less dramatic than the consequence of not being able to read it. The revelations about the text of *Ariel* and the journals opened the floodgates: accusations of censorship and suppression soon developed into a full-blown psychodrama, in which the dead Plath and the still-living Hughes became archetypes of Sapphic self-destruction and chauvinistic manipulation. Burning manuscripts leads, among other outcomes, to scorched reputations. The controversy over subsequent biographies of Plath exacerbated the situation, and, by the early 1990s, when Hughes was poet laureate, it had generated its own critical literature. In 1998, Hughes wrote his own, long-verse account of their relationship, *Birthday Letters*, a myth in a mirror, marbled with the aggrieved release of saying

'I remember'. Their lives are reproduced in other books and a film.

In such a morass of conflicting and unsettled accounts, there is still one lost work. In 1962–3 Plath was working on a second novel, provisionally entitled *Double Exposure*, or *Double Take*. She told her mother that she intended to use her recent, painful experiences (much as she had done with *The Bell Jar*), and apparently 130 pages of the manuscript were written. According to Hughes, these disappeared at some time before 1970. It is a frustratingly vague verb: lost? shredded? burned? The critic Judith Kroll saw an outline for the novel, and it is generally held that it featured a husband, wife and mistress. The manuscript, it seems, has its own ghost: the librarian of Smith College Rare Books Department had to take an unprecedented step and make clear that they did not possess the manuscript, nor was it housed with them under a seal to prevent its contents being made public too soon.

Though various biographers, aficionados and devotees would dearly love to apply another prism to the myriad lives of Ted and Sylvia, we might pause to consider, as well as its possible revelations, the hypothetical literary merit of the work. The 'double' in both prospective titles has itself a twofold resonance: the reduplication of the wife in the mistress, and the schizophrenic fissuring of the man into husband and adulterer. Plath's work always had certain elements of the Gothic. The mere title suggests a work that might have been a fusion of *The Strange Case of Dr Jekyll and Mr Hyde* and *The Doppelgänger*.

A sense of the self shattering into competing elements is thought to typify certain psychotic and depressive states of mind, and suicide can be read as a rational effort on the part of one facet to extinguish the others. Did Plath's novel embody these multiplied impulses? Her doctor had worried that giving her anti-depressants to dispel her apathy might unleash the self-confidence to harm herself. Hughes is also implicated in this tragic fracturing: he dissolved into smithereens of 'I', 'her husband' and 'TH' when he subsequently described the creative work of her last days. *Double Exposure* is, perhaps, a suicide note that, in its physical act of writing, defers an action more finally than rasping a tongue over a gummed envelope. Was she, like Nietzsche, keeping herself alive through immaculate imaginings of self-destruction?

Double Take implies a Freudian moment of confusion and realization, when the world suddenly reveals a glitch in its smooth operation; *Double Exposure* refers to a photographic anomaly where one image is superimposed on another, as if the wife and mistress were somehow merged. She would be taken, and exposed. The titles alone conjure a work of more subtle texturing and novelistic layering than the earlier, auto-biographical writing.

Hughes himself is now dead: the Plath–Hughes estate keeps the flame for two great poets. Never has the potential, ulterior capacity for that flame to become an agent of erasure been so obvious.

Georges Perec

(1936–82)

Is postmodernism – that most elusive, contradictory and elliptical of literary movements – capable of creating a work of
epic scope? Reading the works of Georges Perec, as well as
thinking about those projects he left incomplete, the strong
temptation is to answer: absolutely. Perec's work is an
extravaganza of styles, where vaudeville is mixed with prayer,
and parlour-games have cabbalistic significance. The fabric of
the world he evokes is as complex as humans are, as multi-
farious as language is.

Perec first came to prominence in 1965 when his debut
novel, *Things*, won the Renaudot Prize. He was an orphan,
whose parents had died during the Second World War (his
father, in active service; his mother in Auschwitz), and spent
his days working as an archivist in a scientific research institute, where he prepared elaborate catalogues and dealt with
tedious bureaucracy. Far from plunging him into the doldrums, his day-job formed an important apprenticeship for
his work with a new and sophisticated literary movement:
OuLiPo, l'Ouvroir de Littérature Potentielle, the Workshop
of Potential Literature.

OuLiPo counted among its members Harry Mathews,

Raymond Queneau and Italo Calvino. Its aim was to develop new literary forms, usually where freedom of expression was obtained through the most rigorous mathematical strictures. An early attempt by Perec was the radio-play *The Machine*, where a poem by Goethe was subjected to pseudo-scientific analyses and permutations. It includes an example of the arithmetical substitution game S+7, where each noun is replaced with the noun seven places on in the dictionary. It tries to capture the spirit of the poem, through interminable readings and ritual numerology, dwindling back from DoubleDutch to silence and mystery.

La Disparition (1969) sets itself an almost unbelievable condition. It resurrects the lipogram, a work where one letter is forbidden. Perec wrote the entire novel without once using the commonest letter, *e*. It is a thriller about the missing Anton Vowl. One testament to Perec's ingenuity is that the earliest reviewer managed not to notice the absence of *es* at all. His masterpiece, *Life: A User's Manual* (1978), is a compendium of new forms of intricacy. It is set in a single Parisian block of apartments. Throwing a 10 × 10 matrix over the building, the focus moves from point to point, chapter to chapter, following the Knight's Tour chess conundrum (where a single Knight must touch each and every square on the board only once). From the ground-floor curio-dealer Marcia to the garret-dwelling Smautf, it is a snapshot and a history, a Boccaccio-style anthology of stories, with djinns, Holy Grails and jigsaws. Perec's demands on himself are formidable. There is a compulsory lexicon of words to include, a library to plagiarize. It was his *Moby-Dick*, his final attempt to get over what he called his 'wanting-to-be-Flaubert'. Strange tactics, unusual angles, radical trajectories: little observations vivify each strict strategy, albeit momentarily.

These stories are not trifles. Nor are they dry, anodyne puzzles, but profound examinations of how thoughts, stories and lives are structured; a synthesis of order and clutter. *Life:*

A User's Manual captures living like no other book, in all its poignancy, bravado and surreptitious comedy.

Perec's last novel, '53 Days', is a homage to the low-brow detective stories he loved. Like Dickens' *The Mystery of Edwin Drood*, it is unfinished and thus forces the reader to become a more actively investigative collaborator. It begins in an unspecified port in North Africa, where the narrator, a mathematics tutor, is contacted by the Consul apropos of the disappearance of an expatriate crime writer, Robert Serval. Serval, the pseudonym of Stéphane Réal, has left instructions that, in the event of anything untoward occurring, the narrator is to be given his unfinished manuscript, *The Crypt*.

The Crypt is set in the mist and hail of the far north, and involves the murder of a naval attaché, whose car runs off the road and explodes. The detective is convinced that another crime novel, *The Magistrate is the Murderer*, contains the crucial clue to unravelling this tale of industrial espionage.

As he sits sipping sherbet and cheap wine among the hunters' ivory-tusks and giant-tortoise shells of this sweltering, dictatorial former colony, Veyraud has to determine if the Nordic fragment is some convoluted allegory that explains the disappearance of Serval. Does *The Crypt* encrypt local details: do the brothel or the police thugs have some parallel or translation? As he uncovers, or thinks he uncovers, a conspiracy by the Consul concerning the theft of a statue of Queen Zenobia, he finds himself compromised at every turn. The finger of suspicion eventually points at him, even though he is the only person he is sure is innocent.

Perec only completed the first eleven chapters, but left copious notes about how the riddle would be solved. The narrator realizes the book is effectively his own gravestone: then we are shifted, abruptly, to another voice. A manuscript, entitled '53 Days', about a mathematics tutor who thinks an unpublished novel about an attaché murdered in his car has some secret reference, has been found in the car of a businessman and former Maquis member, who has disappeared. He is called Robert Serval.

So the mania begins again, the edge is breached, with a sequence of Chinese boxes and exponentially increasing interpretations. Perec's final joke can be seen in his working drafts. It ends in the ochre sands of Morocco, where the solution turns out to be a writer called GP, who has accepted a challenge to create this book. Instead of a Pandora's Box, full of wartime suffering and hatred, the last casket is a jack-in-the-box. It is called '*53 Days*' in reference to the time it took Stendhal to write *Charterhouse of Parma*, and boasts several ingenious allusions, Stendhal-related constrictions and subtle traces of the whole elaborate charade.

But all we have is a scattered skeleton of possibilities. Synopsis cannot convey the exquisite texture of reading Perec. His drinking buddy, Harry Mathews, refused to hear how many ploys and pranks were buried in the book, in order to have the pleasure of stumbling on these hidden text-mines; and we can barely recapture the inspiration of the final form in these now melancholy drafts.

Perec did not complete several other projects: his inventory of everything he ate in a year, *Beds I Have Slept In*, the script of an 'adventurous movie' involving 5,000 Kirghiz horsemen. But the most tantalizing, since he spent a lifetime pondering it, is *L'Arbre*, or *The Tree*.

Like a grain of sand niggling and accumulating inside an oyster, the idea of writing a family genealogy obsessed Perec: but no pearl was produced. The riddling Perec is self-effacing at the best of times, and even the final surprise appearance in '*53 Days*' was left unwritten. He wrote up various ideas, about the Peretz and Beinenfeld branches, his rich uncle's pearl brokerage, the strange interconnections of family relations. Would he, with both parents lost to Hitler, have dared to look square on at the worst of the twentieth century?

Conclusion

What better symbol for the facile optimism of the 1980s than the spinning mirror of the Compact Disc?

The CD seemed like a heaven-sent solution to the problem of preserving recorded sound. Magnetic tape was prone to snarling. Vinyl deteriorated from the first minute it was played, as the stylus roughly ground down the very fabric of what it was supposed to be playing. They were no less frail than the earliest wax cylinders.

The CD was different; a futuristically gleaming circle, digitally encoded, replayed by the softest caress of a laser. Adverts showed them being smeared with jam and dunked in dishwater, and yet the information burned on to them did not suffer in the slightest. Of course, there were caveats about dust, magnets and scratches, but, with moderate care and attention, the CD fulfilled a millennia-old human dream: perfect imperishability.

Or so we were led to believe. In the early years of the twenty-first century, CD users started to complain that the discs were becoming erratic. Moreover, they were subtly changing colour, from silver to gold: a phenomenon which became known as 'bronzing' or, more prosaically, 'CD rot'. At first, the industry retorted by saying that all the stunts and pranks featured in adverts were not to be taken seriously, and that clear guidelines about damp, heat, electrical fields and not touching the surface of the disc made it obvious that the CD required a little special handling.

When, however, CDs that had been kept in their packaging since purchase also showed signs of deterioration, another explanation had to be found. A protective lacquer was dropped on to the disc to seal it, and, it was suggested, in some cases the centrifugal force had insufficiently coated the CD. This allowed air – specifically, oxygen – to penetrate to the aluminium layer containing the data. The aluminium was oxidizing, just as copper turns to verdigris. In short, the CDs were slowly charring. Permanence eluded us again.

At the same time as the CD was being busily marketed, a remarkable discovery was made at Herculaneum, the town buried in 79 CE when Vesuvius erupted. During the excavation of a building later known as the 'Villa dei Papiri', or House of the Papyrii, archaeologists realized that the burned bundles previously thought to be grain bags were actually ancient manuscripts. The force of the pyroclastic explosion had carbonized them in their entirety.

Normally, the organic elements in papyrii mean that they gradually corrode. The intense heat of the Vesuvius eruption had eradicated those compounds. The blackened scrolls were disinfected. The very same catastrophe that had destroyed the town had preserved the manuscripts.

Reading them, however, was a painstaking process. The heat had rendered them friable, only just holding out against their own disintegration into ashes. Slowly, in preservative solutions, they were unwrapped. X-Ray and digital photography gradually revealed differences between the black of ink and the black of burned papyrus. Computer enhancement clarified the image, and a text thought lost for ever was read again.

To date, the library at Herculaneum has not offered us a copy of the *Margites*, or a play by Agathon, or a collection of poetry by Gallus. Many of the texts were already known: the idea that such a library would lack *The Aeneid* or *The Iliad* would have created more mysteries than it solved. Many Epicurean tractates, hitherto unknown, have been clawed back from the edge; and many more scrolls remain to be deciphered. Similarly, at Vindolanda on Hadrian's Wall in Northumberland, a refuse pit which previous generations of archaeologists dug through enthusiastically in search of combs or brooches or statuettes has been revealed to contain wooden writing tablets, preserved in the peaty soil. They had been indistinguishable from dirt. Letters, requisitions and more copies of Virgil have been identified, but, as yet, no great new ancient work.

The papyrus and the CD, the codex and the web-page: human ingenuity strives, not only to find a permanent medium for its culture, but to reclaim that which was fixed on a more fragile form. It is a struggle we cannot win.

The Second Law of Thermodynamics – the law of entropy – proves that there is no perfect way to change energy from one form into another. In any transformation, a dissipation occurs. Two billiard balls click, and the momentum transfers from one to the other, with a slither lost in the click and the heat or the momentary abrasion between the balls. If we look beyond our own tiny section of the universe's history, the picture appears bleak.

The coronosphere of our sun will eventually edge forwards, engulfing Mercury, frazzling Venus. In thousands and thousands of years, Earth will scorch like an insignificant piece of paper. As the Bible says, the skies will roll up like parchment. Perhaps by then, like a long-lost science fiction story, future humanity will have fled to a safer, moist and rocky planet, with a Noah's Ark of knowledge. This only defers the inevitable. All matter will eventually be spread as fine, interstellar dust, or concentrated in a black hole's gorged interior. Loss is not an anomaly, or a deviation, or an exception. It is the norm. It is the rule. It is inescapable.

Why, then, do we strive? In trying to preserve what makes us human, we prove our own humanity. A German proverb says *einmal ist keinmal* – once is never. This is not true. Something does not lose its meaning, or its significance, just because it ceases to be. Just as any human life reverberates, causes change and affects our thinking and feeling even after the death of the individual person, so does our culture, that accumulation of countless lost lives. We struggle unsuccessfully against oblivion, and the struggling itself is our success.

And on the pedestal, these words appear:
'My name is Ozymandias, king of kings,
Look on my works, ye Mighty, and despair!'
Nothing else remains. Round the decay
Of that colossal wreck, boundless and bare
The lone and level sands stretch far away

Percy Shelley, 'Ozymandias'

Index